Speaking for Themselves

Speaking for Themselves

Pasó Por Aquí
Series on the Nuevomexicano Literary Heritage
Edited by Genaro M. Padilla and
Erlinda Gonzales-Berry

Speaking for Themselves

Neomexicano Cultural Identity
and the
Spanish-Language Press,
1880–1920

Doris Meyer

University of New Mexico Press
Albuquerque

For Richard,
Kathy,
and Barbara

℮

Library of Congress Cataloging-in-Publication Data

Meyer, Doris.
Speaking for themselves: Neomexicano cultural identity and the
Spanish-language press, 1880-1920 / Doris Meyer. — 1st ed.
p.   cm.
Includes bibliographical references and index.
ISBN 0-8263-1749-9
1. Mexican American literature (Spanish)—New Mexico—History and criticism.
2. Mexican American newspapers—New Mexico—History—19th century.
3. Mexican Americans—New Mexico—Ethnic identity.
I. Title.
PQ7078.5.N6M49 1996
860.9'868720789—dc20
96-4526

CIP

Contents

Note from Series Editors

As scholars in an emerging field of literary and cultural studies, we, the editors of this series, frequently found ourselves discouraged, for our work was impeded by the lack of primary materials. We suspected that there were many more texts available than reference tools would have us believe. It soon became apparent that those materials indeed existed; they had, however, been glossed over by literary historians who either were ignorant of the existence of a strong Hispanic literary tradition in this country, or else did not deem it a legitimate entry for their histories. Because it had been produced in Spanish and, as such, remained "eccentric," it was beyond the scope of their canonical efforts.

As a partial solution, we proposed to the University of New Mexico Press a series that would "offer profound recognition of the Hispano contribution to arts and letters in the region." Ours was to be a labor of recovery and dissemination. We would publish two or three titles per year and each volume would be edited and introduced by a prominent scholar in the field of Hispanic culture and literature. Since then, our plan has expanded to make room for critical and analytical texts, and we are very pleased to add Doris Meyer's book, *Speaking For Themselves: Neomexicano Cultural Identity and the Spanish-Language Press, 1880–1920,* to our growing list of publications.

Meyer is indeed a pioneer in the area of "recovery" work. Her articles on the creative literature published in the Spanish-language press in New Mexico began to appear in the early seventies. At that time she was one of a handful of scholars mining this rich yet virtually untouched source of Hispanic print discourse. After a hiatus, which took her in new research directions, Meyer returned to New Mexico to continue her labor of earlier years. As she acknowledges in her Preface, newspaper research is lonely work. How fortunate we are that she endured. The fruits of her toil, gathered within the covers of this serious and intelligent text, represent a significant contribution to the field of U.S. Latino cultural studies and, specifically, to the study of the distinctive nuevomexicano cultural-aesthetic legacy.

Preface

This book exists because I was moved to revisit an area of scholarship I had explored two decades ago, this time with a much keener awareness of how texts must be read in context. When I first went to New Mexico in the summer of 1973 to look for evidence of a Hispanic literary tradition in the territorial period, I had no idea how engrossing this search would become nor how my fascination with the state and its mixture of cultures would draw me back years later. Spanish-language newspapers that were abundant in New Mexico after 1880 would be my principal source material, given that very few other texts had been printed there in Spanish before the 1900s. For two consecutive summers back in the 1970s I traveled in a rented car from one end of New Mexico to the other, reading old newspapers in museums, courthouses, state archives, and university collections. Librarians and archival custodians helped me beyond measure, as did many other New Mexicans to whom I spoke about their state's cultural history and the life of its earlier Spanish-speaking inhabitants who often called themselves *neomexicanos*. But my day-to-day work was, for the most part, solitary and exhausting as I read roll after roll of microfilm and occasional original issues of old newspapers in Spanish. Pieces of the neomexicano cultural picture jumped out of every issue, but bringing them together into focused images involved sifting back through piles of notes, hoping that I had jotted down something I remembered seeing earlier because, if not, it would be a nightmare to find again in the labyrinth of fragmented and widely dispersed newspaper holdings. I xeroxed as much evidence of literary activity as I could, only to find later that the photocopies faded badly when exposed to light.

After two summers of reading newspapers I had amassed quantities of poems, editorials, stories, articles—significant evidence of a neomexicano literary tradition in the late nineteenth century that had been overlooked in American and Hispanic literature courses and left out of literary histories of the United States or of Spanish America. In these long forgotten texts I found certain patterns of cultural expression that captured my interest, especially the way in which Spanish-speaking New Mexicans in the territorial period articulated their identity vis-à-vis the Anglo-American culture that had forced its way into their midst in the mid-nineteenth century. I noticed that concerns raised by the neomexicano population in those days were still being expressed a century later, and it became increasingly clear that early neomexicano newspapers were an important antecedent to the Chicano literary expression of the 1960s and 1970s. I thus set out to share certain aspects of my research with the academic community in the hope that the significance of this earlier period would be more widely recognized. In New Mexico's late afternoons, the luminous vistas of piñon and juniper-covered mesas ringed by majestic mountains energized my work and I found myself projecting onto those landscapes the images of a Hispanic past that had long been buried in faded newsprint.

The early 1970s in New Mexico and across the Southwest was a time of Chicano consciousness-raising and self-empowerment. In academia this translated into a rapid growth in research, scholarly activity, and pressure from students to incorporate Chicano studies into the curriculum. The ethnic pride expressed by community activists did not necessarily foster a corresponding unanimity regarding strategy and objectives in the public arena. In New Mexico, for example, some Hispanics were sympathetic to the militant crusade of Reies López Tijerina, whose followers protested the government's usurpation of community land grants by occupying the Rio Arriba county courthouse in June 1967. Other more traditional neomexicanos, who tended to call themselves Spanish-Americans, rejected Chicano radicalism and preferred to exert their influence from within the state political machine, which had regularly elected Hispanic officials at the local and national levels. This intracultural disagreement also had its parallel in the earlier territorial period.

The creative literature and critical discourse that came out of the radical phase of *chicanismo* in the 1960s and 1970s unanimously condemned the intolerance of an Anglo-dominated society in which minorities had historically been denied a voice in defining the American experience. In response to this injustice, Chicano writers mythologized a geospiritual homeland called Aztlán and projected a future in which *la raza* would proudly claim its cultural equality in America. Popular writers like Alurista and New Mexico's own Rudolfo Anaya were inspired by the Amerindian roots of the mestizo Hispanic culture in the Southwest and by folklore and folk heroes. However, at the same time, very little research was being done on the literate culture of the preceding era that Luis Leal, a leading critic in this field, defined as the transition period (1848–1910).[1] Some Chicano scholars simply accepted the notion that the lack of voices from previous generations of Spanish speakers in the United States meant that either there had been no significant literary expression or it had not survived the oppression of colonization and neglect of time.

In this heady atmosphere of here-and-now Chicano activism, the articles I began to publish in various literary and historical journals were noticed by only a handful of scholars in the field, such as Joseph Sommers, Charles Tatum, Juan Bruce-Novoa and Raymund Paredes. I am grateful for the encouragement they gave me back in the 1970s and for the welcoming friendship of Sergio Elizondo and Rolando Hinojosa, who were literary leaders in a burgeoning field of Chicano poetry and prose. I eventually wrote six pieces that were published in *The Bilingual Review*, *New Mexico Historical Review*, *New Scholar*, and *Hispania* between 1975 and 1978. Each article grew out of topics suggested by the one before; as I wrote, my focus widened to include issues outside the normal scope of literary criticism. This was inevitable considering the way in which neomexicano writers of the transition or territorial period lived and conceived of a writer's role in society. A century ago in New Mexico, art for art's sake was a rarity. Hispanics who wrote generally focused on sociopolitical realities of the day, and the genres that interested them did not fit neatly into the belletristic definition of literature. What they wrote and published spontaneously in the Spanish-language newspapers did, however, reflect the lives they lived and the cultural dynamics of their time.

I could have pursued further research in the Southwest, but in the late 1970s I became interested in the conjunction of Latin American women's literature and feminist critical theory and I took advantage of a unique opportunity to do a project in that emerging field. This inevitably led to other topics that absorbed me for the next fifteen years, not the least being a major shift in scholarly approaches to reading literature and history in a postmodern, postcolonial context. I should also add that early on it became clear to me that, as an East Coast academic whose father's German name obscured my mother's Hispanic heritage (and maiden name, Xiques), I would be at a continued disadvantage doing research at long distance in a highly politicized field like Chicano studies.

So I put my fascination with neomexicano culture aside and went in other directions. Some years later, however, I decided to design and teach a course on "Hispanic Cultures in the United States." Preparing for this, I reconnected with recent scholarship on the Hispanic Southwest and noticed that there was still much to be done on neomexicano newspapers. I thought of all my old notes still holding parts of the cultural puzzle that had not been deciphered elsewhere, and it occurred to me that extending my research into the early twentieth century might prove fruitful. In the summer of 1991, with the help of a college grant, I went back to New Mexico to take up where I had left off.

Out of that research and later follow-up visits came new discoveries and eventually the idea of this book. At first, I planned simply to bring together my earlier work and add additional chapters. However, after writing the first new piece, I realized that everything I had published in the 1970s had to be rethought and reinterpreted. Not only did I need to include new findings from the newspapers I had gone back to read, but I wanted to incorporate insights inspired by contemporary critical perspectives, particularly the interdisciplinary approaches of discourse analysis and cultural studies. This book therefore goes far beyond my earlier work in an effort to interpret these uniquely representative but fundamentally quotidian texts in the context of their time. It reflects my assessment that cultural identity was the core issue faced by the neomexicano community in the period under examination and that the Spanish-language newspapers offer dramatic and convincing evidence of how it was understood and expressed by neomexicanos themselves.

Looking back over the years, I would like to condense what could be a long list of acknowledgements into a few lines and thank some of the many people who contributed to this project by helping me find the materials I needed, by answering questions, or by doing favors that I can never adequately repay. Theodore S. Beardsley, director of the Hispanic Society in New York, suggested long ago that I look into this topic and I am grateful to him for that fruitful idea. The late Myra Ellen Jenkins of the New Mexico State Records Center and Archives gave me the benefit of her wisdom and experience on many occasions in the early years; and Al Regensberg, also of the State Records Center and Archives, readily produced archival materials on many occasions and, at my request, traced Luis Tafoya's genealogy. Orlando Romero, at the History Museum of the Palace of the Governors in Santa Fe, helped me find early newspapers and recently gave me the pleasure of seeing a newly acquired copy of one of the oldest extant Spanish-language papers in New Mexico, *El Payo de Nuevo México*. My gratitude also goes to Ashley Powell Hanson and James MacDonald of Shain Library at Connecticut College, who always managed to locate needed information enthusiastically and efficiently, and to Peter Blodgett of the Huntington Library, who helped me with Benjamin Read manuscripts in the Ritch collection. I also want to thank the librarians and curators at the Southwest Collection of the University of New Mexico in Albuquerque, the New Mexico State Library and the Palace of the Governors photographic archives in Santa Fe, New Mexico State University in Las Cruces, and at numerous smaller library collections around the state who have shared their knowledge with me. The R. F. Johnson Faculty Development Fund and the Weller Chair stipend at Connecticut College made it possible for me to travel to do research in New Mexico on several occasions and a sabbatical leave in 1994–95 enabled me to complete the task of writing.

Although this book achieves a kind of closure after more than twenty years of interrupted work, it will not be the last word either by myself or other scholars who will build on its findings. I hope that it contributes to productive discourse on the ethnic reintegration of America's cultural past and that it will stimulate more interest in print journalism as a source of cultural expression. For the ethnic minorities who energetically maintained an alternative press against formidable odds, it was a way for them to speak for themselves in a country that was not always as welcoming as it professed to be.

The diversity of Hispanic lived experience from California to Florida, from Texas to New York, and points between makes it imperative that the focus of research be narrow enough to accommodate cultural uniqueness without losing sight of connections between groups and with the rest of the American population. Large collaborative undertakings, such as the recent four-volume *Handbook of Hispanic Cultures in the United States*, have made vast bodies of resource material available to scholars and have enhanced the perceived significance of this important field. Also underway are collaborative projects to document all Hispanic literature in U.S. periodicals (the U.S. Hispanic Literary Heritage Project at the University of Houston) and to bring together in one database the complete periodical holdings in the state of New Mexico (the New Mexico Newspaper Project at the University of New Mexico). Research in graduate schools and by individual scholars is uncovering new information regularly, and much of it bridges the gap that has existed too long between Hispanic experience in the United States and in Latin America. The future is brighter in many ways than it was when my work began.

Essex, Conn.
September 1995

Speaking for Themselves

1

Introduction

Neomexicanos and Their Newspapers

"Cultural identity . . . is a matter of 'becoming' as well as of
'being'. It belongs to the future as much as to the past. It is not
something which already exists, transcending place, time, history
and culture. Cultural identities come from somewhere, have
histories. But, like everything which is historical, they undergo
constant transformation. Far from being eternally fixed in some
essentialised past, they are subject to the continuous 'play' of
history, culture and power. Far from being grounded in a mere
'recovery' of the past, which is waiting to be found, and which,
when found, will secure our sense of ourselves into eternity,
identities are the names we give to the different ways we are
positioned by, and position ourselves within, the narratives
of the past."

Stuart Hall, "Cultural Identity and Diaspora"

The Spanish-speaking residents of New Mexico in the late nineteenth century commonly referred to themselves as neomexicanos,[1] a cultural identifier that both situates them and differentiates them from other Hispanics in
the Southwest. As a cultural community within a given space and time,
neomexicanos experienced their historical situation in a unique context, not
to be confused with that of the tejanos or californianos or other Spanish-
speaking groups in the United States in the same period. I begin by emphasizing cultural differences within the larger Hispanic or Latino population in
the United States in order to underscore the otherness of neomexicano experience. However, I also want to suggest that we need to go "beyond ethnicity,"
to quote Werner Sollars, and look at the complexities of the socialization
process or "the cultural construction of the codes of consent and descent"
that have influenced how Americans of diverse ethnic backgrounds have accepted or defined their Americanness.[2] Rather than debate why some ethnic

3

groups have been denied a voice in American society, it may be time to listen more closely to what those voices that managed to speak out had to say about becoming part of this country.

The span of forty years that this book addresses, 1880–1920, is a critical period of transition in the history of the American Southwest that can be looked at globally and locally. I have chosen to focus on one region, New Mexico, and one segment of its population, the neomexicanos, who were a mestizo people of Indo-Hispanic origins living primarily in the northern Rio Grande Valley and surrounding mountains. This region has been the homeland of neomexicanos for more than four hundred years, and in this environment they developed a cultural identity that has evolved and endured over time, until this day. The historical period my study addresses is arguably the one in which neomexicanos experienced most intensely a dialectical process of resistance and affirmation that shaped their understanding of what it was to be American. Three decades after being invaded and occupied by U.S. troops, Hispanic New Mexicans were still struggling to obtain the equal treatment they had been guaranteed as American citizens. Their increasingly close contact with Anglo culture from 1880 to 1920 made them see themselves in a "different mirror," as Ronald Takaki has described the historical reality of America's many cultures whose identities evolved within a new society.[3] For neomexicanos, this was an unsettling, transformational period. In the remote borderlands of the Southwest, they were at a crossroad, or, to quote Chicana author Gloria Anzaldúa's poetic phrase, they were in the curious position of finding themselves "at home, a stranger."[4]

New Mexico was a frontier zone before the Spanish arrived, and it remained a modern frontier into the early twentieth century, long after the historian Frederick Jackson Turner proclaimed the frontier's demise in 1893. If we define the notion of a frontier in such a way that it encompasses the Hispanic, Anglo-European, and indigenous experiences in the Americas—as do David J. Weber and Jane M. Rausch in a recent book on this subject—frontiers are "geographic zones of interaction between two or more distinctive cultures" or "places where cultures contend with one another and with their physical environment to produce a dynamic that is unique to time and place."[5] As a site of historical conflict and cultural accommodation between nomadic and Pueblo Indians, between Spaniards and Indians, and, at the turn of the last century, between neomexicanos and Anglo Americans, New Mexico has been a quintessential frontier zone.

New Mexico has also been a commercial intersection where trails met and cultures intermingled in mutual interest and self-interest. In the Spanish colonial period Santa Fe was the northern end of El Camino Real, which led down to El Paso del Norte and across harsh desert terrain to Chihuahua and eventually all the way to Mexico City. In the Mexican period, after 1821, New

Mexico was an East–West hub, with the Santa Fe Trail coming from Franklin, Missouri, and the Old Spanish Trail heading toward California. The very name of this remote area, "*New* Mexico," was first used by the Spanish explorers and Franciscan missionaries in the sixteenth century to designate the land to the north as "*un otro México*," similar to, but different from, the Old Mexico to the south.[6] Culturally a part of both Latin America and the United States, a site of contact and blending with indigenous Indians, New Mexico has been a space of multicultural difference and synthesis, or, to borrow a term from Juan Bruce-Novoa, an "inter-space" in which nationalism gives way to pluralism and the possibility of "a fuller polyglot expression."[7]

The different cultures that have collided with and adjusted to one another in this New Mexican frontier zone have inspired writers and artists for centuries. As early as the 1500s, literary texts in Spanish recorded the cultural dynamics of New Mexico's history. The earliest descriptions of the unknown land to the north and its native peoples were written by the explorer Alvar Núñez Cabeza de Vaca, who traversed what is now the southern portion of the state in 1535. A few years later, Fray Marcos de Niza and his scout Estebanico, of African descent, journeyed north from Mexico to assess the potential of the lands described by Cabeza de Vaca. Estebanico had gone ahead and was killed by Zuñi villagers, whereupon the Franciscan friar turned back, never reaching the land he later imaginatively constructed in his chronicle as the fabled Cíbola, the projection of Eurocentric myths and his own wishful dreams of wealth. From Fray Marcos's reports came the stimulus to send Coronado's expedition of 1540–1542 and other subsequent explorations that produced more accounts in Spanish of the land and its people. In 1598 Juan de Oñate, whose father had fought with Cortés and whose wife was Moctezuma's granddaughter, led the first group of settlers to New Mexico with the blessings of the Spanish viceroy in Mexico. Accompanying him was Gaspar Pérez de Villagrá, a military captain and a graduate of the prestigious University of Salamanca. Villagrá composed an epic poem about the expedition entitled *Historia de la Nueva México* [History of New Mexico], which appeared in Spain in 1610 and has been called "a gem among the early records of American history,"[8] and "the first published history of any American commonwealth."[9] This work, however, has rarely been recognized for its historical value and its authenticity, no doubt because it was written in verse and in the Spanish language.

Stuart Hall, in the introductory epigraph, reminds us that cultural identity is an ongoing process of *becoming*, not a set of qualities existing eternally as the normative essence of a people's character or values. A cultural community evolves in and is transformed by history in such a way that its cultural identity is constantly negotiated or repositioned between what came before and what lies ahead, between continuity and difference, affirmation and dissent. Hall's postmodernist view of the politics of identity enunciation stresses the way the subject (collective or individual) constructs meaning from experience;[10] inherited cultural values constantly engage with a present set of realities that demand cultural modification or accommodation to retain the subject's vitality and integrity. Should the cultural integrity of a community be eroded by foreign invasion or enforced dependency, displaced or distorted by the imposition of other cultural norms, then cultural identity itself is endangered. When difference becomes unacceptable within the dominant culture and leads to exclusion of colonized groups, the possibility of a free society is negated.

The cultural experience of neomexicanos over the course of hundreds of years comprises many narratives in which they are both the colonizers and the colonized. In the early colonial period the Spanish church and state oppressed the Pueblo Indians and brutally tried to stamp out their religious practices, which eventually led to the Pueblo Revolt of 1680. In the next hundred years neomexicano settlers and the Pueblos accommodated to one another and often cooperated to fend off raids from nomadic Apaches, Utes, or Comanches with captives taken on both sides. The geographic proximity of Indian and Hispanic cultures in the same isolated homeland, the inevitable blending of their blood and religious beliefs resulting from the imposition of Catholicism, and the particular nature of neomexicano society in which the typical Spanish caste system was no longer viable had the effect of differentiating the neomexicanos as a people. After Mexico won its independence from Spain in 1821, it governed the province of New Mexico for twenty-five years, but this was not long enough for the neomexicano population to develop a strong sense of loyalty toward or identification with the Mexican Republic per se.[11] After Mexico lost nearly half of its land mass to the United States in 1846, neomexicanos were quite easily invaded, colonized, and exploited by their American conquerors.[12] Worse still, they were treated like foreigners even though they were living on the land that had been theirs or their ancestors' for centuries. It is true that even before the territorial period, neomexicano *ricos* had begun to bilk their poorer neighbors of their land rights; some of them collaborated with large-scale Anglo interests to carry out this injustice with relentless efficiency. The long delay in granting statehood to New Mexico in 1912 can be attributed to a power struggle that once again pitted colonizers against the colonized but this time in a much more complicated socioeconomic and political environment. In the 1990s, with an awareness of how individual subject positions influence narrative points of view, we can appreciate how history has been colored by perspective and we can thus envision many different ways in which the neomexicano story might be told.

Discourses of cultural identity are always plurivocal, but in the case of

New Mexico, in the period in question, hearing Hispanic voices demands an ear for multiple modes of articulation and an ability to distinguish among diverse tonalities. Witnesses of the past—especially those relegated to silence by virtue of their class, gender, race, or economic condition—rarely left behind evidence of their "take" on history. We do not know, for example, the thoughts of the average Mexican citizens who were in the plaza of Las Vegas, New Mexico, on August 15, 1846, when Colonel Stephen Watts Kearny summarily absolved them of their allegiance to Mexico and made this pledge on behalf of the U.S. government:

> I shall not expect you to take up arms and follow me, to fight
> your own people, who may oppose me; but I now tell you, that
> those who remain peaceably at home, attending to their crops
> and their herds, shall be protected by me, in their property, their
> persons, and their religion; and not a pepper, not an onion, shall
> be disturbed or taken by my troops, without pay, or by consent of
> the owner.[13]

We do not know how much skepticism was expressed by those present, but it is more than likely that some neomexicanos in the plaza that day converted their thoughts and feelings about Kearny and his troops into poetry or song. With the fossilization of the Spanish empire and the isolation of New Mexico from the centers of Hispanic culture, native-written texts were rare and illiteracy was widespread. Oral narrative and verse was the accepted way for experience to be transmitted from day to day, and from one generation to the next, in communal anonymity. In the early twentieth century ethnographers, linguists, and literary historians began to document this vibrant popular tradition, yet only a portion of it has been preserved to this day.

Although there were lamentably few printed books in Spanish in which neomexicanos spoke for themselves before the 1900s, there *was* another important forum for public commentary within and about the Hispanic population, and that was the local print media. The history of journalism in New Mexico begins in 1834, when newspapers had already become an influential part of daily life in the eastern United States and in the metropolitan centers of Mexico.[14] New Mexico was still a province of Mexico when the first printing press arrived in Santa Fe and the first newspaper, *El Crepúsculo de la Libertad*, was reported to have been printed. No issues survive; however, there are copies of the second and third known newspapers, *La Verdad* and *El Payo de Nuevo México*, both government gazettes published for a short time in Santa Fe during the years 1844–45, prior to the American invasion. The first English-language newspaper, the Santa Fe *Republican*, appeared in 1847, and in the 1850s and 1860s three more Spanish-language periodicals had brief lives, with seven more appearing in the 1870s. A Jesuit publication, *La Revista Católica*, first appeared in 1875 and was later moved to El Paso in 1918, but because its perspective was that of the Eurocentric Catholic clergy in New Mexico and not that of the secular community, and because its concern with local news was minimal, I did not find it that useful. Nor were many bilingual papers published in the territory a fruitful source of information for this project; newspapers that divided their weekly pages between English and Spanish tried to appeal to a wider audience, but by doing so they often sacrificed their journalistic identity along with the space to give in-depth coverage, thus failing to do justice to local issues in either language. Of course the very existence of bilingual papers points to a desire to double readership and reap larger profits.

My concern in this book is not with bilingual or English-language papers in New Mexico, but with the Spanish-language press, which jumped dramatically in number of publications in the last decades of the century. In the 1880s, seventeen new periodicals were begun, and in 1890, forty-four followed suit. Overall, New Mexico produced more Spanish-language newspapers in the nineteenth century than any other region of the Southwest. The climate that encouraged this expansion of press activity, the role the press played in New Mexican social and intellectual history during this era of transition, and particularly the impact it had on the evolution of neomexicano cultural identity is the subject of this book.

In his 1969 seminal work, *The Territorial Press of New Mexico, 1834–1912*, Porter A. Stratton amply documents and describes the history of New Mexican journalism with particular concentration on the Anglo-American journals and their editors. When discussing the Spanish-language press, however, his observations are less detailed and insightful because an Anglocentric bias limits his ability to lend it equal consideration in the cultural history of the territory. Nonetheless, Stratton's work was an important foundation for my own investigations and I recommend it to the reader interested in knowing how the press evolved and how it reacted to and impacted upon the events leading up to statehood in 1912. In this context Stratton makes some general observations that obtain for both Spanish and English-language newspapers in territorial New Mexico: for example, the fact that many lasted only a short time can be explained by the economic difficulties of sustaining a newspaper with low readership, recalcitrant subscribers, high advertising rates, and the lack of outside printing contracts. Newspapers were often propaganda vehicles for political campaigns and thus tended to disappear after elections, but the relative ease with which an owner-editor could start one up with a characteristic blend of optimism and opportunism meant that when one ceased publication, another would grind into operation. The Washington hand press that was commonly used on the western frontier was a time-consuming and labor-intensive device that was not replaced until the end of the century with the more costly steam-driven press because the number of sub-scribers—usually no more than a few hundred for the average paper that only charged a few dollars for a year's subscription—could not justify the expense. News reporting in a typical four-page layout was allocated differently, with items of territorial and local interest given much more attention than national and international news. Provincial customs also led to an unpolished use of language and a rhetorical lustiness that could lapse into mudslinging and rowdy editorial battles. On the whole, however, newspaper editors had an above-average education and a wider range of business and cultural experiences than most of their neighbors; as public figures with a high profile in the community, they were conscious of their power to shape public opinion. Since their trade depended on reader response, they took pride in knowing their constituencies well and cultivating their support. As Stratton points out for both English and Spanish-language papers, "the core of these papers became the editorials, which were made interesting by the prestige and insight of the editors and their strongly partisan support of political allies."[15] The independent "new journalism" of Joseph Pulitzer and the *New York World* in the 1880s would take longer to move west.

Politics and the press have been mutually dependent but distrustful of one another since newspapers first joined the power structure as the fourth estate. In a freewheeling frontier society, the press could take the moral high road and influence public policy or follow the low road and sell out to vested interests. In New Mexico between 1880 and 1920, there were ample reasons for Hispano and Anglo journalists to be tempted by one course or the other and only minimal ethical standards to rein them in.[16] Although some papers professed an independent stance, objectivity was not the norm and editors usually declared their allegiances on the front page and without ambivalence. At stake during these early years of uneasy bicultural coexistence were issues of crucial importance that would determine when and how the territory would join the union of states, who would wield economic and political power, and how the major ethnic groups would adjust to one another within this negotiation for power. According to historian Marc Simmons:

> The entire history of New Mexico from 1850 to the present is
> interwoven with attempts by the Indian and Hispano popula-
> tions to come to terms with an alien Anglo society. Through
> principles supplied by the Declaration of Independence, they
> have tried to win equality while remaining different and have
> sought liberty to pursue a time-honored way of life. That history
> also includes a long story of the Anglo-American's adjustment to
> things that are uniquely and engagingly New Mexican.[17]

For this reason, New Mexico remained different, unlike other emerging western states where Hispanic and Native American cultures would be relegated to isolated and marginated communities. The evolution of cultural identities during these years would shape the future of the state of New Mexico.

The cultural dynamics of this era cannot be understood without a sense of the numbers of Anglo immigrants who poured into the territory to take part in the economic boom that was anticipated when the first railroad lines reached New Mexico in 1878. Prior to 1870 the Anglo population in New Mexico was relatively small, consisting mainly of U.S. military troops and some traders and trappers who had come west on the Santa Fe Trail earlier in the century. Census figures show that after 1870, and particularly after 1900, the increase in immigrants from the East was considerable:[18]

Year	Total Pop.	Born in N.M.	Indian	Born Other Parts of U.S.
1870	91,874	82,193	?	2,760
1880	119,565	92,271	9,772	9,471
1890	160,282	116,216	15,044	26,080
1900	195,310	143,216	13,144	38,469
1910	327,321	184,749	20,573	119,406

Immigration from Mexico, by comparison, remained relatively steady: between four thousand to six thousand per year until 1910, during the revolution, when the numbers doubled, and then doubled again by 1920 when they reached almost twenty thousand.[19] The Anglo influx was proportionately much larger, however, and its cultural impact was not offset by the Mexican nationals fleeing the turmoil in their country. Neomexicano legislators in the 1870s apparently foresaw the changes the railroad would bring to their way of life and some mounted opposition to the construction plan proposed by the Atchison, Topeka and Santa Fe Lines, but in the end legislation favorable to the venture was passed.[20]

With the railroad came a new era of development. Yankee fortune hunters were hungry to seize the opportunity of the "open" frontier, which Frederick Jackson Turner idealized ethnocentrically as a progressive march of democratic civilization westward, transforming society and consolidating the economy and thereby promoting "the formation of a composite nationality for the American people."[21] Small and large investors in ranching, agriculture, and mining were followed by lawyers, merchants, missionaries, and a slew of unsavory parasites who thrived in the rough-and-ready frontier envi-

ronment. For neomexicanos, this massive influx of foreigners with a different social, political, and economic structure, a different language, religion,
values, and ethnic origins, and a completely different understanding of land
rights—which was the critical element of neomexicano day-to-day existence—
would inevitably lead to conflict and hostility on many fronts. First, Colonel
Kearny, and then the Treaty of Guadalupe Hidalgo, promised Mexican citizens living in the conquered Southwest that they would enjoy the full rights
of U.S. citizenship—that their lives, property, and religion would be protected under the Constitution—but the promises were not fulfilled and those
who chose to stay and become citizens were ill-equipped to claim their due
under a different national system of law and custom.

One scholar has suggested that two New Mexicos—Anglo and Pueblo-
Hispanic—existed between 1885 and 1925:

> One of "what is," that of the pragmatist-realist, concerned with
> material things, reflecting the economic and political order; the
> other, that of the mind and spirit, of "what might be," concerned
> with non-material realities, reflecting human yearning for truth,
> brotherhood and eternal meaning in the universe.[22]

Although such broad characterizations can be misleading, there is abundant
historical evidence of a clash of cultures and value systems that reached its
culmination in the bicultural negotiation and accommodation that produced
the New Mexican Constitution of 1910, which brought both New Mexicos
together to achieve the goal of statehood in 1912. This bipartisan-negotiated
document pledged to protect the rights of neomexicanos guaranteed under
the Guadalupe Hidalgo accord and to recognize the equal status of their culture by making New Mexico an officially bilingual state—the only one in the
United States. Such an agreement would not have been possible had not the
Hispanic population in New Mexico been almost ten times larger than that
of Texas or California at the time. Nor would it have occurred without the
Spanish-language press, which kept the concerns and demands of
neomexicanos in the public eye and constantly reinforced neomexicano cultural identity in the struggle for interpretive power in New Mexico.

Joshua Fishman pointed out, in 1966, that the "naturalization" process
for immigrants to America since the end of the nineteenth century has carried with it an expectation of de-ethnicization and yet, in spite of this,
"ethnicity is one of the strongest unrecognized facets of American life—in
politics, in religion, in consumer behavior, in life-styles and in self-concepts."[23]
He spoke of "the anomalous half-life of ethnicity in present-day America"
and warned that Americans needed to face the contradictions that this im-
plied. Fishman noted a further irony: for most ethnic groups in America,

their ethnicity only assumed conscious importance (awareness of their "groupness") *after* immigration, thereby suggesting that anti-foreign sentiments in the social core might in fact precipitate a defensive reaction.[24] When we look at the historical case of New Mexico in the territorial period—a situation in which Anglos arrived as immigrants, albeit on American soil—the tables were turned in one sense, but not in another: it was the Hispanic majority who responded with a new awareness of its group identity and the need to resist a de-ethnicizing, culturally rootless Americanization.

Ironically, the Spanish-language press—despite being a harbinger of a new age of mass communication and industrialization—was the primary vehicle for articulating and galvanizing this counter-hegemonic cultural imperative. It was the neomexicano press, in fact, that bridged the gap between tradition and modernity by establishing the intellectual connection between the remembered past and the anticipated future.[25] Particularly noticeable is the way in which the press consciously assumed the role of cultural interpreter and regularly commented introspectively on its social responsibility, even as it struggled to survive in hard times. As expressed by a November 14, 1891, editorial in *La Voz del Pueblo*:

> En fin esperamos que el sufrido pueblo Neo-Mexicano colecte sus mentes y obre con deliberación en materias públicas; que despierte del letargo en que ha dormido por tantos años, y que aprecie el valor intrínseco de una sana y verdadera educación, y que reconosca que el periódico y la literatura generalmente es el camino más seguro para la ciencia y la prosperidad.

> [So we hope that the long-suffering neomexicano community will collect its thoughts and work with deliberation on public matters, that it will awaken from the lethargy in which it has slumbered for so many years, and that it will appreciate the intrinsic value of a healthy and true education and will recognize that the newspapers and literature in general are the surest way toward science and prosperity.]

Ordinary neomexicanos experienced the jolt of massive Anglo immigration on a personal and nonideological basis: they saw communal property threatened by land-grabbing tactics, their families affected by intermarriage, their produce devalued in a more competitive market, or their ways of life disdained by new *patrones*. The historical record and a few surviving personal texts, such as the autobiography of Rafael Chacón,[26] show that Anglo aggression was met with native resistance. Hispanic popular poems contain flashes of this spirit of defiance and some of this poetry is found in the newspapers, showing that the press was not a tool of the Anglo-affiliated Hispanic *ricos* to indoctrinate the masses but a vehicle for autochthonous expression on many levels.[27] In a precapitalist society such as New Mexico's at the end of the century, however, traditional Hispanic ways of life did not prepare neomexicanos to resist en masse the incursions of an aggressive foreign culture, although isolated examples of self-defense and confrontation abound. Thus, the neomexicano press assumed, among other functions, the unofficial role of a public forum and community bulletin board, where an aggrieved citizen or someone with a opinion could speak out. When political infighting threatened to destabilize the Spanish-speaking community caught up in territorial politics, level-headed Hispanic editors drew their readers' attention to the need for unity in addressing the cultural identity crisis they faced.

Educational opportunities for neomexicanos improved after the passage of a comprehensive school bill in 1891, but the neomexicano community could not sustain the same quantity of newspapers published in English (or in both languages) in the territory. A national economic recession in the 1890s contributed to the financial hurdles all papers faced, but other problems included the higher proportion of literate Anglos and their deeply ingrained habit of reading newspapers; the political patronage Anglo papers obtained in the form of government printing contracts that rarely went to neomexicano newspapers; the higher advertising revenues Anglo papers were able to demand; and the unknown number of readers who were literate in Spanish, or in both languages, but chose to read bilingual newspapers. Considering the obstacles in his path, a prospective neomexicano newspaper owner/editor needed a degree of conviction and determination even greater than his Anglo counterpart. There is no doubt that a gap of varying dimensions existed between editors and the average neomexicano, who might have been a farmer, a miner, a laundress, or a storekeeper; newspaper editors were generally more educated, middle-class, male city dwellers who had probably read and traveled more extensively than 95 percent of neomexicano men and women. These differences notwithstanding, an editor needed to communicate with, speak on behalf of, and represent the people in his community or he would not succeed. His own voice, and the news that he and his coworkers printed, had to find appropriate rhetorical strategies to speak to the interests of his constituency; if his advocacy of one political stance or another became too strident, he ran the risk of reducing his readership or shortening the paper's life span, which was already precarious in all likelihood. In essence, the Spanish-language papers— especially those that became well known and were widely read, such as *La Voz del Pueblo*, *El Independiente*, *El Nuevo Mexicano*, and *La Opinión Pública*—were metatexts of the Hispanic community, with a polyphonic resonance that incorporated directly or indirectly the voices of the common people as well as those of the educated elite who formed the power structure of community politics, business, and society.[28] As one might expect in a traditionally Hispanic patriarchal society further reinforced by Victorian attitudes in vogue at the time, females were not expected to participate actively in journalistic enterprises. Despite the fact that women's cultural identity was publicly defined by men, however, their presence is felt in the rhetoric of the press and their subdued voices are heard in the background.

In 1892, Hispanic editors recognized that they should work cooperatively in support of their own professional interests; thus they founded the Hispano-American Press Association, with membership open to Hispanic journalists in New Mexico, Colorado, Texas, Arizona, and California.[29] With a gradual increase in neomexicano literacy and a corresponding improvement in reader support at the end of the century, a successful newspaper like *La Voz del Pueblo* dared to predict, in 1896, a "brillante porvenir" [brilliant future]:

> Hoy con plena satisfacción, *La Voz del Pueblo* anuncia sin temor de contradicción que el progreso de literatura en Nuevo México está en época de verdadera ascendencia, el pueblo ha llegado á reconocer la utilidad incalculable de la prensa para el desarrollo de un país.

> [Today with complete satisfaction, *La Voz del Pueblo* announces without fear of contradiction that literary progress in New Mexico is in a period of true ascendancy, the people have come to recognize the incalculable usefulness of the press in the development of a country.]

The same January 4, 1896, issue noted that over a hundred of its two hundred resubscribers for the year were "hombres pobres" [poor men] and, considering "la escacez de dinero y los limitados medios de gran parte de los que arriba mencionamos" [the shortage of money and the limited means of most of those mentioned], the editors were doubly gratified by the public's response. It is likely that in the changing and expanding New Mexican economy, local and territorial news became ever more necessary to the livelihood of the average neomexicano; thus newspapers were not only read, but avidly listened to by those who needed to have others read aloud to them. Neomexicano newspapers spoke the people's language, basically using the vernacular without excessive embellishments; by doing so, they appealed to many kinds of readers and also reinforced the maintenance of the Spanish language. More and more neomexicanos began to read newspapers; the semiliterate who could barely afford the few cents they cost used the newspapers to educate themselves, slowly picking out the letters and deciphering news about people and places they had never heard of before.[30] Gradually, the Spanish-language press ended the isolation of centuries and reconnected neomexicanos to the world while also helping them preserve their language and culture. As they became more aware of politics beyond their own towns and cities, neomexicanos also saw the utility of the Spanish-language newspapers in making the collective force of Hispano voices heard as the territory moved closer to statehood. Certainly, without the press and the climate of literary and intellectual expression it promoted, the few printed works by neomexicano authors of the late nineteenth and early twentieth centuries, such as Manuel C. de Baca, Eusebio Chacón, Felipe Maximiliano Chacón, and Benjamin M. Read, would not exist today.

Neomexicano newspapers were the de facto literature of their time, and the contemporary reader who hopes to understand their significance must take into consideration the rhetoric of the medium and the context of the message. Like any literary text, newspaper writing is a form of discourse that reflects the institutions of power in society, and it has both a conscious and unconscious effect on the target audience. As part of a social dialogue in New Mexico, the Spanish-language press functioned within an intricate semiotic system, or what Clifford Geertz has called the "webs of significance" that make up a culture at any given time.[31] Embedded in the newspapers are references to other texts—both popular and learned in their origins—that figure in the neomexicano cultural heritage. In order to interpret the role neomexicano newspapers played and the impact they had as cultural texts we must try to understand them as multi-layered constructs that served different objectives in different ways, reflecting a plurality of voices and subject positions. Rather like archaeological sites, the newspapers must be thought of and studied in their problematical "otherness," as communicative sites where we look for clues to the ongoing narrative of identity and not definitive answers or universal truths about a people. Out of the dialogic discourse of these journals—to borrow a familiar Bakhtinian concept—emerge the contours of neomexicano cultural identity which, as Stuart Hall reminds us in this chapter's epigraph, is "subject to the continuous 'play' of history, culture and power."

I have chosen to limit my study to the years from 1880 to 1920 because they were the most dynamic decades of Spanish-language journalism in the Southwest. These years encompass the period of maximum Anglo immigration and bicultural conflict, and also the period immediately preceding statehood, when the two cultures jockeyed for discursive power over the future of the state. They also take into account the immediate post-statehood period, when political antagonisms continued to destabilize the Hispanic population, both intra- and inter-culturally, and the Anglo community edged closer to achieving majority status. The organization of the following chapters is thus roughly chronological; however, I also hope to convey a sense of the coexistence in the newspapers of neomexicano texts from the traditional (anonymous-oral) as well as the modern (individual-written) expressions of cultural identity. The very nature of printed discourse in neomexicano newspapers, where the active and reflective lives of Spanish-speaking New Mexicans came together and found myriad forms of articulation, conveys the uniqueness of neomexicano voices in a way accomplished by no other preserved documentation of the time. By counterposing chapters that focus on both collective and individual forms of expression, I also want to suggest that behind the varied journalistic discourse of the day—from anonymous poems and political reportage to snippets of social news and substantive editorials—were all kinds of subject positions with different "takes" on cultural identity. From the barely literate shepherd, who struggled to read the local paper (or asked others to do so) in order to combat the loneliness of his existence and, more importantly, to understand the economic trends that threatened the price of wool, to the college-educated political boss, who bought a press to promote his campaign in the tabloids, or the well-to-do señora who monitored social and civic affairs, the Spanish-language newspapers served many needs and functions, not the least of which was ensuring the survival of Spanish as a native, not a foreign, language. The most popular and long-lasting neomexicano newspapers were vehicles of self-empowerment serving a society that had only lately discovered a need to defend itself collectively in print vis-à-vis an *other*, often antagonistic foreign culture. The voices speaking out in Spanish-language newspapers showed differences in race, gender, and class within the neomexicano community. Ultimately, however, it was the educated editors, reporters, and correspondents who decided what was printed as "the news" on a regular basis and who made the idea of receiving news *from* and communicating news *to* the outside world not only a familiar but a necessary reality for the consumer. In recognition of their role in introducing and guiding this technological revolution in neomexicano life, I balance chapters on general themes of importance in the newspapers with those on various individuals whose significance in the domain of journalism was both influential and noteworthy.

I do not pretend to offer here a comprehensive analysis of the Spanish-language press, nor will I address all aspects of neomexicano cultural identity. Rather, I have focused on what I found to be key subjects and individuals in the discursive convergence of these elements of neomexicano life during the period in question. An appendix offers profiles of several other newspaper editors who were well known in their time and deserve to be rescued from anonymity.

Spanish quotations in this book are followed by my own English translations. In quoting from the newspapers, I have opted to conserve the original neomexicano Spanish spelling and punctuation in the interest of authenticity; thus, readers are warned to expect unusual spelling, syntax, and punctuation to which no intrusive *sics* are added. In the bibliography I list all the Spanish-language newspapers as well as other works consulted for this study.

I hope this book will draw attention to the neomexicano newspapers not only as a chronicle of their time and a mirror of their culture, but also as a reaffirmation of the connectedness of all human experience, and particularly of the American experience. For those who think of the western frontier only in the romanticized Anglocentric version of much American historiography, it is time to reconsider what the frontier experience meant from a southwestern Hispanic perspective. For young Latinos today who believe that the mandate to preserve Hispanic cultural identity in the United States began with the political consciousness-raising of the 1960s, it is important to know that earlier generations were struggling toward that goal. For all who believe that the United States and Latin America are divided by the Rio Grande, it should be common knowledge that the Southwest is part of the Hispanic homeland, a cultural and spiritual geography that transcends international borders. In their polyvocal blending of memory, experience, and imagination, the narratives of cultural identity of our diverse Latino communities are becoming integral chapters of a larger American story now being rewritten.

2

Anonymous Voices
in Verse

Aurelio M. Espinosa, whom neomexicanos considered one of their most accomplished native sons, was born in Colorado to New Mexican parents in 1880. He graduated from the University of Colorado, and then earned a doctorate of philosophy from the University of Chicago in the early 1900s. The first scholar to study and document the Spanish language and folklore of New Mexico, Aurelio Espinosa rose from roots in the rural Hispanic villages of the Southwest to become an internationally recognized professor at Stanford University, with many publications on linguistics and folklore to his credit. In retrospect, he stands out as a link between the high culture of American universities and the popular culture of his people, between the Spanish-speaking villages of the Southwest and the Anglo-Germanic traditions of academia. His research in the area of comparative folk literature won him a grant to spend six months in Spain in 1920, where he collected some three hundred samples of traditional folklore, after which he wrote for the *New Mexico Historical Review* of one early discovery: "The reader can imagine the joy and surprise I received when I heard this, my first peninsular Spanish find . . . and recalled the similar, almost identical version that I had heard when a child from the lips of my mother."[1] At a time when Eurocentric universities barely recognized the value of Latin American culture or the history of Hispanics in the United States, Aurelio Espinosa brought the scholarly world's attention to bear on his homeland with this observation: "In the field of popular poetry, New Mexico is a veritable mine of folk-loristic materials, important both as traditional legendary material and as new native product."[2]

The abundance of popular poetry that Espinosa pointed out in the early 1900s reflected the neomexicano folk customs of composing, singing, and reciting verses that had been preserved for centuries despite contacts with Native American and Anglo cultures. These oral verse traditions came to the

Americas with the earliest Spanish colonizers and were preserved with great vitality in northern New Mexico, the most remote outpost of New Spain's northern frontier.[3] In a cultural climate where literacy was the province of the clergy and viceregal officials, ordinary neomexicanos depended on a network of community relationships that valued the verbal arts to transmit knowledge and define their cultural identity. From the custom of passing popular ballads from one generation to the next evolved the habit of extemporizing verses about current events of a political, social, or personal nature. Anyone might be moved to recite or sing verses on any occasion. The best *cantadores*, or popular poet-troubadors, were held in high esteem in the community, and all ages enjoyed hearing them *echar versos* [sing or recite poetry] accompanied by violin or guitar at one of the *tertulias* [social gatherings] that brought friends together and punctuated a routinely harsh and isolated existence. On the long treks to trade their goods, neomexicanos would break the monotony by listening to the humorous songs and spontaneous verse commentaries of the caravan bard.[4]

Aurelio Espinosa had grown up in this environment and was intimately familiar with neomexicano language and culture. His first articles were published while he held his first job teaching Spanish at the University of New Mexico, and in 1911 the New Mexico Historical Society brought out his first major work, *The Spanish Language in New Mexico and Southern Colorado*, which was followed by numerous studies on the Hispanic folklore of the same region. His work was an affirmation of the historical uniqueness and validity of neomexicano culture just as the territory was about to achieve statehood; it was also an implicit denial of Mexican cultural influence at a time when the revolution was gathering momentum and creating unrest along the border. The way Espinosa saw things, neomexicano popular poetry was essentially Spanish not Mexican:

> The *versos* are the philosophy of the people and express in beautiful and rhythmic verse the feelings and ideas of the Spanish people. The real character of the Spanish race may be very well studied in the popular *copla*. In it are expressed its joys and its sorrows, its hopes and its skepticism, its sentiments, feelings and ideas. In short it expresses the life of the people in artistic form.[5]

Espinosa's hispanophilia was not uncommon in academia in the early part of this century, where all things Spanish were considered superior to their Latin American counterparts. But his theories of folklore also reinforced a racial bias shared by many upper-class New Mexicans whose families could trace their ancestors back to the first Hispanic settlers and who thus claimed to be of pure Spanish descent when, in fact, their connections to Mexico and its

Indo-Hispanic peoples were incontrovertible. Although later scholars have criticized Espinosa's interpretations, his fieldwork was groundbreaking for his time and he was widely admired for his efforts to document and preserve neomexicano folk poetry. Ironically, as John R. Chávez has pointed out, "the myth of Spanish New Mexico had its positive side" because it allowed Spanish-speaking New Mexicans to feel proud of their cultural heritage and thus worked against assimilation by the dominant American culture.[6]

While Espinosa was teaching in California, he would write to friends in New Mexico and ask them to send him as many popular *versos* as they could collect.[7] He knew that the cultural landscape of his homeland was changing rapidly and that the customs of the *viejos* would not be practiced the same way by future generations. Cognizant of the need to gather the treasure wherever it could be found, he wrote in 1926: "I confidently believe that it would be difficult to find a New Mexican of Spanish descent who could not recite or sing at least a half dozen of them. The local newspapers printed in Spanish often publish a few of them and a small collection could be compiled from these newspapers alone."[8] As he knew from personal experience, Spanish-language newspapers of the late territorial period were the only public place where popular poetry of the "native product"–type was preserved in print. Some of these poems were authentic folk poems widely known in the Hispano community, but most of them were composed topically in the popular mode by native poets who, for a variety of reasons, preferred to remain anonymous.[9]

Unlike their Anglo and bilingual counterparts, Spanish-language newspapers published anonymous poetry with frequency and regularity, some doing so in every issue. Considered from various stylistic and thematic perspectives, this poetry functions as a kind of popular commentary on life at the time. Originally a form of discourse composed by and for the neomexicano community, it became increasingly politicized and dialogic with the arrival of Anglos in New Mexico.[10] An early example can be found in *El Clarín Mejicano* (August 10, 1873), published in Santa Fe, in a piece entitled "La influencia de los Greenbacks" [The Influence of Greenbacks]; this anonymous poem acknowledges with satiric and prophetic good humor the power of American currency in the economy of post–Civil War New Mexico, concluding,

| Sin dinero no es nada | [Without money, neither the wise man |
| Ni el sabio, ni el literato | Nor the well-read is worth anything.] |

Using traditional forms of poetry, neomexicanos could affirm their own culture and respond to the new culture in their midst in a medium that was both highly flexible and uniquely expressive. The public nature of the burgeoning press in Spanish, which coincided with a growing number of intercultural relationships in territorial society, increased the likelihood that Spanish-speaking Anglos would read it as well.

In the cultural dialectic of a society in transition, the anonymous poetry in neomexicano newspapers cannot simply be dismissed as "low" or "mass" culture. According to Antonio Gramsci, a "broader history of culture" must include the "common sense" of popular folklore that does not belong to any one class but is "the document of its historical reality."[11] Historians and literary critics have tended to leave the study of popular folklore to anthropologists and linguists, but it is clear from the example of neomexicano newspapers that the literate reader of the time appreciated anonymous, folk-style verse as much as anyone. It would be folly to think that the acquisition of literacy somehow obliterated the taste for the popular medium; to the contrary, as an authentic form of indigenous expression, it was intentionally used by the press to engage its audience and to represent its most active complaints and concerns. In the case of the American Southwest in general, where printed materials in the nineteenth century rarely conveyed Hispanic viewpoints,[12] scholars have much to learn from popular poetry. As the tejano scholar Américo Paredes, reminds us, some ballads tell a truer story than official chronicles.[13]

For purposes of definition and example, I would like to discuss four types of popular poetry found in neomexicano newspapers: (1) adversary-style political verse, (2) *corrido*-style narrative verse, (3) *canción*-style lyric verse, and (4) the work of one prolific anonymous writer in the 1890s. I will focus here on the period from 1880 to 1900, which was especially rich in published poetry. The relationship between popular poetry and historical events in many of these examples will help bring to the fore the anonymous voices of neomexicanos in modes of expression that are integral to their cultural identity.

Adversary-Style Political Verse

This style of popular poetry, generally in the traditional octosyllabic meter, dominated many pages of neomexicano territorial newspapers, especially in more politically engaged cities like as Santa Fe, Las Vegas, Las Cruces, and Albuquerque. It was a type of verse guaranteed to draw reader attention. Papers competed in their verse battles in much the same way two frontier ballad singers might have disputed the title of local *maestro*.[14] What the poems lacked in originality or artistry they made up for in their enthusiasm for satiric insult. Considering that politics and the verbal arts were both favorite pastimes among neomexicanos, a political campaign made the poetic juices flow and in this context brevity was not considered the soul of wit.

Two long political poems published within a week of each other in major northern New Mexico newspapers in 1890 offer an example of this type of popular verbal sparring in the acerbic campaign spirit of the time. Antonio Joseph, a Taos-born Democrat who had first been elected as New Mexico's territorial delegate to Congress in 1884, was seeking reelection for the fourth time. He had the backing of the influential paper *La Voz del Pueblo* (recently moved from Santa Fe to Las Vegas), whereas his Republican opponent for the second time, Mariano S. Otero, a prominent banker and one of the wealthiest men in the territory, was supported by the more conservative *El Nuevo Mexicano* (Santa Fe).[15] The following poem in support of Antonio Joseph, published in October 1890, plays to the contentious political atmosphere of the time, aiming not to *portray* reality so much as to *create* a climate of victory for the candidate with combative imagery typical of this "down-and-dirty" style of adversarial verse. In this case, both Joseph and Otero were native political bosses and purported associates of the notorious Santa Fe Ring—a group of Anglo and Hispanic businessmen whose investment schemes and manipulation of the justice system, usually at the expense of the poor Hispanos, brought them wealth and power.[16] The poem quoted below accuses Otero of trying to buy votes. Only the last half of the long, anonymous composition is quoted here:

Santa Fé, gallardo y serio	[Santa Fe, genteel and serious,
Dá la muerte al invasor,	Deals the invader a deadly blow,
Y hace que caiga el imperio	And causes his empire to fall
Dándole a Joseph honor.	Giving the honors to Joseph.
San Miguél con harto brío	San Miguel with great force
Y segura gentileza	And sure-footed grace
Del opulento caudillo	Smashes the wealthy boss
Aplastará la cabeza.	With a blow to the head.
San Juan, con sus armas blancas	San Juan, with its cold steel
De defensa y dignidad,	Ready to defend with dignity,
Va quebrando las palancas	Tears down fortifications
Dando al pueblo libertad.	And liberates the people.
Sierra, con ufano grito	Sierra, with a proud shout,
Por Joseph sus voces dá	Rallies support for Joseph
A pesar que Marianito,	Despite the money
Sus monedas gastará.	That Marianito spends.

Socorro, con voz valiente	Socorro, with a valiant voice,
Pone en hombros el pendon,	Shoulders the banner,
Y con razon suficiente	And rightly calls
Llama á Joseph campeon.	Joseph a champion.
Taos, á su turno vuela	Taos quickly responds,
Dando á Joseph admision,	Helping Joseph to win
Porque en verdad no recela	Because it really does not fear
Del otro la oposicion.	Opposition from the other side.
Valencia, descuartizado	Valencia, carved into quarters,
Promete dar mayoría	Promises the majority
Al genuino delegado	For the genuine delegate
De la fiel Democracía.[17]	Of the Democratic party.]

A typical response from the Republican side, quoted in part below, employs the traditional rhymed *décima* form—widely used in New Mexico at the time—and is found in *El Nuevo Mexicano*, also in October 1890. In spite of the vigorous attack that Otero partisans launched to unseat the incumbent, Antonio Joseph won reelection. The opposition's poem tried to undermine Joseph's strength by saying that, contrary to his campaign claim to defend neomexicanos, he intended to give behind-the-scenes support to a bill proposed in Congress that would deny jobs and votes to non-English speakers. The anonymous author appeals to the Hispano's strong sense of ethnic loyalty by drawing attention to the candidate's Portuguese background and accusing him of not respecting the neomexicano's language and culture. The sarcasm and insults were typical of similar campaign poems:

Este justo parangon	[This paragon of the law
Que tanto presume el taco	Who presumes to be so great
Se porta como un bellaco	Is conducting himself like a fool
Y tiene la pretencion	And he has the intention
De quitar toda ocasion	Of taking away the right
De ser empleado y jurado	To be employed or on a jury
A todo el que no ha logrado	From anyone who has not
El inglés aprender bien,	Learned English well,
Sin hacer caso de quien	Without paying any heed
Tanto bien le ha procurado.	To those who have voted him in.
. . . .	. . . .
¡Que bonito delegado	What a lovely delegate
Tenemos en el congreso!	We have in Congress!
Un hombre de tanto seso	A man with so many brains

Que ni un burro le ha ganado!	That not even a burro beats him!
Por esta vez ha logrado	But this time he has managed
Calumniarnos de manera	To slander us to the point that
Que el congreso si quisiera	Congress might be willing
Este acto pasaría,	To pass this act,
Y este pueblo quedaría	And the people would be
Sin derecho que valiera.	Deprived of their rights.
. . . .	. . . .
Joseph, como portugues,	Joseph, being Portuguese,
Aborrece el castellano,	Hates the Spanish language
Y quiere que el mejicano	And wants Mexicans
No hable ya mas que el ingles.	To speak only English.
La verdad de este caso es	The truth is that
Que este maldito procura	This no-good fellow
Todo aquello que, sin duda,	Will try anything
Nos acarrea perjuicio,	To cause us harm
Y lo hace solo por vicio	And he does it because he wants
De hacernos mal con usura.[18]	To profit from our injury.]

Neither one of these poems is of any transcendental literary value, nor should their accusations be mistaken for the truth in all cases. Culturally, however, they reflect the Hispanic penchant for poetic sparring and the passion for politics that characterized the Spanish-speaking community after the American invasion. A tradition of cultivating the verbal arts, combined with the competition for power in a volatile socioeconomic climate, bred a division within the Hispanic political community that may have been good for selling newspapers, but undermined neomexicanos' ability to stand united as an ethnic group. In this particular contest between powerful bosses with well-entrenched interests on each side, a new populist party (the United People's Party) was the beneficiary and it managed to grab a significant, if short-lived, foothold in territorial politics.

Another typical example of adversary-style verse was the diatribe launched against *La Unión de Albuquerque* by its competitor, *La Opinión Pública,* in August 1892, when the *Unión's* editor, Augustín Barón, called "El Padre Trompo," printed a libelous attack on the editor of the *Opinión,* Pedro García de la Lama. The amount of space the *Unión* devoted to this dispute is not known, as only one issue survives, but if the *Opinión* responses are indicative, it was a major feature for several months, both in prose and verse. *La Opinión Pública* of August 27, 1892, printed a long front-page poem accompanied by a crude drawing of the priest-editor Barón looking like a nefarious carpetbagger. (Barón was a non-native, non-Anglo.) One stanza will suffice to convey the tenor of this verbal battle:

A ese extraño advenedizo	[That strange newcomer
de Italia o del Turquestán;	From Italy or Turkestan,
que envuelto en una sotana	Who landed in this Territory
negra como el mismo mal,	Wrapped in a cassock
arribó a este Territorio	Black as evil itself,
con el fin, es la verdad,	Whose motive, in truth,
de desplumar a sus neófitos	Is to fleece his followers
tomando como antifaz	Wearing a disguise,
y careta de mentira	The better to fool them,
para mejor engañar,	And the deceiving mask
el grande nombre de Dios,	Of God's great name,
el púlpito y el Misal:	The pulpit and the missal:
a ese infeliz Padre Trompo	Does that old Padre Trompo,
de cuerpo de orangután,	With his orangutan's body
de cabeza de lechuza	Head of an owl
y de instintos de chacal:	And jackal's instincts,
¿qué importa, preguntamos,	Care, we may ask,
la política de acá,	About politics here?
que se eleve ó caiga Pedro	Whether Pedro rises or falls,
y que triunfe ó pierda Juan,	Or Juan wins or loses?
si lo que él sólo pretende	If his only intention
es engullir y medrar?	Is to devour and prosper?]

In this poem, as in the one directed against Antonio Joseph, there is a strong appeal to neomexicano clannishness, with the implication that newcomers (not including recent immigrants from Mexico who were ethnically related) should not be trusted. Both poems appeal to an attitude of Hispano ethnocentrism that was probably exacerbated by their finding themselves on the cultural defensive in territorial society, despite holding a numerical majority. Neomexicanos had lived with foreigners in their midst for decades, but the increasing numbers and power of Anglos and the economic benefits of holding office in the territory turned politics into a cutthroat business. When it came specifically to relationships with Anglos, however—insofar as the press reported them—Hispanos expressed no strong xenophobia or ethnic chauvinism; indeed, evidence in the press indicates that cultural accommodation was more the rule than the exception between neomexicanos and Anglos, despite ongoing conflicts over land, language, religion, education, and Anglo racial prejudice that forced most neomexicanos into a defensive and subordinate position. From the perspective of the Hispanic middle and upper classes, the prospect of statehood and full American citizenship was a desirable objective that mitigated against overt hostility. Among the less privileged who had to fight the land-grabbers and struggle to survive in the new cash-based economy, political allegiance came down to local alliances, and where injustices were felt, resistance was more pronounced. One is tempted to say that affirmation or resistance to Anglo invasion was class-based, but evidence in the newspapers indicates that intercultural relationships were not so neatly polarized.

As an ethnic group that had been the dominant native population until the invasion of 1846, Hispanic New Mexicans faced a complex and difficult psychological adjustment for which centuries of sporadic interaction with neighboring Indian populations did not prepare them. Contact with Anglo culture was entirely different. In spite of numerous conflict situations, interethnic strife was effectively submerged by party politics and by economic alliances across ethnic lines because, as Carolyn Zeleny wrote over fifty years ago, "large numbers of the Spanish-Americans were incorporated into the political spoils system which the Santa Fe Ring and its political descendants controlled."[19]

As the stakes for election to congressional delegate and representative territorial posts rose, physical and verbal violence also escalated to the point that assaults and libel suits became common.[20] Where politics was concerned, journalism had a desperado-like quality: if you could get away with it, it was okay. One must also take into account a public thirst for controversy that encouraged yellow journalism; detailed reporting of political skirmishes ensured a faithful readership just as it did in other parts of the country. Since aggressiveness was a frontier way of life, it should not be surprising that editorial ethics were as loose as they were, despite many calls for reform within the professional ranks.

Not all editors relished the anonymous backbiting and feuding for which no one could be held accountable. One of several articles against this appeared during election week in 1890, when Joseph and Otero were concluding their campaigns. Published by *La Voz del Pueblo* (Las Vegas) on November 8, 1890, it reads in part:

> El anónimo, es asesino y ladrón, el más ruin y cobarde de todos los ladrones y asesinos, ataca de lejos, desde donde no puede ser conocido ni atacado: roba con ganzúa, cuando todos duermen: insulta en la sombra para que no le vean el rostro; el anónimo es el único criminal que puede en todos los casos, celebrar su odioso triunfo, antes de cometer la vil acción.

> [The one who writes anonymously is an assassin and thief, the lowest and most cowardly of all thieves and assassins. He attacks from afar, from where he cannot be recognized or attacked himself. He robs with a picklock when everyone is sleeping. He insults from the shadows so his face cannot be seen. The anonymous writer is the only criminal who can in all cases celebrate his odious triumph before committing the vile act.]

The adversary-style of anonymous verse was under fire as malicious and dishonorable even as it flourished. In one sense, it contributed to the survival of a folk tradition, but its anonymity also became a cloak for partisan politics and rhetorical invective rather than an expression of the collective folk spirit. Its most avid readers, after all, were those with vested interests for whom politics spelled potential loss or gain. The illiterate neomexicano probably heard similar verses or composed a few himself, but he was not the political junkie that avidly bought the newspapers. Despite the fact that it gave a bad name to anonymous versifying, the custom of publishing adversarial political poems would continue until the early 1900s, when codes were established by press associations to curtail yellow journalism.[21]

Corrido-Style Narrative Verse

Of all the anonymous verse forms found in New Mexico, the *corrido* is the closest to the heroic epic of the Spanish Middle Ages. The name comes from the verb *correr*, meaning to run or to flow: the *corrido* tells a story, quickly, dramatically, and without adornment. It can be epic, lyric, or narrative, but most typically it is inspired by something tragic involving a well-known person; there were many, for example, inspired by the Mexican Revolution of 1910.[22] Américo Paredes, who brought the tejano *corrido* of Gregorio Cortés to public attention, noted that this type of popular poem, like earlier frontier ballads in Spain, flourished in small, self-contained communities vitally concerned with their own immediate survival.[23] The *corrido* probably originated in Mexico and along the lower Rio Grande Valley in the early nineteenth century, where border conflict prior to the Mexican American War stimulated its development. It later moved into New Mexico, where there was already a tradition of singing *romances*, *coplas*, and *décimas*, and became a widely used verse form there until about the 1930s. From today's vantage point it appears less and less certain that the old *corridos*, even the most oft-recited ones, will be preserved for posterity. Oral entertainment has given way to visual technology for which the future is more compelling than the past. Thus, the *corridos* found in Spanish-language newspapers deserve notice for their value as literary and historical testimony that might otherwise not have survived.

Corridos were published in neomexicano newspapers less frequently than other anonymous verse forms; yet they sometimes appeared when popular sentiment was sufficiently aroused. The characteristic content and structure of the *corrido* are: a memorable event of heroic proportions; a call to witness the event; the event's definition and description; and a final farewell. An octosyllabic metrical form is favored for the narrative, although some flexibility is allowed.

One particularly shocking event that provoked several *corrido*-style responses in the newspapers was the murder of Faustino Ortiz, a Santa Fe policeman whose mutilated body was discovered on March 28, 1890, in the mountains near the city, three weeks after his disappearance. Violent and brutal crimes were common at the time and were reported regularly in the press, but only a few were accompanied by published *corridos*, generally submitted anonymously by friends or relatives who were poets in spirit if not in artistry. No fewer than three *corridos* of protest were published between April and September 1890 relating to the Ortiz crime, which was not solved until 1897.[24] One of them is blended with the traditional *décima* format, in which each consecutive line of the initial quatrain concludes one of the four ten-line stanzas that follow. It was enclosed in a letter to Santa Fe's *La Voz del Pueblo* and signed "Un amigo de Faustin Ortiz." Its faulty spelling, lexical poverty, and graphic descriptions of brutality betray the simplicity of the author's background. In the body of the poem the narration of the crime is interspersed with ambivalent feelings of Christian forgiveness, on one hand, and an urge for revenge, on the other. Appealing to the popular Hispanic legend of the holy child of Atocha, it begins and ends as follows:

I

Santo Niñito de Atocha,
descubre al cruel asesino,
perdonadle mi señor,
y dadle Gloria aunque indigno.

. . . .

[Holy Infant of Atocha,
Find the cruel assassin,
May the Lord pardon him,
And give him Glory undeserved.

. . . .

III

Año de mil ochocientos,
noventa si hablo con tino
el día primero de Marzo
desapareció Faustino
se hisieron las dilijencias
por ver si se allaba vivo
cuando milagrosamente
descubrió su cuerpo un niño
hallando asesinado
el dia veintiocho del mismo
y yo siempre arrodillado
pidiendote Santo Niño
para que sea castigado
descubre al cruel asesino.

. . . .

In the year eighteen hundred
ninety if I remember well
the first day of March
Faustino disappeared
investigations were made
to see if he was still alive
when miraculously on
the twenty-eighth of that month
a child discovered his body
which had been assassinated
and I am here on my knees
asking you, Holy Child,
to find the cruel assassin
so he can be punished.

. . . .

V

¡oh! cual serian los conflictos	oh! how my friend Ortiz Faustino
de mi amigo Ortiz Faustino	must have suffered
al ver que aquel asesino	to see that assassin
con puñales lo estocaba	stabbing him with a blade
y tal vez con un martillo	and perhaps he used a hammer
le deshizo las quijadas	to crush his jaw
sus dentaduras quebradas	break his teeth
y su lengua como un higo	and turn his tongue into a fig
sus narizes y sus ojos	his nose and eyes
despedasados lo mismo	destroyed the same way
su cabeza hecha zecinas	his head broken to cinders
oh Dios lo demas no digo	oh Lord I won't say more
Conduelete por su muerte	Have pity for his death
y por el gran sacrificio	and for his great sacrifice
perdonadle sus pecados	pardon his sins and
y dadle gloria aunque indigno.[25]	give him glory he may not merit.]

Several *corridos* can be found in the press that were written by youthful would-be poets. In *La Revista de Taos* (July 10, 1902), for example, there is a long, anonymous poem composed by a fourteen-year-old in memory of a nineteen-year-old stranger in town who took his own life without anyone knowing why. The editor of the paper said he was publishing the verses to encourage the young author. What moves today's reader is not the awkward style but the profound sorrow and dismay conveyed by the youngster, who tries to gather a personal lesson from the tragedy. The poem ends this way:

A! que caso terrible	[Oh! what a terrible thing
es este que ha pasado.	has taken place.
Que este desgraciado joven	That this poor young man
la vida se haya quitado.	took his own life.
Es caso muy admirable	It's a remarkable thing
el que ha pasado nuevamente,	that has just occurred
Y nos servira de esperiencia	And it will be a lesson
para todos los vivientes.	to all the living.
Cuando se nos va a olvidar	When we tend to forget
lo que ha pasado,	what has happened,
Nuevamente que este	Just think once again
joven desgraciado	about this poor fellow
En el condado de Taos	Who took his own life
la vida se halla quitado.	in Taos County.

Dios les de consolacion
a todos sus parientes,
Y nos guie por buen camino
a todos los vivientes.

May God give consolation
to all his relatives,
And guide all us survivors
along the path of goodness.]

There were many similar verses in the newspapers in honor of a deceased family member—some of them signed, some not; some written by a third party at the request of one less poetically inclined; but all of them remembering ordinary folk, not legendary heroes, as epic-style *corridos* commonly do.[26] Their presence in the paper confirms that average neomexicanos were reading the papers and using them to inscribe their personal identity in new ways, perhaps understanding the print medium as a prestigious way to enhance the public tribute that a traditional poem, sung among friends and family, inherently intended. The straightforward quality of these poems about death and the way in which personal grief is shared with the community reflect how Hispanic cultures have traditionally confronted this experience more openly. If frontier violence tended to shorten lives, these poems achieved the brief immortality of remembrance on the printed page.

Cancion-Style Lyric Verse

Arthur L. Campa, a Mexican-born scholar writing in the generation after Aurelio Espinosa, explained that "a *canción* may appear in any verse-form that strikes the composer's fancy, and while the theme may be lyrical for the most part, there is a long range of subjects that may be treated."[27] He draws a distinction between genuine *canciones* "which show real folk invention" and "those which are definitely *cultos.*" Guidelines for distinguishing between the two are not rigid, but elements such as vocabulary, phraseology, and tone serve as clues.

True folk *canciones* that came to life out of popular traditions and were shaped by nameless voices over generations are not likely to be found in the newspapers. Some of them originated in Mexico, and others were native to New Mexico. These lyrical ballads, about love, nature, religious faith, family, and the homeland, were generally sung to accompaniment by violin or guitar at the many dances and social events that were an integral part of Hispanic life both before and after the Anglos arrived. According to Campa:

> Perhaps no other form of folklore so well expresses the true spirit
> of a race as the folksong. The words give the sentiment; the music
> adds the feeling. Around the house, at work, in social gatherings,
> may be heard strains of the *canción popular*. It is a medium
> through which the individual gives vent to the outpouring of his
> soul![28]

31

Those who submitted verses to the papers were generally individuals who aspired to imitate the spirit of folk poetry and may have had other personal reasons for sharing their *canciones*, either signed or anonymous. A few of these poems were quite good, but far too many were the work of amateurs whose ego was much bigger than their poetic talent. The complaints of neomexicano editors, inundated by the work of would-be poets, are reminiscent of the satiric comments of seventeenth-century Spanish writers like Cervantes or Lope de Vega; verse writing and reciting in both eras was such a popular pastime that *pobres* and *ricos*, old and young, would give it a try whenever the spirit moved them. Humorous articles and counter-verses were published in the papers, pleading for a stop to amateur submissions. One such article in the Santa Fe paper, *La Aurora*, published in 1884 under the title "Tijereteo: remedios para la versomanía"[29] [Scissor-snipping: remedies for verse fever], ended with the plea, "Have pity on the public!" Another newspaper in Socorro printed the following announcement in gentle mockery of a naive aspiring author:

Las estampillas del poeta

Un individuo nos escribe diciendo que nos remite unos "bersos" y diez centavos en estampillas postales como recompensa de nuestros servicios al publicar su composición. No dice el lugar de donde escribe ni firma los "bersos," por cuyo motivo, y no deseando nosotros aprovecharnos de los laureles que pudiera conquistar el incógnito poeta con los partos de su numen, asi como porque no acostumbramos cobrar por inserciones de esa clase, no damos cabida en nuestras columnas a la mencionada producción de ese "bate", que si nos mandara su nombre le devolveríamos sus estampillas.[30]

[The Poet's Stamps

An individual has written and sent us some "berses" and ten cents in postage stamps to cover our expenses for publishing his composition. He doesn't say where he's from, nor does he sign his "berses," and since we don't want to benefit by the laurels that this unknown poet might earn with the fruits of his genius, and since we aren't accustomed to charging for insertions of this type, we will not publish the work of this "boet." If he will send us his name we'll return his stamps.]

Many over-the-transom verses were similarly rejected by editors who had little patience with what one of them called "una gentil manía" [a nice little mania].[31]

Some of the more interesting anonymous *canciones* from Spanish-language newspapers are printed below to give an idea of the variety of inspiration and subject matter. Each one attests in a different way to fundamental aspects of the neomexicano cultural identity and thus portrays common experience. A number of them allude to the influence of other Hispanic literatures and, in their intertextuality, suggest the density of cultural traditions and the pen of a more educated author.

The purity of feeling in the following simple *canción*, published in *La Crónica del Río Colorado* in 1882, recalls Spanish lyric balladry in its expression of faith in nature as a refuge for the lonely. The fact that it conveys the perspective of a farmgirl who feels empowered and liberated by an unfettered contact with nature is an intriguing aspect of this otherwise traditional-style folk song:

Canto de una joven campesina	**[Song of a young farm girl**
Cuando el sol brilla	When the sun shines
No sé lo que es miedo	I don't know what fear is,
Libre avecilla,	Free as a little bird,
Cantar yo puedo.	I can sing my song.
La selva hojosa	The leafy forest
No me da espanto	Does not scare me
Y aunque medrosa	And despite my timidity
Me anima el canto.	Song heartens me.
Me anima el brillo	I'm heartened by the rays
Que el sol derrama,	That the sun sheds
Y el pajarillo	And by the little bird
Que está en la rama.	Sitting on the bough.
Me anima el cielo	I'm heartened by the sky
Que luz da al día	That brightens the day
Del ave el vuelo	By the flight of the bird
La sombra mía.	And by my own shadow.
Y hasta el gemido	And even by the moan
De la tojosa	Of the wild dove
Cuando en su nido	When she sings
Canta llorosa . . .	Plaintively in her nest . . .
Cuando el sol brilla	When the sun shines
No sé que es miedo	I don't know what fear is,
Libre avecilla	Free as a little bird
Cantar yo puedo.[32]	I can sing my song.]

The following *plegaria*—or prayer—modeled after the popular *canción "a lo divino"*, but more cultured in vocabulary and phraseology, shows the intimate relationship between Hispanics and Catholicism. It also reveals, at the end of the third stanza, the author's familiarity with Gustavo Adolfo Bécquer, the most popular of all nineteenth-century Spanish poets. Many poems with a spirit of religious veneration similar to this one, published in Santa Fe in 1884, can be found in the neomexicano press:

A la Virgen

Ya es tiempo, virgen santa,
Que mi harpa corrompida
Plegaria enternecida
Consagre á tu loor:
Ya es tiempo que abandone
Los goces terrenales,
Por otros celestiales
Que espero de tu amor.
Yo sé que eres muy buena,
Muy noble y generosa;
Yo sé que eres piadosa
Con el que acude á tí;
Por eso arrepentido
De todos mis pecados
Tus célicos cuidados
Imploro para mí.

¡Oh virgen sacrosanta
Del mundo redentora!
Tu la única señora
De cielo, tierra y mar;
Escucha de tu siervo
Las cantigas sencillas
Que absorto y de rodillas

Murmura ante tu altar.

Si mi alma fué perversa,
Profana, escandalosa
Si en noche tenebrosa
Pasé mi juventud,
Yo quiero que el ocaso
De mi existencia oscura
Sea puro como es pura
La faz de la virtud.

Con toda la confianza
Del inocente niño,
Te entrego mi cariño

[To the Virgin

It is time, holy virgin,
That my aged harp
Dedicate this prayer
Of devotion to you:
It is time for me to abandon
The pleasures of this world
For others more heavenly
That I aspire to through your love.
I know of your goodness,
Great nobility and generosity;
I know of your pity
For one who turns to you;
Thus in true repentance
For all my sins
I implore for myself
Your heavenly protection.

Oh blessed virgin!
Redeemer of the world!
You the only queen
Of heaven, earth and sea;
Listen to the simple songs
Of your servant
Who in wonder and on his
        knees
Murmurs before your altar.

If my soul has been perverse,
Profane, or scandalous,
If I spent my youth
In the shadows of the night,
I want the evening
Of my dark existence
To be as pure
As the face of virtue.

With the confidence
Of an innocent child
I give you my love,

Mi corazon y fé;	My heart and my faith;
De nuestro triste mundo	I will distance myself,
De todo vale nada	Forever, beloved mother,
Por siempre, madre amada,	From this sad world
Lejísimo estaré.	That has no worth.
Suplícote tan solo,	I only beg you,
Castísima María,	Purest Mary,
Que dés al alma mía	That you give my soul
Tu santa proteccion.	Your blessed protection.
Afin que por mí rezo	And thus I pray
De lágrimas bañado	Bathed in tears
[not legible]	
Me otorgue su perdon.[33]	That you give me your pardon.]

Another *canción,* in traditional octosyllabic quatrains, refers to the way some young Spanish speakers were beginning to adopt aspects of Anglo culture in the late territorial period. Many such satiric poems mocked the youthful fashion trend of the time that often led to inept self-expression in an alien language. With a lighthearted but clear rebuke, this poem calls for ethnic pride and loyalty. Note how the male speaker chides his "linda paisana" [pretty native girl] for using English, perhaps in anticipation of finding an Anglo suitor. Given the fact that intermarriage between neomexicanas and Anglos had existed in New Mexico since the early 1800s, the poem has a realistic ring to it. There is little doubt that young people of both sexes were among the first to be lured by "foreign" modes of speech and conduct, and the leap from the betrayal of language to the abandonment of blood ties seemed increasingly plausible and threatening to the Hispanic community:

Mi gusto	[**My preference**
No me hables ¡por Dios! así . . .	Good heavens! Don't talk like that! . . .
¿Por qué me hablas al revés?	Why talk to me all backwards?
Di con tu boquita "sí";	With your little mouth, say "sí";
Pero no me digas "yes."	But don't tell me "yes."
Si no quieres verme mudo,	If you don't want me to be silent,
Saluda "¿cómo estás tú?"	Say "¿cómo estás tú?
Yo no entiendo tu saludo	I don't understand your greeting
"Good morning, how do do?"	"Good morning, how do you you do?"

¡No por Dios! linda paisana,	Good gracious, no! lovely paisana,
No desprecies nuestra lengua,	Don't disdain our language,
Sería en ti mal gusto y mengua	It would be bad taste and foolish
Querer ser "americana."	To try to be "Americanized."
Que yo, a las mexicanitas,	To me, the Mexican girls
Las aprecio muy de veras;	Are what I like the best;
Trigueñas o morenitas	Darkskinned or darkhaired,
Me gustan más que las hueras.[34]	I like them better than blonds.]

As Luis Leal has pointed out, the use of Spanish and English is found in numerous popular poems throughout the Southwest in the transition period of 1848–1910, anticipating a rhetorical device that would be very important in later Chicano poetry.[35] In the Spanish-language newspapers in New Mexico, however, such examples constituted only a small number of the poems published, which indicated that Spanish was still the primary vehicle of communication rather than a mix of the two languages.

The next anonymous *canción*, in ten-syllable meter, appears more *culto* than its topic would initially suggest. Perhaps its author knew the Spanish poet José de Espronceda and the "outcast" poems he wrote in the romantic mold. In New Mexico, where the outlaw was a real not a romantic figure, this poem from *La Voz del Pueblo* in 1893 has more historical validity:

El bandido	**[The bandit**
Tantos males los hombres me han hecho	Men have done me such ill
Que he perdido la fe y la esperanza;	That I've lost all faith and hope;
He jurado exterminio y venganza,	I've sworn to exterminate and avenge
Y mi voto fatal cumpliré.	And I'll keep my fateful vow.
Despreciado del género humano	Disdained by the human race,
El encono desgarra mi pecho	Malevolence fills my breast
Y por eso bandido me he hecho	And so I've become a bandit
Respirando venganza y rencor.	Breathing vengeance and rancor.
Soy el rey del desierto apartado,	I'm king of the lonely desert,
Mi puñal ejecuta sus leyes,	My knife administers its laws,

Soy más grande que todos los reyes Y la tierra me ve con pavor.	I am the greatest of all kings, Everyone looks at me with fright.
Nunca tiembla el puñal en mi mano Para herir a la víctima inerte, Antes bien me recreo en su muerte	My knife never trembles When it wounds its victim, Rather, I take pleasure in his death
Y me gozo al mirarla expirar.	And enjoy watching him expire.
Cuando ruge con ímpetu el trueno Y retiembla la tierra de espanto, Sólo se oye en las rocas mi canto,	When the thunder roars loudly And the earth shakes in fear, Only my song is heard in the hills
Y á mis pies viene el rayo á morir.	And lightning dies at my feet.
De cien bravos se forma mi banda	A hundred brave men in my gang
Y obedecen mi altiva mirada, Solo allá en mi cabaña apartada, Aparece mi rostro feroz.[36]	Obey my haughty gaze, Alone and in my desert cabin, I show my fierce countenance.]

Another *canción*, in octosyllabic rhymed verse, expresses the connection between Hispanic identity and the city of Santa Fe, the oldest capital city in the country. In the 1880s and 1890s numerous bills were introduced unsuccessfully in the territorial legislature, aimed at transferring the seat of government to the more modern city of Albuquerque on the new railroad line where business interests stood to profit.[37] The force of history and the will of the people defended Santa Fe, as pledged in this poem from 1891 of which only four stanzas are reproduced here:

A Santa Fe

Villa gentil tan amada,
De tan excelsa memoria,
Ninguna en antigua historia
Puede serte comparada;
Del indígena habitada
Cuando el español llegó
Que por siglos gobernó
La patria así conquistada;
Por nadie será humillada
La que el tiempo consagra.

[To Santa Fe

Exquisite and beloved city,
Of such noble memory,
None in ancient history
Can be compared to you;
Inhabited by indigenous people
When the Spanish arrived
And governed for centuries,
Thus conquering the fatherland;
No one will humiliate
What time has consecrated.

Has sido la capital,	You have been the capital,
Cabeza del territorio,	Head of the territory,
Ridículo e irrisorio	It would be ridiculous
Es querértela quitar;	To want to change this;
Tu puedes manifestar	You can prove
Que tienes la preeminencia,	Your preeminence
Y del pueblo la conciencia	And the people's awareness
Jamás eso permitiera;	Will never permit it.
Por derecho y conveniencia	By right and by agreement
Es Santa Fé la primera.	Santa Fe is the first.
Algunos legisladores	Some legislators,
Por vil lucro o por rencor,	Out of greed or resentment,
Pretenden que está mejor	Are trying to justify
Inmolarte a sus furores;	Sacrificing you to their will;
No temas, pues los favores	Do not worry, the people's
Del pueblo están de tu parte,	Sentiment is on your side,
Y el enemigo dañarte	And the enemy cannot harm you
No lo podrá aunque lo quiera,	Even though he may try,
Pues que reza tu estandarte	Since your banner proclaims
Que Santa Fé es la primera.	That Santa Fe is the first.
España te prefirió	Spain selected you
Como asiento de gobierno	As the seat of government,
México, igualmente cuerdo,	Mexico, equally wise,
Lo mismo ratificó;	Ratified the same;
Igual cosa decretó	So decreed in like measure
El Gobierno americano	The American government
Confirmando por su mano,	Confirming by its signature
Y dejándote en la esfera,	And leaving it to be
Que proclama cotidiano	Proclaimed daily
Que Santa Fé es la primera.[38]	That Santa Fe is the first.]

The Poetry of X.X.X.

Between 1893 and 1900, fifteen poems and a number of verse translations from English and French literature appeared in *El Nuevo Mexicano* that were signed simply "X.X.X."[39] Judging from the artistic quality of these poems and the similarities among them, X.X.X. was probably a single individual of considerable knowledge and talent who was on the paper's editorial staff. The fact that he chose not to sign his work may be explained by his professional status, by his preference for the freedom that anonymity offers, or by his identification with the concerns of the citizenry at large. It seems evident that he enjoyed being the people's bard.

Unlike the typical bard, however, X.X.X. was literate and sophisticated, a poet and translator[40] with an outlook that transcended local affairs. Many of his verses were inspired by Washington politics, the Spanish-American War, and the Boer War in Africa. In a modern context, X.X.X. was a poet of the New Mexican people in relationship to the world at large. The spirit of his poetry offers testimony to the end of an era of isolation for New Mexico and the beginning of a larger collective profile and responsibility.

Notwithstanding his cosmopolitan concerns, X.X.X. consistently chose to use the traditional forms of Spanish balladry, almost exclusively the octosyllable in quatrains or *décimas*. His regard for the masterworks of popular verse can be seen, for example, in a gloss that he wrote to the famous *redondilla* by the Spanish poet, Luis de Góngora ("Aprended, flores, de mi"),[41] and in his "Coplas nuevas de don Simón," a reworking of a familiar New Mexican folksong.[42]

The range of X.X.X.'s interests is vast, from environmental crisis in "Versos al agua, a propósito de la sequía"[43] [Verses to water, inspired by the drought] to unsolved crime in "Sobre la muerte del Coronel Fountain" [On the death of Colonel Fountain].[44] What gives unity to his themes is a concern with contemporary topics that affect the people of his homeland. In one poem, he dramatizes the injustice of the federal program to educate Indians that in fact Anglicizes them and abandons them as misfits among their own people.[45] Another poem, after Congress once again denied New Mexico's petition for statehood in 1898, expresses the collective popular sentiment that the territory was like a beggar, unjustly turned away from the rich man's door over the issue of free silver, rejected in the East. The introductory quatrain of this *décima* conveys the sense of repeated rejection that New Mexicans had come to expect:

Lo de siempre

No quiso el Tio Samuel
Admitirnos como estado,
Y al Nuevo Mexico fiel
El Congreso ha rechazado.

Por achaques de la plata
Que aquejan a la nación,
Una grande oposicion
Nuestros planes desbarata,
Nuestra aspiracion la mata
Sentimiento tan novel

[Same as always

Uncle Sam refused
To admit us as a state
And faithful New Mexico
Has been rejected by Congress.

The ups and downs of silver
That plague the nation
Provoked great opposition
Defeating our plans,
Killing our aspirations
With this new attitude

Y hacemos triste papel	And we in our sad role
El estado pretendiendo,	Hoping for statehood
Pues nos quedamos diciendo,	Say once again
No quiso el Tío Samuel.	Uncle Sam refused.
Medio siglo hace cabal	A half-century has passed
Que el estado prometieron	Since statehood was promised
Y ni antes ni ahora cumplieron	And neither then nor now
Su promesa tan formal;	Was the solemn promise kept;
No fue promesa verbal	It was not a verbal promise
Sino consta en un tratado	But written in a treaty
Bien escrito y redactado	Duly set down
Que aprobaron dos naciones,	And approved by two nations,
Y aun rehusan los Solones	And still the lawmakers refuse
Admitirnos como estado.	To admit us as a state.
Cual harapiento mendigo	Like a ragged beggar
De la puerta nos despiden	Sent away from the door,
Y en contra nuestra deciden	They decide against us
Sin proceso ni testigo;	Without trial or witness;
Nos hizo falta fiel amigo	No faithful friend was there
Que con palabras de miel	With honeyed words
Nos jure por San Miguel	To swear by St. Michael
Que si hay congreso platista	That a silver congress
Dará entrada al estadista	Would bring statehood
Y al Nuevo Mexico fiel.	To faithful New Mexico.
La esperanza es el consuelo	Hope is the consolation
De las almas afligidas.	Of afflicted souls.
Que al sentirse doloridas	Who in their pain
Dirigen su vista al cielo;	Direct their gaze to heaven;
No se logró nuestro anhelo	Our desire was not achieved
En el caso ya pasado	In the recent case
Pero se verá logrado	But it will be successful
Y tendrá nueva atencion	And will be considered again,
Esto que está sin razón	This cause that without reason
El Congreso ha rechazado.[46]	Has been rejected by Congress.]

A final example deals with the participation of New Mexican volunteers in the 1898 war against Spain in Cuba.[47] This was not the first time neomexicano soldiers had defended the American flag: veterans of Civil War battles waged on New Mexican soil were still alive when X.X.X. wrote this poem. A strong feeling of national patriotism pervades his verses, showing that the loyalty of Spanish-speaking volunteers was not diminished by having to fight this time against Hispanic brothers. Democracy and freedom were the issues being defended in this war, not ethnic heritage. Only the first and final few stanzas are reproduced here:

A los voluntarios de Nuevo Mexico

Dejais el plácido suelo
Del país neo-mexicano
Y os dirigís con anhelo
A la tierra del cubano.

. . . .

Por la patria combatís
Su estandarte no se humille,
Y si triunfais o morís,
Vuestro valor siempre brille.

¡Soldados neo-mexicanos!
Mostrad arrojo y lealtad,
Y ayudad á los cubanos
A alcanzar su libertad.

Que retorneis esperamos
A Nuevo México ufano.
Y plácemes os daremos
Con apretones de mano.

El que se expone a la muerte
Por amor á su nación,
Es un hombre digno y fuerte
Y merece galardón.[48]

[To the New Mexican volunteers

You leave the peaceful soil
Of your New Mexican home
And head with hope
To the land of Cuba.

. . . .

You fight for your country,
Do not shame its banner,
Whether you win or die
Your valor will always shine.

New Mexican soldiers!
Show boldness and loyalty
And help the Cubans
Obtain their freedom.

We await your return
To proud New Mexico.
We will give you our thanks
With handshakes for all.

He who risks death
Out of love for his country
Is a worthy and strong man
And he deserves recompense.]

Although the poetry of X.X.X. is traditionally neomexicano in its popular style, his sophisticated global outlook places him in a modern context, looking ahead to the twentieth century more than to the past. As an enunciation of Hispanic identity in this era of transition, X.X.X. represents a unique and hopeful synthesis of community and individual perspectives, tradition and modernity.

The vitality and diversity of the poetry found in Spanish-language territorial newspapers illustrate how neomexicanos modified and adapted the traditional custom of versifying to articulate their cultural identity at the end of the nineteenth century. Poetry in the popular mode was a familiar discursive strategy with which to negotiate an unfamiliar borderland between the Hispanic world of their colonizing forbearers and the Anglo world in which they were now the colonized. The isolation of the neomexicano past helped preserve the intensity of folkloric customs and their connection to everyday life; now, in a turbulent era of contact with a foreign culture that threatened to change their world forever, neomexicanos found themselves adapting to new circumstances while also vigorously defending the customs of their cultural heritage.

The samples of poetry in this chapter demonstrate that neomexicanos were aware of the forces that threatened their collective identity through political maneuvering, linguistic contamination, and ethnic prejudice. Given the stressful bicultural situation and the aggressive nature of the poets of the era, it is notable that very little anti-Anglo sentiment is expressed in the newspapers. To the contrary, as X.X.X.'s poetry shows, the Hispanic author/editor/poet avoided interethnic conflict while still retaining a strong sense of loyalty to his Hispanic community. This accommodative but independent spirit characterized the late territorial period and can be explained by the unusual circumstances in which neomexicanos had become citizens of the United States:

> It would be expected that assimilation would proceed more extensively in the opposite direction and that the Spanish-Americans would adopt the culture of the Anglos, the dominant group in their new mother-country. There are several reasons, however, why their rate of assimilation has been extremely slow. The Spanish-Americans differ from the immigrant groups in this country in two respects. They did not join our population individually or in families of their own free will, but they were incorporated into the country en masse through conquest, and as a result have not been motivated to become Americanized. In addition, their culture was deeply rooted in the region in which they lived, and its continuity was not disturbed by the process of annexation. Their culture was moreover highly integrated and well adjusted to the conditions of life the region presented, and offered sources of satisfaction outside the realm of material prosperity.[49]

Until the past few decades, literary and cultural histories of the Southwest have given the impression that nineteenth-century New Mexico was bereft of literary expression.[50] This misconception, along with the definition of what constitutes cultural history, is now changing. Room must be found to accommodate anonymous voices whose self-effacement, in the folk tradition, has given symbolic voice to many. Through the medium of popular poetry, which resists cultural assimilation, neomexicanos not only retained their identity as a community but also engaged in an active dialogue with the forces that threatened to deny their validity. The fact that this poetic testimony has been conserved in the neomexicano newspapers of the transition era is evidence that the newspapers were not a discourse of the elite, but spoke for and to the common people as well.

Banditry, Politics, and Poetry
in Old Las Vegas

Vicente Silva, whose misdeeds have been chronicled in both Spanish and English, was a native New Mexican who settled in Las Vegas, in San Miguel County, around 1875.[1] By all appearances, he was a peaceful family man and a saloon keeper. Unknown to the general public, Silva's saloon was also a meeting place and hideout for a gang of outlaws called La Sociedad de Bandidos de Nuevo Mexico [The Society of New Mexican Bandits]. The society was actively captained by Silva from about 1888 to 1893. After that date, he dropped out of sight, and it was rumored, and later verified, that he had been murdered by his own men.[2] During the spring of 1894, more than a dozen members of the Silva gang were tried and convicted in district court in San Miguel County for being party to assorted crimes and murders. They were sentenced to imprisonment in the state penitentiary and, in one case, to death by hanging. Extensive press coverage accompanied each stage of the arrests and trials, as was the custom of the day.

Incidents of crime had risen to such extreme levels in Las Vegas in the 1890s that townspeople were afraid to venture out at night on the suspicion that the police were complicit with criminals and unwilling to enforce the law. Local sentiment was vocal in demanding reform, and newspapers regularly deplored what appeared to be an uncontrollable problem.[3] At the height of the violence in 1891, an anonymous poem entitled "Duerme la justicia" [Justice sleeps] appeared in *El Sol de Mayo*:

En este país desgraciado	[In this unfortunate land
Las leyes no se ejecutan.	Laws are not enforced.
Los criminales disfrutan	Criminals enjoy
De renombre ensangrentado;	Bloody renown;
Su crimen queda ovidado	Their crimes are overlooked
Y el castigo merecido	And the proper punishment
Rara vez es recibido	Is rarely received

Por el delito de muerte.	For committing murder.
Está la justicia innerte	Justice is inert
Y las leyes en olvido.[4]	And laws forgotten.]

Three years later the *Las Vegas Daily Optic* reported that the situation had reached outrageous proportions:

> That a carnival of crime has reigned in this county [San Miguel] for several years has not been unknown to every citizen of it. Commencing in fence-cutting, it progressed to barn-burning, and culminated in murder, while it also degenerated into larceny, both petty and grand. For the number of crimes committed the apprehensions and punishments have been deplorably and criminally small. In fact, they have been so few, and the number and enormity of undetected and unpunished crimes have been so great, that there has come to be entertained a general feeling that no one need hesitate to commit any crime for fear of punishment.[5]

Some of the banditry rampant in Las Vegas at the time was undoubtedly perpetrated by Anglo lawbreakers who had gravitated to New Mexico after the Civil War, making a living from petty crime and thievery in a society where the justice system was not as regulated as back East. But a good deal of the lawlessness involved native New Mexicans and much of it had to do with interethnic conflict over landownership in and around Las Vegas.

Founded in 1835 on the eastern side of the Sangre de Cristo mountain range, along the Santa Fe Trail that brought the first commercial traders from the East, Las Vegas grew in a few decades from a small outpost into a bustling commercial town, "the Mecca of all the cattle and sheep men for hundreds of miles around."[6] When the Atchison, Topeka and Santa Fe Railroad reached Las Vegas in 1879, many more Anglos immigrated to the New Mexican territory, hoping to profit by the accessibility to new markets and products that rail transport made possible. As the population increased and altered Las Vegas's cultural composition, a new Anglo section grew up on the east side of the Gallinas River, while the traditional plaza in Old Town or West Las Vegas remained the focus of Hispanic life. Among Anglo speculators coming into San Miguel County were investors in large-scale cattle ranching, which depended on the acquisition of huge tracts of land for grazing. To get control of ranch lands that they fenced with barbed wire, Anglo investors maneuvered the legal system and manipulated local farmers who had worked the land for generations. Some wealthy neomexicano families, owners of individual land grants who wanted to retain the influence they had long enjoyed in the Hispanic socioeconomic community, collaborated with Anglo power brokers in this era of rapid change:

> A small group dominated the economic and political upper circles. A surprisingly stable association of lawyers, politicians and speculators known as the Santa Fe Ring was the most powerful clique. According to Governor Edmund G. Ross, the Ring formed around Stephen B. Elkins and Thomas B. Catron, two lawyers who adopted "the language and habits of the country in order to accomplish the objects of their ambition." The two began by dealing in land grants and moved from this base to other enterprises "till the affairs of the Territory came to be run almost exclusively" in their interest.[7]

The land being fenced by large corporations as private property included parts of a nearly 500,000-acre communal holding known as the Las Vegas Grant. The Hispanics who had farmed and grazed their livestock there, in individual and community arrangements, adhered to traditional customs of ownership that had been established under the Spanish and Mexican governments and later were guaranteed to them by the United States under the Treaty of Guadalupe Hidalgo in 1848.[8] These neomexicano communities basically functioned within a peasant economy, in which the land and available water sustained the community as a whole in accordance with a complex pattern of social relationships and usage customs. In contrast, the Anglo notion of a market economy, in which land is a commodity to be privately possessed and developed to produce a marketable surplus, presupposed a completely different ethical and cultural framework. Interaction between these two views of land use inevitably led to conflict in which the small Hispano farmers and stock owners who had been self-sufficient within their communities were increasingly outmanipulated, displaced, and forced to seek wage labor elsewhere. This left them vulnerable to market fluctuations in the cash economy, and gradually their lack of education and marketable skills led to joblessness and poverty.

Out of frustration and anger that had economic, political, and ethnic overtones, a neomexicano vigilante group called the Gorras Blancas [White Caps] began to make destructive night rides around Las Vegas and surrounding counties in 1889.[9] Its white-hooded members cut fences, burned crops and buildings, tore up railroad tracks, and generally terrorized unsympathetic landowners. They had the tacit support of many townspeople and the grudging acknowledgment of the local press that injustices had been committed.[10]

Juan José Herrera, a native New Mexican and the local leader of the Caballeros de Labor [Knights of Labor], was known to be the organizer of the

Gorras Blancas, but his populist zeal tapped into what was already a well-developed sense of outrage and dispossession felt by *los pobres* in San Miguel County. Herrera had spent about twenty years in Colorado, Wyoming, and Utah acquiring an above-average education and experience with labor organizations defending workers' rights. Juan José, a strong-willed individual, and his two brothers, Pablo and Nicanor Herrera, were known to be political agitators in Las Vegas and reputed to be capable of violence. Herrera himself did not admit to being behind the Gorras Blancas, but it was widely rumored that the two organizations were one and the same in Las Vegas. The night rides that began in 1889 soon disrupted the whole county and had the land developers thinking twice about fencing new tracts.

With this local base of resistance, San Miguel County became "a logical birthplace for territorial Populism."[11] In 1890, a new political party called the United People's Party [El Partido del Pueblo Unido] took advantage of the instability and discontent sowed by the Gorras Blancas and the Caballeros de Labor and put forward a platform whose key issues were land-grabbing and political corruption. According to Robert J. Rosenbaum:

> A mixed bag of Las Vegas *políticos* signed the call for the convention. White Caps Herrera and his brother Nicanor joined the young ambitious native Democrats Félix Martínez and Nestor Montoya. Anglo Knights of Labor and Anglo lawyers and businessmen of the Democratic Party mingled with renegade Republicans unhappy with county leadership. *Jefes* like Lorenzo López saw a chance to increase their power. Idealism, dissatisfaction, patronage and power spurred the alliance of old antagonists. Opposition to the Republican Party as run by Eugenio Romero in San Miguel and Thomas Catron in Santa Fe was the only point of agreement among the leaders of the party that capitalized on the White Cap outbreaks.[12]

Lorenzo López, son of a wealthy local grazier, was a powerful political boss in the Republican party, like his brother-in-law, Eugenio Romero.[13] By the time the new party was formed, López had fallen out with Romero, but because he controlled a significant block of votes, he was elected county sheriff over Romero's objections.

The new party had both Anglo and Hispanic members and it incorporated elements of the national Populist party in its rhetoric relating to anticapitalism and agrarian rights, but it was also a phenomenon particular to New Mexico and to San Miguel County. The Republican newspaper, the *Las Vegas Daily Optic*, referred to it disparagingly as a "mongrel association of dissimilar elements."[14] Contrary to the *Optic*'s predictions, the People's Party registered some major victories in the 1890 elections, and in 1892 it helped reelect congressional delegate Antonio Joseph who defeated the powerful Thomas B. Catron. The party was also behind the establishment of a U.S. Court of Private Land Claims, which first met in 1892 but did not resolve all the land grant disputes until over a decade later, with many of them eventually denying Hispanic claims for lack of a clear title. Nonetheless, the success of Populism in these years marked "a turning point in New Mexico biparty politics," loosening the grip of the Republican party, with its lock on federal appointments, and consolidating awareness among native New Mexican voters that they could have an influence in modifying the way progress would be interpreted in New Mexico.[15] The unity achieved by the new party among neomexicano *políticos*, however, did not last more than a few years.

After the Populist successes, the Gorras Blancas and Caballeros de Labor diminished in importance. Both groups, however, fomented enough anti-railroad labor agitation to stir up a heated journalistic debate and to consolidate opposition to their power in the form of an organization called La Sociedad de los Caballeros de Ley y Orden y Protección Mutua [The Society of Knights of Law and Order and Mutual Protection], formed in late 1890. It was led by Republicans Eugenio Romero and Manuel C. de Baca, who also founded *El Sol de Mayo* in May 1891 as an official organ of the Society. Not to be outdone, a month later Juan José Herrera acquired ownership of *El Defensor del Pueblo* in Albuquerque, whose editor was the Mexican-born liberal Pedro García de la Lama. Herrera used the paper to respond to attacks by *El Sol de Mayo* and also to expand the activities of the Caballeros de Labor to other parts of the territory. For about a year, the two papers hurled insults and accusations at each other while also printing some interesting literary material for neomexicano readers who were able to look beyond the diatribes. In March and again in July of 1891, the conservative Jesuit paper *La Revista Católica* entered the fray; it denounced secret activities of the Gorras and accused the Caballeros de Labor of being a front for them, to which Herrera responded with a vehement denial and slanderous attacks on the Jesuit clergy in *El Defensor del Pueblo*.[16] This, in turn, provoked an outraged response from a group of Catholic citizens in Santa Fe, among them Ring members Thomas Catron and Antonio Ortiz y Salazar, and also prominent men like Adolph Bandelier and Benjamin Read, who denounced Herrera and his newspaper as a "scandalous, vicious and immoral publication, representing nihilistic tendencies unworthy of a civilized community."[17] *La Voz del Pueblo*, run by liberal Democrats Félix Martínez and Enrique H. Salazar, joined the journalistic battle with front-page criticisms of *El Sol de Mayo* for being too stridently opposed to the Gorras Blancas. In February 1892, *El Sol de Mayo* counterattacked with a series by Manuel C. de Baca, entitled "Noches tenebrosas" [Dark nights], that dramatically recounted the past crimes of the Gorras Blancas, with help from the Caballeros de Labor, and described how Lorenzo López had gone from being a victim of the fence-cutters to becoming one of their members: "esperaba que uniéndose á ellos calmarían el deseo de su ambicion á mandar y por último se vengaria de Romero, á quien por envidia se imaginaba que era su enemigo" [he hoped that joining them would placate his desire to command and that he would finally take revenge on Romero whom he imagined out of envy to be his enemy].[18]

The intense political rivalry between Eugenio Romero and Lorenzo López, in conjunction with the atmosphere of violence that continued to prevail in San Miguel County, led to suspicions that there was active collusion between politicians and bandit gangs.[19] A future governor of New Mexico and long-time resident of Las Vegas, Miguel A. Otero, Jr., would later write:

> Politics were red hot in both San Miguel and Santa Fe counties, and frequent murders were being committed on all sides. In fact, the year 1892 will always be remembered, not so much on account of political murders as for what should be termed "gang murders." The causes might well be termed *political,* for all these "button gangs" grew out of political organizations gotten up by certain leaders, who looked with favor on assassinations and killings of all kinds, whenever any objectionable politician appeared on the horizon to interfere with plans. In San Miguel County we had the Vicente Silva gang, while in Santa Fe County the Alliance League was the authorized Republican gang, and the Democrats had a "button gang" of rather secret nature, but openly opposed to the Alliance League.[20]

To what extent Vicente Silva and his Sociedad de Bandidos were actually involved in party politics is hard to gauge, but it appears that there was considerable politically motivated violence. Some members of the Silva gang belonged to the Caballeros de Labor,[21] and they probably rode with the Gorras Blancas. According to Otero, Silva's Society of Bandits was formed as an adjunct to the local branch of the People's Party and was manipulated behind the scenes by López:

> The true facts are well known to everyone in San Miguel County, that the Gorras Blanco [*sic*], La Sociedad de Bandidos de Nueva [*sic*] Mejico, and the Partido del Pueblo Unido were one and the same, and all under the leadership of Don Lorenzo López, the sheriff of the county, at that time. His political ticket was known as Partido del Pueblo Unido (The United People's Party), but the other two organizations were the powers behind the throne.[22]

Otero's assessment of Lorenzo López as the kingpin behind these organizations has not been universally accepted.[23] The name of Juan José Herrera appears in many historical studies as the organizer of the Gorras and the "Gran Capitán" [Chief Captain] of the Caballeros, but his political power in Las Vegas is more questionable. Certain incriminating facts about Lorenzo López cannot be overlooked: Three of his deputies in Old Town confessed to being members of Silva's gang,[24] and Sheriff López himself was frequently criticized for allowing known criminals to flaunt guns and evade prison.[25] Penalties for those who sided with the enemy were severe: a member of Silva's organization, Patricio Maes, was murdered by his cohorts when he broke the gang's vow of secrecy and announced, in a letter to the editor of *El Sol de Mayo* in October 1892, that he was switching from López's Pueblo Unido party to Romero's Socieded de Caballeros de Ley y Orden.[26] It was also reported in *El Nuevo Mexicano* and in Las Vegas papers that López, in his desire to control local politics, had traveled to other parts of New Mexico recruiting for the Gorras Blancas.[27] The degree of collusion between López, Herrera, and Silva may never be known, but it is significant that one of Silva's own bandits left behind some additional incriminating testimony.

On May 5, 1894, *La Voz del Pueblo* reported the sentencing of eight members of the Silva gang and included a transcript of the court proceedings. As the judge condemned Procopio Rael to the longest prison term (ten years), he indicated that Rael was an active member of the Caballeros de Labor and possibly also of the Gorras Blancas:

> Ud ha sido muy conspicuo en las filas de una organización, la cual ha prostituido su propósito original, pervirtiéndolo en el ultraje de inaugurar terror sobre una comunidad de la cual Ud. ha sido un miembro, y desenfrenadamente menospreciando la ley con la esperanza de que la secrecia que guardaban y el crecido número de socios que componían su organización le serviría de protección.

> [You have been very prominent in the ranks of an organization that has prostituted its original objective, perverting it by the outrage of terrorizing a community of which you have been a member, and freely scorning the law with the hope that the secrecy that you kept and the growing number of members that your organization comprised would serve as protection for you.]

Two weeks later, on May 19, 1894, *El Sol de Mayo* published the following poem by the accused, Procopio Rael, as he was about to be transferred to the state penitentiary in Santa Fe:

Adios mi Padre y mi Madre,	[Goodbye my father and mother,
Echenme su bendicion	Bestow on me your blessing,
Que por andar de asesino	For having been an assassin
Me boy para la pricion	I am going off to prison
Adios mi querida esposa,	Goodbye my beloved wife
En quien yo nunca pensé	About whom I never thought
Acuerdate de tu esposo	Remember your husband
Que se ba pa Santa Fé	Who is leaving for Santa Fe
Adios "Pueblo" agradecido,	Goodbye grateful "People's Party,"
Que yo memorias les dejo	I leave you the memories
De las maldades que hicimos	Of the evil deeds we committed
Por consejo de Lorenzo.	On the advice of Lorenzo.
Parese que no hay justicia	There seems to be no justice
Entre Jueses y Jurados	Among Judges and Juries,
Me mandan á la pricion	They are sending me to prison
Por haber asesinado.	For being the assassin.
Yo me boy con la confianza	I go with the confidence
Según lo dira la gente,	As the people will say,
Que recordaran de mi	That they'll remember me
Y el que ahorcamos en el puente.	And the one we hanged on the bridge.
Yo no me ciento ni solo	I don't even feel alone
Porque eso es lo que queria	Because that is what I wanted,
Deje mis padres y esposa,	I left my parents and wife
Por cumplir con la Pandia	To go along with the gang
Adios Don Lorenzo Lopez,	Goodbye, Mr. Lorenzo López,
Siempre recuerde de mi	Always think of me
Para cumplir las promesas,	To fulfill the promises
Que yo á Ud. prometí.	That I made to you.
El Moro[28] va por la vida	The Moor is going for life,
Que era el mejor traisionero	Since he was the biggest traitor,
Ya se perdio la esperanza	The hope is already lost
De asesinar á Romero.	Of assassinating Romero.
E Silva siempre recuerdo	And I'll always remember Silva
Por ser hombre muy valiente,	Since he was a very brave man,

Fué Capitan de nosotros	He was our captain
Y robo á toda la gente.	And he robbed everyone.
Procopio Rael es mi nombre	Procopio Rael is my name,
Mi historia queda vigente,	My story is now known,
Puede que en estos diez años	It could be that in ten years
Se olvido todo á la gente.	People will forget it all.
En fin madre de mi corazon	Finally, mother of my heart,
Hoy me veo atribulado,	Today I feel very sorry
Por no tomar los consejos	For not having taken the advice
Que desde tiempo me has dado.	That you gave me long ago.]

The poem is essentially a farewell, or *despedida*, not unlike the many popular poems that appeared in neomexicano newspapers to mark the final departure of a loved one. In Rael's case, he was leaving the circles of family and community for what would be a symbolic public death, and his farewell verses, although contrite, appeal to a higher justice for retribution. Rael admits his guilt, but takes pains to point an accusing finger at his two superiors: Lorenzo López and Vicente Silva. López, he says, not Silva, was the top man, and he alludes specifically to a plot to assassinate Romero, which coincides with Otero's description of political gangsterism and with the political rivalries known to exist in Las Vegas at the time.

Rael's parting accusations explain why *El Sol de Mayo* published the poem, probably in hopes of discrediting López, who was still county sheriff. The lack of any response seems to confirm the general perception that political corruption existed at the highest county levels. It is unlikely that the poem is a forgery considering its language and style, which were commensurate with Rael's limited education, and also the established custom of including verses by local residents in the Spanish-language papers.[29] Even the most amateur poet like Rael would have felt it natural to share his poem with others as a kind of public testimony and final plea for understanding. Although editors sometimes rejected material of low quality, they were inclined to indulge contributions like Rael's—perhaps even encourage them—if they had some immediate political value.

Another member of the Silva gang composed poetry with somewhat more literary talent than his compadre Rael. Germán Maestas was twenty-six years old in the spring of 1894, and was serving a three-month sentence for robbery when he learned that Rosita Durán, the woman he had "married" but had never bothered to make his legal wife, had left him and married the foreman of a sheep ranch. The irate Maestas escaped from the county jail, tracked down the couple, and, while Rosita ran off, cornered his rival and shot him to death in the presence of several witnesses.[30] Maestas was well known around Las Vegas for his violent deeds, but Vicente Silva had set an even worse example when it came to relationships with women: Silva had murdered his wife's brother and then brutally killed her when he thought she might be a witness against him. In his 1896 biography of Silva, Manuel C. de Baca recounts Germán Maestas's crime and re-creates a conversation between him and his victim, prior to the murder, in which Maestas taunts the cowering ranch foreman for taking Rosita's word that she was free to marry him: "Ha, ha, ha! Conque la serpiente engañó Eva y Eva á Adán, eh! Cual de estos papeles te gusta para representar, amigo mío?" [Ha, ha, ha! So the serpent deceived Eve and Eve did the same to Adam, eh? Which one of these roles do you prefer to play, my friend?] Hearing no defense, Maestas continues: "Quiero acabar contigo; la ofensa que me has hecho es intolerable; la mancha que has puesto sobre mi frente solo se lava con sangre" [I want to finish you off; the offense you have committed against me is intolerable; the stain you have left on my forehead can only be washed with blood].[31] After the murder, Maestas rode off in pursuit of Rosita, but was hunted down by the authorities and captured within a few days. The court found Germán Maestas guilty of the murder and sentenced him to hang on May 25, 1894.

Interviews with the condemned prisoner were reported at length in both Spanish and English-language newspapers. In a final declaration published in *La Voz del Pueblo* the day after his execution, Maestas explained that he had resisted arrest until Sheriff Lorenzo López arrived because he felt he could trust López to protect him from lynchers. Maestas talked freely about his act, claiming that he shot in self-defense, only after the victim reached for his gun. His crime, he maintained, was really the fault of his faithless wife. The intolerable threat of female autonomy and the disruption of established gender roles frequently led to domestic violence on the western frontier, just as it does in our day. In traditional Hispanic gender constructs, however, the adulterous wound to male honor condoned a husband's violence against his wife, and this appeared to be Maestas's self-justification in jailhouse interviews:

> Lo que tengo que decir, es una declaracion espontánea para que el público, o á lo menos la mayoria, sepa que no soy un asesino tan depravado como se me ha pintado, o para que á lo menos, ya que no pueden salvarme la vida se dignen ofrecer una plegaria por el bien de mi alma. No niego, continuó, que yo maté á Pedro Romero, pero lo hice bajo circunstancias, las cuales si hubieran sido tomadas en consideracion por el jurado, nunca habria fallado en primer grado como lo hizo. Mi mujer, dijo el reo, ha sido la causa principal de todo esto. . . .[32]

> [What I have to say is a spontaneous declaration so that the

public, or at least the majority, may know that I am not as depraved an assassin as they have made me out to be, or so that at least, since they can no longer save my life, they might be so kind as to say a prayer for my soul. I don't deny, he continued, that I killed Pedro Romero, but I did it under circumstances which, if they had been taken into consideration by the jury, never would have sentenced me to the first degree as it did. My wife, said the prisoner, has been the principal cause of all this. . . .]

Whether out of sympathy, indignation, or simply the undying fascination with notorious public figures, the public thronged to Maestas' hanging. People bought tickets and came from as far as Colorado Springs to watch the Silva gang member climb the steps of the scaffolding in the plaza in Old Las Vegas on May 25. *La Voz del Pueblo* did not disappoint its readers, hungry for details:

> El prisionero anduvo con paso firme y no levantó la vista ni siquiera para echar una ojeada á los que le rodeaban. Parecía estar profundamente impresionado, y en su semblante se notaba que el infeliz sufría indecible agonía en aquellos momentos tan aciagos de su vida.[33]

> [The prisoner walked with a firm step and did not raise his eyes even to glance at those who surrounded him. He seemed to be profoundly moved, and in his face you could see that the poor fellow was suffering untold anguish in those very sad moments of his life.]

The same issue that described Maestas's last moments also included a poem with the heading "A Rosita Durán, por Germán Maestas, su Marido" [To Rosita Durán, by Germán Maestas, her husband]:

Goza de tu libertad	[Enjoy your freedom,
Que el quitártela es injusto,	To take it away from you is unjust,
Que aunque yo viva á disgusto	For although I may be unhappy
Mi mal remedio tendrá.	My woe has a remedy.
De tu inconstante fortuna	Of your inconstant fortune,
Mi vida te has de quejar.	My dear, you will surely complain.
Grande horror te ha de causar	It will be horrible for you
El ver clisada la luna;	To see the moon eclipsed,
Pues no se ha visto ninguna	Since no woman has shown
Lo que hoy en ti se verá,	What will be seen in you today,

Pues tu con grande crueldad	Since in your great cruelty
Hoy me has echado al olvido,	You have forgotten me today,
Conociendo tu muy bien	Knowing full well
Que yo he sido tu marido.	That I have been your husband.
Teniendo mi libertad	If I had my freedom,
Puede costarte la vida	It could cost you your life
Mantente con el dichoso	Stay with the fortunate one
Inter yo salga de aqui;	Until I leave here;
Que puede ser para ti	The crime could be for you
El delito lastimoso.	A painful one.
Si otro fuera el victorioso	If another had been the victor
Y yo fuera el abatido,	And I the defeated one,
Fuera tu gusto cumplido	You would have been happy
Verme difunto a tus piés;	Seeing me dead at your feet;
Pueden ser penas despues	The pleasures you have had
Esos gustos que has tenido.	Could later bring anguish.
Para morir nací.	I was born to die.
Yo nunca he de ser eterno,	I'll never be eternal,
Que aunque yo vaya al infierno	But though I may go to hell,
Vengaré mi agravio, sí,	I'll most surely avenge the insult,
Haciendo un ejemplo en ti,	Making an example of you
Como el vulgo lo verá;	As the people will see;
El mundo se asombrará,	The world will be amazed,
Y el que leera esta historia	And for him who reads this story
Todito esa vanagloria,	Every bit of that vanity
Pesar se le volverá.	Will turn into woe.
En fin, ingrata mujer,	And so, ungrateful woman,
Me has hecho perder la vida	You have made me lose my life
Por quererte defender	By wanting to defend you,
Hoy me hallo en una prision	I find myself today in prison
Esperando el fatal dia	Awaiting the fatal day
De mi triste ejecucion.	Of my sad execution.
Se llegará el veinticinco,	The twenty-fifth will come,
Sin justicia y sin razon;	Without justice, without cause;
Pues tu has tenido la culpa,	Since you have been to blame,
De Dios espera el perdon.[34]	Look to God for pardon.]

The condemned Maestas cannot forgive Rosita Durán, and while he protests the injustice of his fate he vows vengeance—sentiments he also expressed to reporters who interviewed him in his cell.[35] Compared to the tone of resignation in Rael's poem, Maestas's mood is defiant and emotional and thus the impact of his verses is stronger. The role Rosita actually played in this domestic triangle is left unresolved; her story was apparently not considered newsworthy.

The authenticity of these outlaws' poems is heightened by their style and content. Both authors use traditional Hispanic versification, vernacular language, and references to events that had recently transpired and were well known by the public. The structures of the two poems are similar, for both are farewells that seek self-justification by assigning some or most of the blame for criminal acts to others. Seen through their verses, both Rael and Maestas acquire human dimensions and seem far less cold-blooded than they do in Baca's melodramatic history of the Silva gang.

Both these young neomexicanos were essentially common outlaws with what might be considered an uncommon poetic urge unless they are understood in the context of their own culture. Rael and Maestas utilized the folk customs of their Hispanic heritage—which Billy the Kid, Dave Rudabaugh, Black Jack Ketchum, and other Anglo outlaws in New Mexico did not share— to protest an alien system of justice. Composing verse on momentous or even commonplace occasions was a natural form of self-expression for them, not a result of formal training. Through poetry they affirmed their cultural identity and authorized their individual voices, soon to be publicly silenced. Their poems offer valuable insights into the multicultural history of the Southwest, as Américo Paredes has shown in the well-known case of Gregorio Cortés, another Hispanic outlaw.[36] One wonders what might have been written about the territorial period in New Mexico if more neomexicano voices, documented in verses such as these, had been heard and recorded.

By the time Maestas met his end in the spring of 1894, the brief political marriage of disparate interests in the Pueblo Unido party had dissolved into bitter factionalism once again. Spanish-language newspapers in Las Vegas, like *La Voz del Pueblo* and *El Independiente*, frequently commented on the high price that would be paid for neomexicano disunity in the new bicultural environment. They also continued to include the testimony of common folk, like a certain Cristobal Sánchez of Ocaté, New Mexico, who wrote a long and personal poem directly to President Cleveland in protest of his economic policy. The poem reads in part:

Soy un rudo borreguero	[I am a lowly sheepherder
el que trata de esplicar	who is trying to explain
por que siendo tu el primero	why you as the head man
que me tratas de arruinar	are trying to ruin me,
con tu corazon de fierro	with your iron heart
nos va a sacrificar.	you are going to sacrifice us.

La borrega y su producto	Sheep raising and its product
que mal nos puede acarriar	which can hurt us badly
es la sostencion del hombre	is the way we make a living
y la Industrial principal	and the principal industry
que Nuevo Mexico tiene	New Mexico has
para poder avanzar.	to be able to advance.]

A decrease in the price of wool on the national market and a depression economy could ruin a rural neomexicano farmer who had previously depended only on local demand for his product. Seasonal wage labor, with village menfolk traveling to work in mines and beet fields in Colorado or in other parts of the West, was the economic solution to which many families reluctantly resorted. Women stayed behind in the Hispanic village enclave, tending to the needs of the home, seeking out service jobs in the neighboring Anglo community, and maintaining the traditional patterns of culture. The adjustment to accommodate modernity stretched the traditional fabric of neomexicano lives.[37]

Life was changing in northern New Mexico, but as the poetry of both lawbreakers and law-abiders shows, the cultural viability of neomexicano life did not easily succumb to Anglo notions of progress nor to the political factionalism or socioeconomic dislocation that accompanied it.

4

Mexicano/Neomexicano:

The Writing of José Escobar

Alongside the vigorous oral tradition of popular poetry in late nineteenth-century New Mexico there existed a more learned literary tradition that was also given voice in the Spanish-language newspapers. Although the number of neomexicanos who actively participated by reading, writing, or studying the literary arts was small in comparison to the Spanish-speaking population as a whole,[1] Hispanic New Mexico did not lack an intellectual community. Some middle- and upper-class neomexicanos enjoyed the benefits of higher education, travel, and contacts with literary circles outside the territory. Well-read individuals familiar with the classics of Europe and the Americas formed literary societies that occasionally included female members, and some who had a knowledge of foreign languages even translated poems and stories by popular English, French, or German writers into Spanish. Among these frontier literati were a few newspaper editors and regular reader-contributors who raised their newspapers' level of discourse and reflected their own engagement in a wider cultural dialogue.

One of the better Spanish-language papers published in Albuquerque in 1892, *El Defensor del Pueblo* featured a by-line called "Alrededor del Mundo: Crónicas de Literatura, Ciencias y Modas" [Around the world: literary, scientific, and fashion news], signed by "Zig-Zag," a fairly common pen name in Mexico in the nineteenth century.[2] Interestingly, it was addressed to "Simpáticas lectoras" [Dear female readers], showing that women were perceived as the principal readership for these topics, which were quite varied indeed.[3] The feature starts out in the first person commenting on the local weather or a recent holiday, and then quickly transports the reader to Mexico, France, Canada, Italy, or Spain with information about books, authors, discoveries, exhibitions, locales of interest—all in some depth of detail. In one issue "Zig-Zag" identifies himself as from "mi querida México" [my beloved México]; otherwise he maintains an anonymous but chatty intellectual demeanor. One gets the impression that he writes as much for his own literary and social indulgence as for the edification of his readers.

"Zig-Zag" was the pen name used by José Escobar, a Mexican national born and educated in Zacatecas, who came to the New Mexican territory in the early 1890s as a political exile during the Díaz regime in Mexico. Journalists and writers were among the first to protest that Díaz had turned from a reformer into a dictator. When they were unable to write freely in Mexico, they headed north to what they commonly referred to as "México de Afuera" [Mexico beyond the border], seeking freedom of speech and support for a revolution. Some fomented armed rebellion along the Rio Grande border in subversive activities and exile periodicals; others, less radical, looked for work as journalists in various parts of the Hispanic Southwest. Clues to Escobar's history as an opposition journalist in Mexico are found primarily in his writing, although a small volume on the history of journalism in the Mexican state of Chihuahua mentions a José Escobar in Villa de Casas Grandes who had to cease publishing a paper called *El Cantón Galeana* because "tuvo dificultades con las autoridades locales" [he had difficulties with the local authorities].[4] Whatever the circumstances of his exile, Escobar came to New Mexico some time around 1891, allied himself with liberal causes in the territory, and stayed on for a number of years.

Escobar clearly had experience as a journalist by the time he arrived in New Mexico. He was well informed about the literature and arts of Europe, and he had developed a style of writing that showed innate abilities in his native language and a knowledge of the most recent literary trends in Mexico and Latin America. The first paper where he worked was *El Defensor del Pueblo* in Albuquerque, the newspaper owned by populist agitator Juan José Herrera, the controversial leader of the Caballeros de Labor who left Las Vegas after being accused of collaborating with the Gorras Blancas. Escobar worked for *El Defensor del Pueblo* for about five months in the winter of 1891–92. He was most probably introduced to the owner by Pedro García de la Lama who edited the paper for Herrera in 1891; García de la Lama was vehemently opposed to the Díaz regime and had even published an editorial—significantly dated July 4, 1891—specifically referring to Mexico and defending a citizen's right to murder an oppressive dictator. Escobar's association with the paper was short-lived, however, and in the spring of 1892 he left and started up his own pro-Populist and Democratic paper, *El Combate*, in July of that year. It was not long before Escobar won professional recognition in the territory and was referred to as "[un] periodista bien conocido en este territorio por su aptitud y capacidad" [a journalist well known in this territory for his ability and talent].[5] He took an active part in the Hispanic-American Press Association,[6] and in the eight years he was in New Mexico Escobar edited at least eight Spanish-language newspapers—all of them superior to the run-of-the-mill product of the time. The short duration of these papers, or his tenure with them, is an indication both of the financial difficulties endemic to the trade and of Escobar's proclivity for speaking out on political issues that tended to raise the hackles of local party bosses.

In addition to his journalistic trade, Escobar was a creative writer, a prolific author of poetry in a learned style that appeared in his own and other newspapers in New Mexico. I have found twenty-four poems signed by him, all apparently written in New Mexico, some reprinted in several different newspapers. Escobar dedicated many of his verses to women and appears to have been a bachelor with a keen eye for lovely, literate ladies who, it seems, tended to reject him. In one poem, he recounts being deeply disillusioned in Mexico by his efforts to help his country and also by a woman he loved there, resolving thereafter that "en la vida la misión del poeta solamente es llorar" [in life the poet's mission is only to cry]. Such was his romantic poetic persona, but there was much more to Escobar than his affective side. He also wrote several short stories inspired by historical and legendary themes, and he was the author of an early history of New Mexico that has not survived intact.[7]

The lack of other information about José Escobar makes the newspapers he edited and the pieces he wrote for them the primary sources from which to reconstruct his personal and professional life.[8] Journalism and politics occupied his working days; writing poetry must have been a private refuge and an outlet for his creative and emotional nature. With one exception, his verses are subjective and completely apolitical, and most of them date from his early years in New Mexico, which may indicate that he had less and less time for poetry as he became more involved in the local milieu. During one of his last editorial stints, at *El Nuevo Mundo* in Albuquerque in 1897, he wrote again as "Zig-Zag"—this time in long editorial pieces about contemporary issues I will discuss at the end of this chapter.

Escobar was a Mexican expatriate who only spent a short time north of the border, but he became deeply enmeshed in the New Mexican Hispanic community in the critical decade of the 1890s. Being a mexicano evidently did not preclude a strong sense of identification and affiliation with neomexicanos, as his cultural loyalties were not restricted by national boundaries. According to another expatriate, Pedro García de la Lama, "aunque nuestra patria es México, amamos á los hijos de Nuevo Mexico, porque los consideramos como hermanos"[9] [although our fatherland is Mexico, we love the sons and daughters of New Mexico, because we consider them our brothers and sisters]. This crossover attitude, blending an experience of Mexico de Afuera with that of Mexico de Adentro, anticipates the perspective of some contemporary Chicano writers who emphasize the commonality of Hispanic culture in the Rio Grande borderlands area. It also shows that the "high" culture in neomexicano society was multivocal and not as strongly Anglo-oriented as has been suggested.

The last indications of Escobar's professional affiliations are in Socorro in 1898, where he edited a short-lived paper called *El Combate*.[10] That he chose to use this title, which was also the name of a leading anti-Díaz newspaper in Mexico, both for the first and the last papers he edited in New Mexico, suggests that Escobar's ideological commitment had not waned. Indeed, his denunciation of local corruption probably cost him his job more than once, as this characteristic quote implies: "A los caprichos de los bosses políticos se debe la corrupción de las elecciones, el progreso de los 'blancos' y la decadencia de los nativos" [The caprices of political bosses account for the corruption of elections, the progress of "whites," and the decline of the natives.] A last poem published in a Las Cruces newspaper in 1898 indicates that he was heading back to Mexico for personal, legal, or political reasons[11]—the nature of which is yet to be discovered.

Escobar as Poet

José Escobar's poetry appealed to neomexicano readers because it combined popular universal themes with aspects of the more modern, less grandiloquent style of romantic poetry. In this, Escobar was following the already established trend of Latin American poets in his day who initiated the *modernista* movement. As one critic has said: "Pensar que el modernismo eliminó el romanticismo, equivale a desconocer la poesía. . . . El romántico alienta en la entraña mientras la superficie se moderniza"[12] [To think that modernism did away with romanticism is not to understand poetry. . . . The romantic finds inspiration from within while he modernizes on the surface]. Like many Mexican poets of his generation, Escobar owed much to the legacy of early European romantic writers like Espronceda, Hugo, Lamartine and also to later, more intimate romanticists like Spain's Gustavo Adolfo Bécquer and Rosalía de Castro. But his immediate source of inspiration was Mexican, not European. Escobar's generation of writers in Mexico acknowledged the cultural leadership of Manuel Altamirano and the important literary review, *Renacimiento*, which combined a nationalist orientation with a respect for the best in the foreign literature of the time.

Poems by modern Mexican writers were often reprinted in the newspapers that Escobar edited, and in his "Crónicas" he praised their work. For example, one commentary introduces the work of Mexican poet Manuel Gutiérrez Nájera to New Mexican readers and includes one of his poems. Of his compatriot, who frequently used the pseudonym "El Duque Job," Escobar says: "es un escritor tan fácil y fecundo que no hay día que la prensa de Allende el Bravo no engalane sus columnas con las inspiraciones de ese poeta"[13] [he is such an approachable and prolific writer that not a day goes by without the press Beyond the Rio Grande adorning its columns with his inspirations]. Escobar, like many of his Latin American contemporaries, was indebted to Gutiérrez Nájera and consciously imitated his work.[14] A brief selection of Escobar's poems will illustrate this and other influences that shaped his styles and themes.

The first poem Escobar published in New Mexico was a sonnet, a form he later abandoned in favor of more flexible poetic structures. There is an ingenuous, tentative quality to this piece, which presents a familiar romantic theme: separated from the woman he loves, the poet turns to nature for consolation. His interlocutor is a little swallow, a privileged go-between in whose warbling the poet seeks responses to his questions. Many elements of the poem are reminiscent of Becquerian postromantic verse; they later reappear in his other poems, which show more autobiographical detail and more confidence in defining a personal style.

A Pepa

Ave que llegas de región lejana,
ven hasta mí y cuéntame si viste
aquella niña suspirando triste
o si alegre cual siempre está y
    galana.

Colgaste, dí, tu nido en su
    ventana?
El rayo de sus ojos percibiste,
sus besos perfumados recibiste
o te trató con saña
    sobrehumana?

Ven golondrina, ven que en tu
    gorgeo
escuchar sus palabras cariñosas
a veces triste y conmovido creo.

Mas si otro amor hoy forma
    su recreo,
calla entonces tus notas
    armoniosas
y cállame también su devaneo.

[To Pepa

Bird arriving from afar,
come and tell me if you saw
that little girl sighing sadly
or if she was happy and lovely as
    ever.

Tell me, did you hang your nest in
    her window
and did you see the light in her eyes
or receive her perfumed kisses,
or did she treat you with
    superhuman anger?

Come swallow, come, in your
    warble
I hear, sadly and with
emotion, her loving words.

But if another love now
    amuses her,
hush your harmonious
    song
and silence, too, my illusions.]

(Socorro, N.M., January 29, 1892)[15]

Still in the imitative vein, another early poem demonstrates Escobar's admiration for one of the great modernist poets in Mexico, Justo Sierra. Escobar's verse is enriched by imitating Sierra's indigenous thematic flavor as well as his more innovative decasyllabic versification. The juxtaposition of a Sierra and an Escobar poem (here without translations) will illustrate how much Escobar owes to his compatriot. The subject of both poems is a lover's invitation to his *niña,* a typical appellation in romantic poetry where the female is infantilized, reduced by the male imagination to a helpless, sometimes capricious child. The promise of a warm tropical night implies an exotic if not erotic rendezvous that Sierra's gemstone imagery—lacking in Escobar's poem—intensifies. Escobar's version, on the other hand, reveals a refined sense of musicality. The lilting rhythm and repetitive phrasing of his verses gracefully mirror the rocking motion of the mariner's *barcarolas.* Where Sierra's mysterious conclusion attributes a magical, fairylike quality to the frightened *niña* who runs away crying, Escobar sustains a static vision of a virgin goddess. In this, Escobar shows a thematic conservatism that distinguishes him from many modernist poets who were intrigued by themes of enchantment and the supernatural:

Playera[16]	**Primaveral**[17]
Justo Sierra	*Imitación de Sierra*
Baje a la playa la dulce niña,	Venga la Virgen de mis amores
Perlas hermosas le buscaré	La luz de alba se acerca ya
Deje que el agua durmiendo ciña	Venga y corona de lindas flores
Con sus cristales su blarco pie. . .	Para su frente mi amor tendrá
Venga la niña risueña y pura	Venga y escuche la melodía
El mar su encanto reflejará,	De los zenzontles y del turpial
Y mientras llega la noche oscura,	Venga, y alege la niña mía
Cosas de amores le contará.	Con sus encantos el florestal.
Cuando en Levante despunte	Venga y admire entre la
el día,	bruma
Verá las nubes de blanco tul,	Los rayos de oro del igneo sol,
Como los cisnes de la bahía,	Venga, y admire como en la espuma
Rizar serenos el cielo azul.	Quiebra sus iris el arrebol.
Enlazaremos a las palmeras	Entre la sombra de los manglares
La suave hamaca, y en su vaivén	Su blanca hamaca colocaré
Las horas tristes irán ligeras	Y mientras duerme con mis cantares
Y sueños de oro vendrán también.	Y mis amores la arrullaré.

Y si la luna sobre las olas
Tiende de plata bello cendal,
Oirá la niña mis barcarolas
Al son del remo que hiende el mar.

Mientras la noche prende en sus velos
Broches de perlas y de rubí,
Y exhalaciones cruzan los cielos
¡Lágrimas de oro sobre el zafir!

El mar velado con tenue bruma
Te dará su hálito arrullador,
Que bien merece besos de espuma
La concha nácar, nido de amor.

Ya la marea, niña, comienza;
Ven, que ya sopla tibio el terral;
Ven y careyes tendrá tu trenza,
Y tu albo cuello rojo coral.

La dulce niña bajó temblando,
Bañó en el agua su blanco pie;
Después, cuando ella se fue
   llorando
Dentro las olas perlas hallé.

         (Enero 1868)

Cuando la tarde llegue silente;
Cuando se apague del sol la luz;
Y las estrellas en el oriente
Temblando brillen sobre el capuz,

Juntos iremos a mi cabaña;
Cabaña blanca, nido de amor
Do no hay rencores, odio ni zaña,
Ni sombras negras, ni atroz dolor.

Juntos podremos niña hechicera
Cuando la luna brille en el tul
En mi barquilla blanca y ligera
Cruzar las ondas del lago azul.

Mientras los remos corten las olas
Alzando triste, lúgubre son,
Oirás ¡oh niña! mis barcarolas
Interpretando mi adoración.

Después, bogando, siempre bogando
En pos de sueños y amor los dos,
Cuando tan solo queden
   mirando
Nuestros amores la noche y Dios,

Un beso ardiente do irá mi vida
Entre tus labios recogerás
Y luego, niña, niña querida,
Entre mis brazos te dormirás . . .

Ven, pues, bien mío, ven sin tardanza,
Ven que la noche llegando va;
No hagas que muerta vea mi esperanza,
Ven, que mi barca te espera ya.

    (Albuquerque, Febrero 6 de 1892)

The spring of 1892 was, artistically, a prolific period for Escobar. His sense of disillusionment after having had to abandon his homeland is expressed frequently in his poetry, as is the theme of lost love, perhaps in reference to a woman he left behind. From these poems of reflection and regret we can reconstruct some of Escobar's personal history, assuming that the autobiographical clues are relatively accurate. A portion of one such composition follows:

Desde el destierro[18]

A Josefina

I

Hasta el lejano y extranjero suelo
donde calma no encuentra mi dolor
llegan en raudo y caprichoso vuelo
como aves blancas en nublado cielo
las sombras de mi patria y de
    mi amor.

II

Lleno de dulce y triste arrobamiento
recorro el diapasón de mi memoria;
despierta mi dormido pensamiento
y sin querer, recuerdo en un
    momento
todas las horas de mi amarga historia.

III

Con los ojos del alma y del deseo
miro mi hogar y patria
    en lontananza . . .
Y aunque atado me encuentro cual
    Proteo
en mis propios dolores me recreo
que aun al dolor se hermana la
    esperanza.

IV

Miro las selvas de la patria mía
cuajadas de perfumes y de aromas
cuando despierta el sol y llega el día,
y me parece oir la melodía del
    turpial,
del zenzontle y las palomas.
. . . .

[From exile

To Josefina

I

From the distant and foreign soil
where my pain finds no rest
in rapid and fanciful flight
like white birds in a cloudy sky
come the shadows of my homeland
    and my love.

II

Full of sweet and sad rapture
I roam the space of my memory;
sleeping thoughts awaken
and in a moment I unwillingly
    remember
all the hours of my painful history.

III

With soulful and longing eyes
I look toward my home and
    country in the distance . . .
And although tied down like
    Proteus,
I revel in my own sorrows
For hope binds itself even to pain.

IV

I see the jungles of my fatherland
dense with perfumed aromas
when the sun rises and day comes,
and I seem to hear the melody of the
    turpial,
the zenzontle and the doves.
. . . .

XIII

Adios! velero barco . . . ya te alejas!
Ya la noche te cubre con su manto;
a un cisne gigantezco te asemejas . . .
Adios! querido barco, aunque me
    dejas,
aquí te esperaré llorando en tanto . . . !
        (Febrero 19 de 1892)

XIII

Goodbye! white sailboat . . . off you go!
The night covers you with its mantle;
you look like a gigantic swan . . .
Goodbye! dear boat, although you
    leave me,
I will await you here in tears.
        (February 19, 1892)]

In this poem Escobar is obsessed with memories of the past and finds no comfort for his exile in the majestic scenery surrounding him in New Mexico. Although in involuntary exile ("atado me encuentro cual Proteo"), hope is not lost ("aun al dolor se hermana la esperanza"). Nostalgia colors his vision of a idealized tropical homeland ("selvas," "turpial," "zenzontle") toward which the imagined boat sets sail, departing without him. Perhaps the swan, a familiar Parnassian and modernist symbol, is meant to suggest the question mark surrounding his fate. The final image represents the hope of freedom and repatriation. The rhythmic flow of these verses, the idyllic descriptions of nature, and a subtle use of imagery give an overall impression of controlled elegance without excess. Several aspects of this poem are typical of Escobar's poetic oeuvre: (1) the theme of personal dejection, failure, and discordancy in contrast to the beauty, greatness, and harmony of the surrounding world; (2) a description of nature that is decidedly *americana*; (3) a preference for the twilight hour, the hour of nostalgia; and (4) a heightened sense of the melodic and sensorial quality of words. .

When Escobar turns to writing about women, he portrays them as mysterious and unyielding, archetypally seductive yet also tragically flawed. The poet, although rejected, is the faithful and forgiving friend-in-need. His poems depict dramatic confrontations in which the poet observes the woman he loves tormented by a deep personal shame—apparently her own sexuality—that causes her to live a lie and to reject him as well. The following poem shows Escobar's sensitivity to the psychological complexity of the female trapped by an unforgiving society. The irregularity of its one eight-line stanza framed by quatrains dramatizes the reckless, unbalanced nature of the woman he describes:

Perdón[19]

A Jenny . . .

Quieres fingir y ríes; pero en tu risa

como himno funerario de la pena,
una nota estridente se desliza
que te vende, te acusa y te condena.

Para acallar el mal que te tortura
buscas el cieno que te ofrece el vicio,
sin recordar mujer en tu locura,

que el vicio no es ni ha sido sacrificio!

En medio de la orgía desenfrenada,
de su impudicia y asquerosa trama
como vio Baltazar la mano airada

miras que surje tu pasado drama. . .

Y tiemblas; y la copa en mil pedazos

en el suelo se estrella; y luego, luego
entre sangrientos y asquerosos lazos
y entre espirales de verguenza y
   fuego
tu conciencia que duerme, se alza
   y grita!
tu frente ajada palidece y duda . . .

en fuerte convulsión tu amor se agita

y ante esa sombra permaneces muda.

Tu sonrisa sarcástica se hiela
con su provocación y sus antojos
y una lágrima blanca brota y riela
sobre el abismo de tus negros ojos . . .

[Pardon

To Jenny

You want to pretend and you laugh;
   but in your laugh
like a funereal hymn of sorrow,
a strident note slips out
that betrays, accuses and condemns
   you.

To hide the evil that tortures you
you seek out the mud of vice
without remembering, woman, in
   your madness
that vice is not, nor ever has been
   sacrifice!

Amidst the unrestrained orgy
of your lewd and loathful scheme,
like Balthasar who saw the angry
   hand,
you see your past drama emerge.

And you tremble; the glass breaks in
   a thousand pieces
on the floor; and then, then
among bloody and foul dancers
and among spiraling shame and
   passion
your sleeping conscience rises up and
   shouts!
your tarnished face goes pale with
   doubt . . .

in a strong convulsion you feel your
   love

and silently face its shadow.

Your sarcastic smile freezes
with its fanciful provocation
and a white tear falls from
the abyss of your black eyes . . .

Después, como otra nueva Magdalena	Then, like another Magdalene,
te arrepientes ... La sombra te abandona	you repent ... The shadow flees
y el alma que te adora al ver tu pena	and the soul that adores you and sees your pain
olvida tu pasado y te perdona ...!	forgets your past and pardons you ...!]

The tone of this poem, both passionate and compassionate, is unmistakably moralistic: the anguished woman cannot blot out her guilt by more wanton behavior. Biblical references and religious overtones create a sinner–redeemer relationship in which the poet's love promises forgiveness. To the reader of his time, especially if she was female, the gothic nature of this psychological drama warned against sexual freedom and its shameful consequences. In all his poems about women, Escobar reinforced traditional gender roles.

A final example of Escobar's verse, written shortly before his probable departure from New Mexico, is also, to my knowledge, Escobar's only political poem. His other poems of exile might have had political associations for the author, but they are not explained to the reader. This poem was written in direct response to the attacks of unnamed enemies who were opposed to Escobar's editorial policies and were powerful enough to oust him from his position as editor of *El Nuevo Mundo* in Albuquerque in 1897. Poetry was often the vehicle of political attacks, but it was rare for this type of poem to be written in cultured hendecasyllables and to be signed by its author. Those who saw José Escobar's defiant denunciation in the newspaper probably were familiar with the circumstances that provoked it.[20] The vehemence with which he insults his enemies and the dramatic excess of his imagery show that Escobar was a formidable opponent with a powerful ego. Only the first stanzas are quoted here:

¡Esas![21]	[Those!
Ellos podrán con su ruindad cobarde	Their cowardly baseness may
Herirme arteros; infamarme, ¡nunca!	Wound but never defame me!
El sol es siempre el sol, aunque en la tarde	The sun is ever the sun even
Su luz quebranta y sus destellos trunca.	When its light is hidden and its brilliance is blocked.
La grita que ahora alzáis, seres serviles,	The cries you servile creatures
Es la misma de envidia y torpe celo,	now raise are the same as

Que entonan en el fango los reptiles	Those voiced by reptiles in mud
Viendo a las aves escalar el cielo.	When they see birds climb the heavens.
Seguid en vuestra grita; Es necesario	Keep on shouting; there must be
Para que brille el genio, que haya pena;	Pain for genius to shine;
¡Allí está Jesucristo en el Calvario!	There is Christ on the Cross!
¡Allí está Napoleón en Santa Elena ...	There is Napoleon on Santa Elena ...]

Escobar is overzealous in his impassioned response, but his arrogance in this poem is characteristic of many modernist poets: "Para los modernistas el hombre es el centro de la vida; el poeta, el hombre superior, el superhombre .... A fines del siglo la desmedida arrogancia del romanticismo todavía está con ellos. El mayor enemigo del modernista es el crítico"[22] [For the modernists, man is the center of life; the poet is superior, superman. ... At the end of the century, the outsized arrogance of romanticism is still with them. The greatest enemy of the modernist is the critic].

To classify Escobar's poetry as postromantic or premodernist would be to follow a literary taxonomy which, as has often been suggested, might better be ignored.[23] Undeniably, his place among his more illustrious Mexican contemporaries is a minor one, but it is important to note that he was aware of the innovative poetic trends in neighboring Mexico and was an admirer of the modern poets there who, like himself, were nurtured by journalistic discourse and contributed to its perpetuation.[24] It is, in the final analysis, less important to define him as a poet than to see his poetry as evidence of a learned literary presence in New Mexico at a time when journalism, literature, and politics were related aspects of a turbulent multicultural discourse.

Escobar's Prose

The prose material that has come to light is very likely just a small part of what Escobar wrote in his lifetime—which is also true of his poetry. Had it been more customary or less costly to publish books, or had there been more readers to buy them, we might have additional evidence of his and other neomexicano literary expression than what has been found to date in newspapers and on library shelves. Nonetheless, I have been able to locate four short stories—two signed by him and two of very likely attribution—and a group of fourteen essays by Escobar that are enough to give an idea of his talent in this area.

The four short stories appeared within a brief time of each other in *El Nuevo Mundo* (Old Albuquerque) in the spring and summer of 1897, when Escobar was editing the newspaper.[25] They are similar to his poetry in their distinctly nineteenth-century flavor, both in style and subject. All four are historical or legendary tales about miracles performed by the Virgin in different parts of the Hispanic world and the power of religious faith. In tone and composition, they are reminiscent of Bécquer's romantic legends of Spain, and in fact two of them have a Spanish setting.

The first, entitled "Los pescadores" [The fishermen], is the tale of a miraculous rescue at sea of two simple fishermen whose lives are given up for lost in a dreadful storm. The deep faith of the villagers, who pray to the Virgin of Hope daily in a shrine overlooking the sea, saves the two men, and the story concludes as the younger one marries the older man's daughter in a joyous village celebration. The second one, "El rosario de una madre" [A mother's rosary], tells the story of two men whose paths in life are affected by a rosary that one of them discards and the other finds. The rosary, a mother's gift to her son, represents faith lost and later retrieved; it has the miraculous power to transform lives and is the symbolic key to happiness in a devoutly religious society that interprets the Virgin mother as the self-abnegating vehicle through whom Christian rebirth is made possible. The third story, whose title is "La Marinera" [The mariner], also tells of a rescue at sea, but this time the story is based on an incident in 1541, when the Bishop of Panama, Fray Tomás de Berlanga, was returning to Spain aboard a vessel when a gigantic wave threatened to destroy the ship and all its passengers. The prelate's prayers to the Virgin are answered when the wave suddenly diminishes and a chest washes on board that contains an image of the Virgin, called "La Marinera." Once safely home, the bishop builds a sanctuary to the Virgin near Soria. These two middle stories were not signed by Escobar, but they so closely resemble the ones published immediately before and after them as to leave little doubt that Escobar was the author.

The fourth story, "El milagro de la Virgen" [The miracle of the Virgin], is the most interesting because it is told in the first person and recounts an experience Escobar had in November of 1884 in a little town in the area of Zacatecas, Mexico. He says that during his student days at the Commercial Institute of Durango he went on a trip to a village called Sombrerete where he visited a lovely chapel. There he saw a painting depicting a miracle performed by the Virgin of Solitude. The sacristan of the chapel, who had seen the miracle, told him the story. It seems that a wealthy mine owner had a daughter with a fatal illness who was miraculously cured by the Virgin of Solitude, whereupon the grateful miner gave a huge diamond ring to the chapel, which was placed on the statue of the Virgin. One night a thief tried to steal the ring, and the next morning he was found dead with the Virgin's hand grasped in his. As Escobar explains, "Los milagros hechos por ésta imágen se conservan siempre frescos en la tradición del pueblo zacatecano, y son tantos los que se cuentan de esa milagrosa Virgen, que bien pudiera llenarse con ellos las numerosas páginas de un grueso volúmen" [The miracles performed by this image are always kept fresh in the tradition of the Zacatecan people, and so many are the miracles of that Virgin that they could easily fill a thick tome].

Escobar's stories show his own religious faith, but they were also written to celebrate and reinforce the long-standing and deeply ingrained Catholicism of the people of New Mexico. The readers of these stories would have enjoyed learning how other Catholics in Spain and Mexico shared the same faith in the Virgin that had come to New Mexico with the first Iberoamerican settlers. According to Fray Angelico Chavez, who has recorded New Mexican religious history in numerous books, don Diego de Vargas carried with him a statue of the Virgin called "La Conquistadora" when he prepared to reconquer Santa Fe in 1692 after the Pueblo Revolt. That image of the Virgin had been saved by the earliest settlers when they fled the Indian uprising, and was brought back from El Paso by Vargas to be reinstalled in Santa Fe when he was named governor and captain-general. It remains there to this day. The identification of this religious icon with the cultural roots of the Hispanic community in New Mexico is evident in a letter by don Diego de Vargas, dated January 12, 1693:

> It is my wish, and of those with whom I enter, including the soldiers, that they should, first and foremost, personally build the church and holy temple, setting up in it before all else the patroness of the said Kingdom and Villa [Santa Fe], who is the one that was saved from the fury of the savages, her title being Our Lady of the Conquest. And so, with the aid of the soldiers and settlers, the foundations will be laid and the walls of the holy temple raised.[26]

New Mexico's history is deeply embedded in the religious folk customs of its Hispanic people. From the secret societies of *penitentes* in the northern villages to the folk drama of *Las Posadas* [The Inns] and *Los Pastores* [The Shepherds], neomexicano patterns of belief sustained a preference for the dramatic representation of the holy story. Folk plays were reenacted annually and shared by the community in the village church, often a rough adobe structure with interior *vigas* [timber beams] and a simple alter with *retablos* [painted wooden screens], hand-carved *bultos* [figures of saints], and images of the Virgin and the crucifixion.[27] The many folk dramas and stories preserved for centuries among Hispano-Catholics make New Mexico a rich source of popular culture that José Escobar understood and accepted as part of his own Iberoamerican heritage.

That Escobar identified with the people of New Mexico and cared about their culture as if it were his own is evident in the essays he wrote, also under the pen name "Zig-Zag," for a column called "Boletín" [Bulletin] in *El Nuevo Mundo* in 1897.[28] These lengthy editorial-essays, of which I have found fourteen in this newspaper alone, analyze various aspects of neomexicano society at this critical juncture in history. Viewed as component parts of a cultural philosophy that he had developed during his years in New Mexico, they show that Escobar was extremely knowledgeable about all aspects of territorial life and that he was very worried, as were many of his colleagues in the Hispanic press, that the Spanish-speaking citizens of the territory, despite their numerical majority, were rapidly losing ground to Anglos and were being marginalized in spite of being as authentically "American" as their English-speaking neighbors. Escobar's analysis of the reasons behind this is the focus of these essays, which penetrate the core of the relationship between the two cultures, both in an historical and contemporary framework. Although Escobar had initially been affiliated with a liberal Democratic paper in 1892, he had by 1897 aligned himself with the dominant Republican party in New Mexico—not an uncommon switch in a political milieu that was very volatile and driven by personalities as much as by platforms. His perspective in these essays, however, transcends party politics in order to focus on the collective problems of the neomexicano people in their homeland. Escobar is a cultural nationalist when it comes to defending the rights of *la raza*, but this does not mean he is anti-Anglo or fundamentally critical of the United States form of government on a larger level. His essays are, in fact, quite similar to what many of his Hispanic colleagues were then writing. As a consecutive series, they have the virtue of expressing these concerns within a short space of time, of being identifiable as the work of one author who was exceptionally articulate and persuasive in his own language, and of bringing to the fore issues that show blame on both sides of the cultural spectrum in New Mexico.

Briefly, the points Escobar makes are the following: (1) that Washington has not treated New Mexico with justice based on its promises in the Treaty of Guadalupe Hidalgo; (2) that New Mexico has changed drastically in the past twenty years and that neomexicanos are generally worse off than their ancestors as a result of these changes; (3) that the material progress brought by Anglos has not benefited neomexicanos because they have not been educated appropriately or trained as employable tradesmen to become a part of this new culture of progress; (3) that party politics is largely to blame for dividing the neomexicano community and preventing them from working for the common good of *la raza*; (4) that Hispanic newspapers are also to blame because they are too often the pawns of politicians and parties who care more about their election than about the greater good; (5) that those who sign up as subscribers to newspapers do not pay their bills and therefore encourage owners to seek partisan patronage elsewhere; (6) that neomexicanos are contributing to moral decay among the younger generation by being neglectful of their children's after-school activities, allowing them to loiter, smoke, and use bad language; (7) that young neomexicanos, both female and male, are too quick to adopt Anglo fashions and imitate English expressions to the point that they are objects of ridicule both in their own and in the foreign culture; (8) that the eastern press unjustly insults neomexicanos for no apparent reason unless it is their racial makeup; (9) that the neomexicano press could be a valuable educational tool, more so even than printed books, which are less accessible to the local community; and (10) that statehood should be energetically sought by neomexicanos in order to reduce the divisive struggle for power among politicians and to enable Hispanic voters to directly elect the governor and local judges who are now appointed by Washington.

Escobar's analysis paints a bleak picture for Hispanic readers, despite his obvious sympathy for their plight and his identification with them as "nuestro pueblo" [our people], "nuestras masas" [our masses], "nuestra raza" [our race/culture], "nuestros hermanos los latinos" [our Latin brothers]. Escobar is quick to defend the native abilities of neomexicanos and the resources of their homeland, predicting that immigration from the East and trade with Mexico would one day make New Mexico a center for manufacturing and commerce. But he is pessimistic about the future unless the passion for politics and all its attendant abuses can be replaced by ethnic unity grounded in the pride of cultural identity. Escobar places considerable blame on neomexicanos themselves, but he also accuses the federal government of sustained neglect:

> Hágase á este pueblo una poca de justicia: 53 años de vivir bajo la férula del gobierno territorial es mas que prueba, y en vista de nuestros recursos y población, déjense á un lado todos los maquiavélicos planes de la nefasta política y dese a Cesar lo que es del Cesar.[29]

> [Give this people a little bit of justice: 53 years of living under the yoke of territorial government is more than proof, and in view of

our resources and population, put aside all the Machiavellian
plans of wicked politics and rend unto Caesar what is Caesar's.]

It seems that Escobar touched some sensitive nerves among Anglos who
saw his essays as being too "racist," for he was forced out of his editorial job at
El Nuevo Mundo shortly after writing the last of these pieces. A statement
at the end of one of his essays shows his sensitivity to this potential criticism, and he took pains—to no ultimate avail—to disclaim any divisive
ethnocentrism:

> ¡Queremos que se entienda y que se entienda bien: que no
> tenemos preocupación alguna en contra del pueblo norte ameri-
> cano u otra nacionalidad alguna; muy por el contrario, nosotros
> somos los primeros en admirar el practicismo y energia del
> carácter anglo sajón; sabemos además, que vivimos en un país
> cosmopolita y libre por excelencia, regido por sabias leyes que
> son con justicia el asombro del mundo, y creemos que la inmi-
> gracion es fuera de todo duda una de los principales factores del
> adelanto moral y material de todos los pueblos . . . [30]

> [We want it to be understood and understood well: that we
> have nothing whatsoever against the people of North America or
> any other nationality; much to the contrary, we are the first to
> admire the practicality and energy of the Anglo Saxon character;
> moreover we know that we live in a cosmopolitan and free
> country, without peer, ruled by wise laws that are justifiably the
> marvel of the world, and we believe that immigration is without
> a doubt one of the principal factors behind the moral and mate-
> rial advancement of all peoples . . .]

Escobar's parting words upon leaving *El Nuevo Mundo* were an appeal to
his colleagues in the Spanish-language press:

> Déjense de una vez los rencores y caprichos personales; refle-
> xiónese que esa á sido la audaz medida usada por elementos de
> "busos" políticos que siguiendo el adagio de "mas vale mañana
> que fuerza," han por fin arribado con pingüe botín de honores y
> "dólares," en tanto que los principales hombres de nuestra raza se
> han quedado oscuros, olvidados y por añadidura sin sus antiguos
> crecidos capitales.
> ¿Permitirá el patriotismo de la prensa española de Nuevo
> México que esta situacion se prologue por más tiempo. . . . ?
> ¿Permitirán los descendientes de dos razas tan nobles como

altivas, que en nuestra propia casa tengamos "amos" que tratan
ya de imponerse como si fueran de hecho los "dueños absolutos"
de esta seccion del pais. . . . ?

No lo creemos, y por esto esperamos que la prensa hispano
americana estudiará lo mejor y mas conveniente para conseguir
de una vez poner un límite a ese estado de cosas que ni pueden,
ni deben seguir asi por mas tiempo.[31]

[Leave aside once and for all the personal resentments and
whims; realize that this has been the aggressive method used by
elements of political "sharpies" who have adhered to the adage
"better late than forced" with their abundant booty of honors
and "dollars" while the best men of our people have remained
unknown, forgotten, and, what's more, bereft of their former
capital worth.

Will the patriotism of the Spanish press of New Mexico
permit this situation to go on much longer. . . . ? Will the
descendants of two such noble and proud races permit that in
our own house we have "masters" who try to impose themselves
as if they were really the "absolute owners" of this part of the
country . . . ?

We don't think so, and that's why we hope the Hispanic
American press will study the best and most convenient way to
find and end once and for all this state of affairs which cannot
and must not continue as it is any longer.]

José Escobar's work deserves to be acknowledged as a significant contribution to the cultural and intellectual history of New Mexico.[32] With many
other Mexican emigrés who came to New Mexico seeking new opportunities, he discovered that its society was rapidly changing to the benefit of some
and the detriment of others. It is to Escobar's credit that, despite not being a
native son, he used his literary talents to promote the cause of New Mexican
Hispanics who were losing out as a result of the cultural collision. He himself
was very conscious of the distinction—often blurred in his time and ours—
between mexicanos and neomexicanos, and particularly of how Anglos in-
discriminately used the term *Mexicans* when making disparaging remarks
about neomexicanos. Escobar's response in one essay was "Pero acaso,
esa prensa estúpida, se olvida de que aquí todos son ya americanos? No,
no se olvida, lo sabe de sobra. . . . "[33] [But does that stupid press perhaps
forget that here they are all Americans? No, it does not forget, it knows
very well. . . .]

Escobar's ethnic loyalty went beyond borders in an effort to ensure that
neomexicanos would retain their cultural heritage, yet he was also a political

pragmatist in his support of statehood, which held the promise of unifying a community that had been debilitated by territorial colonialism. His writing, both in poetry and prose, shows the breadth of knowledge and awareness found in the neomexicano intellectual community at a time when powerful forces in the East continued to block statehood for New Mexico because they considered the native population unfit to meet its standards for admission.

Newspapering on the frontier could be a challenge in any language. *The Kingston Shaft,* Kingston, New Mexico, August 1886. (Courtesy Museum of New Mexico, neg. no. 14691. J.C. Burge, photographer.)

Composing room of the Santa Fe *New Mexican* and *El Nuevo Mexicano,* 1899. (Courtesy Museum of New Mexico, neg. no. 10560.)

San Miguel Chapel and St. Michael's College, College Street, Santa Fe, 1881.
(Courtesy Museum of New Mexico, neg. no. 1403. William H. Jackson,
photographer.)

Enrique H. Salazar, editor of *El Independiente* of Las Vegas, New Mexico. (Courtesy Museum of New Mexico, neg. no. 14775.)

Nestor Montoya, editor of Albuquerque's *La Bandera Americana*. (Courtesy Museum of New Mexico, neg. no. 87663.)

Felipe Maximiliana Chacón from his book of poetry and prose, 1924.

"The Mexican Band." David Chávez with bass viol. Monticelo, New Mexico, ca. 1900. (Courtesy Museum of New Mexico, neg. no. 58627. Henry A. Schnidt, photographer.)

Benjamin M. Read, neomexicano historian, attorney and legislator. (Courtesy Museum of New Mexico, neg. no. 111958.)

Staff of the Santa Fe *New Mexican* at the turn of the century (left to right): Miss Swope, Henry Pacheco, an unidentified woman, Paul A.F. Walter, Colonel Max Frost, and Elmer Marsh. (Courtesy Museum of New Mexico, neg. no. 15275.)

Print shop of *La Revista de Taos*. Taos, New Mexico, ca. 1910. (Courtesy Kit Carson Historic Museum.)

"In the School Room." Cubero, New Mexico, October 1903. (Courtesy Museum of New Mexico, neg. no. 130423.)

Félix Martínez, publisher of *La Voz del Pueblo,* businessman and statesman. (Courtesy Museum of New Mexico, neg. no. 10292. Frederick J. Feldman, photographer.)

Governor Octaviano A. Larrazolo and his daughters, ca. 1919. (Courtesy Museum of New Mexico, neg. no. 47660.)

Front page of *El Independiente*, Las Vegas, New Mexico, April 18, 1894, with a poem by José Escobar at bottom right. (Courtesy Museum of New Mexico, neg. no. 160911.)

The principal towns of New Mexico during the territorial era.

5

Identity Crisis:

Responses to Negative Stereotyping

"Racial confrontation lay at the root of western history, and it
never went away. Central to the discourse of any succeeding era
were the language of race and struggle between races for territory, for hegemony, for boundary setting, for definition."

—Sarah Deutsch, "Landscape of Enclaves," 130.

Anglo-Americans who first journeyed to the New Mexican territory in the
early nineteenth century carried with them much cultural baggage, not the
least of which was a deeply ingrained disposition to view the native Hispanic
population as an inferior, half-breed society.[1] Early travelers and settlers were
influenced by racial prejudices dating back to the conflict between Protestant England and Catholic Spain in the sixteenth century. The hispanophobia
they inherited from their Puritan ancestors had its roots in the Black Legend
that portrayed Spaniards as a cruel and genocidal people of impure stock
who had mixed with Semitic and African races during the Middle Ages.[2] Propaganda in the early American press and in the Protestant pulpit also de-
monized Mesoamerican Indians and other aboriginal groups, painting
frightful images of their heathen beliefs and savage rituals. Thus it took
no leap of faith for those Anglo-American pioneers to believe that the
mestizo peoples of the Southwest were even more defective than their
Spanish ancestors and to justify their own zeal in expanding capitalism on
the western frontier as the duty of a superior race with a regenerative function to perform.

Most Anglo-Americans who came to New Mexico in the nineteenth century failed to take into consideration factors of history, culture, and geography that had made neomexicano society different from their own. Nor could
they see, as David J. Weber has observed, that living conditions on Mexico's
northern frontier resembled their own on the American frontier in their lack
of refinement and sophistication.[3] The relative ease with which U.S. troops
concluded the Mexican-American War and occupied New Mexico in 1846
merely heightened the Anglo sense of superiority and added to their contempt for the defeated Mexicans, especially in the eastern press. The fact that
the invasion was maneuvered by the politics of Manifest Destiny, artificially

stimulated by a massive propaganda effort, and then unjustly blamed on Mexico was not considered reprehensible.[4]

Since most of the Anglo men who traveled the Santa Fe Trail to New Mexico arrived without wives or families but with all the normal human needs, they tended to judge Hispanic women less harshly than their men. Some early literature claimed that Spanish-speaking females were unusually promiscuous and lured men into sexual liaisons. Historical evidence shows that in the northern New Mexico area between 1821 and 1846 there were at least 122 intermarriages and common-law unions of Anglo men and neomexicano women.[5] The crossing of racial lines in these cases simply appears to confirm, as one historian put it, that "American males allowed their hormones to overcome their ethnocentrism."[6] In some cases intermarriage even made good business sense.

While Anglos, Hispanics, and Native Americans clashed, negotiated, and constantly struggled for self-definition on the western frontier, the print media churned out its own versions of what was happening. Western dime novels, the pulp fiction of the late nineteenth century, played to the prejudices of a chauvinistic American readership with their blatant rhetoric of racism. In these poorly written but very popular tales of adventure that had little to do with actual life experience on the western frontier, Mexicans were "greasers," "half-breeds," or "yellow bellies."[7] Curiously enough, other novels of the period, like the very popular *Ramona* (1884) by Helen Hunt Jackson, showed an obvious class bias by romanticizing a western society made up of feudalistic *dons* and gracious *señoritas*, creating what has been called the "Spanish mission culture," replicated in early Hollywood movies with similar disregard for historical reality. As Philip Ortego observed in his 1973 introduction to an anthology called *We Are Chicanos*, "Mexican-Americans have been characterized at both ends of a spectrum of human behavior (seldom in the middle) as untrustworthy, villainous, ruthless, tequila-drinking, philandering *machos*, or as courteous, devout, and fatalistic peasants who are to be treated more as pets than people."[8]

Negative stereotyping of Hispanics in the Southwest was thus the result of cultural and racial prejudices that festered in American society for centuries and arose from a combination of historical circumstances. That it appeared in so many contexts and was so widely tolerated—particularly among easterners who had no direct contact with Hispanics—shows the extent to which cultural difference was antithetical to the perceived national mandate to Americanize the western frontier. The impact of this climate of opinion on the lives of New Mexico's Spanish-speaking population after 1846 was far-reaching, as the two cultures adjusted to one another over time. It would not be an exaggeration to say that Anglo racial prejudice impacted all classes of neomexicano society and directly affected critical issues of the territorial period including statehood, public education, and landownership, as well as social and political contacts between the cultures. Above all, it influenced the way neomexicanos saw themselves and their relationship to the American community in their new capacity as citizens of a rapidly changing Southwest.

The ill feeling bred by the hostility of the first Anglos—whom the neomexicanos often referred to as *gringos* or *bolillos* [white doughy rolls]—precipitated habits of social separation in many parts of the territory that were reflected in the newspapers as they were in neighborhood geography. In cities like Santa Fe, where there were more families of mixed marriages, this was less evident; the commerce of daily life in the capitol and other larger cities inevitably involved intercultural exchange and negotiation.[9] Many Anglos who came West were tolerant, pragmatic, and even admiring of Hispanic culture; some English-language newspapers rose to the defense of the Spanish-speaking community when they were publicly insulted because certain Anglo business interests rightly perceived that statehood would be longer in coming if negative stereotypes were allowed to define New Mexico's population. However, Hispanic newspapermen saw beyond the political or economic objectives. The practice and rhetoric of negative stereotyping was not just insulting and demeaning to the Spanish-speaking population of New Mexico; it also posed a direct threat to the exercise of their constitutional rights and the preservation of their cultural integrity. Neomexicano newspapers documented the reaction of the native Hispanic community. By their very existence and proliferation, these journalistic texts contested hegemonic discourse and defined a space of resistance.

Legal guarantees from the federal government seemed worth no more than the paper they were printed on, and yet neomexicanos, as United States citizens, clung to the authority of the written law in their own defense. The Treaty of Guadalupe Hidalgo, signed on February 2, 1848, ceded extensive lands on Mexico's northern frontier to the United States, including the area of New Mexico that had been inhabited by Hispanics since 1598. As a people whose homeland had been invaded and occupied by a foreign country and who then became citizens of that country, neomexicanos found themselves in an anomalous situation. They were not immigrants and they were not a minority. Under the terms of the treaty, Mexican nationals residing in the conquered lands were legally guaranteed "all the rights of citizens of the United States according to the principles of the Constitution" (Article 9). The law stipulated that they were entitled to the full enjoyment of their property, their religion, and their culture. It was a treaty that neomexicanos wanted to believe and trust, as statements in the Spanish-language newspapers made clear. But the guarantees of a treaty that was little known outside the territory could not change the prevailing racial sentiments of the time: that Hispanics were second-class citizens, or even worse, foreigners who did not qualify as Americans.

The gap between the letter of the law and the practical experience of intercultural exchange became painfully evident as the New Mexican territory grew and prospered. At stake for neomexicanos by the late 1800s and well into the 1900s was not just the issue of legal entitlements but the vindication of their identity as a ethnic community. In essence, the circumstances in which they found themselves had the dimensions of a cultural identity crisis, not arising from within the ethnic community but rather from factors external to it. It was a crisis that nonetheless threatened to debilitate the collective psyche, and the neomexicano press—the public medium for communal introspection and expression—elected to deal with it head-on.

Over the course of at least three decades, from around 1890 to 1920, the Spanish-language newspapers, speaking for and to their community of readers, took a three-sided approach to negative stereotyping by expressing (1) an awareness of being rejected as an ethnic group on a national level, especially in the context of the ongoing quest for statehood; (2) a strong defensive reaction, critical of unfounded negative stereotyping; and (3) a campaign to transform the image of neomexicanos through education. In prose and verse, editorials and letters to the editors, journalists and ordinary citizens protested the unwarranted stigma of negative stereotyping and offered their analyses of what could be done about it. Although they were writing in Spanish, their opinions were frequently directed outside as well as inside the ethnic community; bilingual and local Anglo papers often echoed their concerns and acknowledged the validity of their complaints.[10] Many members of the Hispanic press interpreted this unwanted, but not unheeded, identity crisis as an opportunity to undertake a kind of group psychoanalysis. A sampling of their ideas demonstrates that a century ago—even before the impact of Mexican immigration to the Southwest during the Mexican Revolution—there was a heightened self-awareness within the Spanish-speaking community and a willingness to discuss sensitive issues that, in themselves, contradicted the pejorative notion that Hispanics were a passive and fatalistic people.

Among articles of the first type is a letter to the editor of *El Nuevo Mexicano* shortly after it began publication in Santa Fe. Printed on the front page on September 13, 1890, the letter, signed only with the author's initials, alleges that the negative image of neomexicanos in the eastern press was being encouraged by Anglo politicians of the Democratic party in New Mexico who wanted to delay statehood. In fact, many Anglo Democrats in the southern part of the territory, influenced by anti-Mexican sentiment in Texas, were opposed to statehood because they feared the potential voting power of the Hispanic majority. Other Democrats, both Anglo and Hispano, were against statehood on the grounds that it would increase the power of the land-grabbing Santa Fe Ring, which was mostly Republican but also included some wealthy Democrats.[11] Most Hispanic New Mexicans, however, favored statehood in 1890, and they knew that degrading images of the native population only increased Congress's reluctance to support an enabling act. The author of the letter takes particular umbrage over a special congressional subcommittee sent to New Mexico to assess the native people's capacity for self-government:

> Este es el colmo de la injusticia, que ya se desborda, acumulada sobre este pueblo por años por unos cuantos demagogos ambiciosos y sin principios . . . Ya es tiempo que nuestra populacion natal sacudiese este yugo que tanto tiempo los ha mantenido en esclavitud política. . . .

> [This is the height of injustice, which is already excessive, heaped upon this people by a few ambitious and unprincipled demagogues. . . . It is time now that our native population shake off this yoke which for so long has kept them in political slavery.]

Numerous political and economic interests were at stake both in Washington and in the territory during the long debate over statehood for New Mexico. In the 1870s and 1880s the issue was deadlocked by sparring between power cliques and by the violence of territorial land wars and Apache raids.

The need to promote unity and defend the interests of the native population was the primary motive behind the founding, in March 1892, of the Hispano-American Press Association. According to Victor L. Ochoa, who became the first president of the association,

> La voz de la prensa Hispano-americana pocas veces es atendida por las autoridades de este país, y no es extraño que las quejas y las protestas se pierdan en el vacío de la indiferencia oficial.[12]

> [The voice of the Hispanic-American press is rarely listened to by the authorities of this country, and thus it is not surprising that its complaints and protests are lost in the vacuum of official indifference.]

One of the first acts of the new association was a joint resolution to censure the territorial governor, L. Bradford Prince, for racist remarks he had made about native New Mexicans in an interview with the *Chicago Tribune* and for his subsequent attempt to bribe the local press into not reporting it. In the words of the resolution:

Que en vista de su conducta hipócrita hacia nuestro pueblo de quien pretende ser el mejor amigo, y quien en ausencia trata desdeñosamente de "greasers," juzgamos que es conducta indigna de caballeros y de hombres honrados. Precavemos á nuestros compatriotas en el territorio y fuera de él que es un hombre que no merece ni sus favores ni su confianza.[13]

[That in view of the hypocritical behavior toward our people of one who pretends to be their best friend, and who in their absence treats them disdainfully as "greasers," we deem his conduct unworthy of a gentleman and honest man. We warn our compatriots in the territory and beyond that he is a man who merits neither our favors or our trust.]

The press association tried to act as a professional forum and ethnic booster group, and it remained active for several years, but the distances between cities and political dissent between editors made the spirit of cooperation difficult to sustain over time.

Two articles written in 1897 express the frustration that neomexicanos experienced when the false stories were still propagated with apparent impunity by outsiders who came to New Mexico. An editorial in *El Nuevo Mundo* (Albuquerque, May 29, 1897), from the pen of José Escobar, who was also active in the press association, lashes out at negative stereotyping, the reasons behind it, and the injustices that it occasioned. With his knowledge of cultural history and current problems, his reasoned arguments, and frequent notes of sarcasm, Escobar vents the outrage of many less articulate neomexicanos. Considering that his readers were primarily Hispanos, it seems that his protest also intended to convey the uplifting subtext to neomexicanos not to abandon their cultural pride. The essay is reproduced here in its entirety, in translation:

Yesterday and Today:

Something about the Past and Present of New Mexico.

If the TUBERCULARS who come to seek health in the benign quality of our climate and the pure breezes of our mountains; if the INTELLIGENT tourists who perform the miracle of studying our people and their customs from the window of a PULLMAN running at a speed of 60 miles an hour had judgment, or even the rudiments of instruction, the eastern press would neither fill its columns with unbelievable tales nor would it feed its innocent readers stories that stupidly and unjustly criticize the limited culture of a people who, instead of feeling shame, should be even more proud of carrying the blood of two illustrious as well as

94

heroic races in their veins, since for their prowess, valor and lineage the Aztecs as much as the Spaniards are worthy of the bronze immortality of the imperishable crown of glory.

Hernán Cortés, Fray Bartolome de las Casas, Nezahualcoyotl, Cuauhtémoc, and a thousand wise men and warriors of the Iberian and indigenous races are the just pride of today's generations who, through the dense fog of centuries, can still admire their epic deeds, feeling their hearts beat with noble and blessed praise.

But let's leave digressions aside. As we said before, the articles, or rather the undeserved invectives, that appear from time to time in the newspapers of the East do not have, in all justice, any reason for being since the tourists that write them (only with the aim of publicizing their travel impressions) are very far from being educated or informed persons. The SO-CALLED WRITERS of this sort are excursionists who travel for PLEASURE and that says it all. These novel critics establish their points of comparison between the best classes of the cities of New York or Chicago and the lowliest of our people, and thus the natural discordance of the TRAVEL NOTES and the lack of foundation of the insults to our race which they accuse of being dirty, ignorant, unattractive, etc., etc. But if these travelers made a just and fair comparison among equal classes of society, then the victory would be ours; since neither now nor ever have our people lived like the ANGLOS in true pigsties located, for example, in the neighborhoods of New York. From the descriptions of these tourists, we are considered more barbarous than the ancient redskins found in this country by the Breton conquerors, and it is just a miracle that they do not consider us cannibals. If these train-bound passengers would like to take the trouble to study even a little the history of these regions, they would understand that the brave native settler who had to devote half his time to struggling for survival and the other half to conducting campaigns against the indomitable Apache and bloody Navajo, who frequently robbed many of his cattle, would not be able to lounge in a comfortable hammock like the settler of today, enjoying the beauties of Lord Byron's poems, the sublime scenes of Shakespeare, the famous parliamentary speeches of the Girondins or those of Gladstone or Bismarck. Take a look back at the past, reflect a bit on the situation of the settler in those times, and then let it be said frankly whether these attacks are just or unjust. The topographic system of this territory isolated it naturally from the large centers of knowledge and culture; its enormous deserts plagued by savages and dangers were a constant obstacle prevent-

ing the governments of Spain and Mexico from doing anything
for the inhabitants of its borders, and nevertheless think of the
memorable New Mexicans like the Archuletas, the Chavezes, the
Bacas, the Armijos, the Gallegos and the Martinezes, and you will
see how false and calumnious these judgments are.

Today everything has changed: the savage does not rob or kill
in the desert; the smoke of the country campfires has been
substituted with that of locomotives, smelters and factories; the
steel veins of the railroad have put us in contact with the great
centers of civilization, and in the formerly arid deserts rise
beautiful and modern towns with all the comforts and advantages that in their laboratories our most illustrious inventors
have known how to cull from the mysteries of progress. The
marvels of Franklin, Tesla and Edison are familiar today to the
native resident of the capitals of New Mexico, who, like his
country men, knows how to applaud and admire them.

But what has been the result of the metamorphosis of New
Mexico? Unfortunately for our race, there has been no improvement whatsoever. The railroads killed the traffic of our old cart
trains; our agricultural products cannot compete with those that
come to us from Colorado and California, and our only present
resource, our wools, cannot face the competition of those imported from Australia and Argentina. Educationally our people
have gone ahead very little, since it is well known that the institutions of public schooling date from very few years back, owing
their improvement, without any doubt, to the diligence of the
intelligent Mr. Amado Chavez, First Superintendent of Public
Instruction in New Mexico. One can see, then, that making a
very cursory study of the past and present, one comes to the
conclusion that the exalted American progress has hardly benefited our popular masses at all. It is urgent that the government
pay attention to what we in general outlines have tried to point
out so that it may investigate how some more practical educational institutions might be set up that could give a better result
to the children and youth of New Mexico, since it has been
noticed by natives and foreigners alike that the Agriculture and
Mining schools are unnecessary. Let's hope that, just as today we
condemn the indifference of the government, we who have
sincerely sought the true progress of our race may someday be
able to praise a means for giving New Mexico a true *pléiade* of
laborious artisans and knowledgeable skilled workers, the only
hope for the salvation of our race which from day to day gets
weaker. If this does not happen, like the former indigenous
owners of this country, the descendants of today's New Mexicans

will also have to emigrate to another land, leaving in the hands of strangers the tombs in which rest those equally brave and honest settlers who, in spite of their ignorance, knew how to receive with open arms those who shortly thereafter would become CORRE-SPONDENTS in order to heap insults upon them in their press and their books.

Escobar demonstrates a populist perspective that roundly rejects the notion that progress is a desirable goal if it benefits only the wealthy. Despite being a man of learning, he condemns the intellectual pastimes of the leisure class if they are accompanied by a disdain for the sweat of the common man. Like many of his Hispanic contemporaries, however, Escobar could be ethnocentric when it came to characterizing the indigenous "redskins" who had raided their lands in generations past and whom he saw as "savages," not, ironically, in the same class as the Aztec peoples whose heritage he proudly claimed. Escobar saved his harshest invective, however, for those of his own profession whose blithe fabulations reinforced false stereotypes in utter disregard of the truth.

A similar editorial, excerpted here in translation from *La Voz del Pueblo* (Las Vegas, Aug. 7, 1897), comments specifically on insults printed in New York and St. Louis newspapers as well as "hundreds of others":

> In the view of the people of New Mexico, and in the opinion of every man who possesses a heart and soul and in whose character there exists nobility, one does not judge a whole people to be bad because they are poor or because they are ignorant, especially when the blame for their ignorance rests with the government under whose protection they live. The person or persons who make such judgments are themselves the best evidence of their own low character, of their own baseness.
>
> For our part in New Mexico we have always admired the intelligence of our Anglo-American compatriots. We always give each and every one of them the support and respect they deserve because we do not blind ourselves with worry or with vanity. Hundreds of Anglo-American citizens are still here today who came to our land poor, discouraged, hungry and even ragged; we, inspired by the generosity that has been ours in New Mexico, extended them a cordial welcome, offering them the best place that our humble homes had. We offered them opportunity, even making them head of our public and private businesses; we gave them to understand with our behavior that we were not experts in the art of making money, but we were men who believed that good treatment of one man by another and the formality of his

word and the sacred nature of friendship were worth more than money. They, carried by their irresistible character trait, put their five senses to accumulating money. We said, enjoy it in good fortune, although it was to our own pecuniary disadvantage. But now in return, many of them have cloaked themselves in the blackest ingratitude, calling us inferior beings, citizens useless to our government, of course always with the idea that money is God, is government, is everything, and we don't possess this God. But we, the people of New Mexico—although we may have been left generally without means and even rights for having been so docile in the past, and although we don't know the art of the rarefied civilization in which only money is valued, and although a large majority of us may not have the means to improve ourselves—we still have one proud satisfaction, and that is that our story proves that we showed our Anglo-American compatriots a pure heart and a generous hand when they needed it or would have perished. Now if they insist on wanting to scorn us, looking at us only with greedy eyes, recognizing us only as good subjects for exploitation, we will tell them without mental reservation, we still have a heritage, and this is the gentility of men with the persistent belief that there are many other virtues worth more than money. We disdain baseness, though it may be cloaked in gold, and we rest much more peacefully with that satisfaction than the civilized gentlemen who accumulate millions using the legislatures and even the national Congress so that their "trusts" or combination of infamies become fatter at the expense of ignorant people such as they consider us to be.

Both articles make the point that neomexicanos have much to be proud of in their Indo-Hispanic history and culture, emphasizing that what the native peoples lack in education and material well-being was largely the fault of the U.S. government, which failed to live up to its promises. Both stress the traditional generosity and moral decency of the neomexicano people and attribute negative criticisms of New Mexico to a lack of understanding of the history and current reality of the territory. Both see Anglo-Americans as blinded by their pursuit of the "almighty dollar". Interestingly, however, neither article accuses Anglo critics of outright racism, which seems to indicate an attitude of conciliation and a realistic awareness of the need to find a middle ground where both cultures could live harmoniously. Both articles reflect the perspective of middle-class, forward-thinking intellectuals who wanted to avoid inflammatory rhetoric. The anger felt by the dispossessed and exploited rural peasants was more likely to be expressed in the verses composed by local bards or even in physical acts of retaliation.

A common insult to Hispanics often found in the eastern press was the suggestion that they were untrustworthy aliens, non-Americans. A *Chicago Tribune* article of February 2, 1889, for example, referred to Hispanics in the territories as "not American but 'Greaser,' persons ignorant of our laws, manners, customs, language, and institutions." Not only their citizenship but their bravery was called into question. According to Cecil Robinson, "Of the words used by early American writers to describe Mexicans, one of the most frequent to appear is the word *cowardly*."[14] This accusation was particularly galling to neomexicanos who had fought on the side of the Union in the War between the States and had volunteered again when President McKinley called for volunteers for the war against Spain in Cuba, serving bravely as members of Teddy Roosevelt's Rough Riders. In that war, ironically, neomexicanos fought against their Hispanic mother country, in defense of an adopted American country whose leaders did not treat them as true and equal sons.[15] The following poem, one of several of a similar nature, appeared in *El Nuevo Mexicano* on May 28, 1898:

Muchas son las opiniones	[Many are the opinions
En contra del pueblo hispano,	Against the Hispanic people,
Y le acusan de traidor	Who are accused of betraying
Al gobierno americano.	The American government.
Haciendo un experimento,	This should be examined
Quedarán desengañados,	And the record set straight,
Que nuestros bravos nativos	That our brave native men
No rehusan ser soldados.	Do not refuse to be soldiers.
No importa lo que se diga	No matter what is said
Y defame de su fama,	Or how their name is blemished,
Pero pelearán gustosos	They will fight willingly
Por el águila americana.	For the American eagle.
A nuestro pueblo nativo	Our native people are accused
Le acusan de ser canalla,	Of being no-good rabble,
Pero no ha demostrado serlo,	But this has not been proven
En el campo de batalla	On the field of battle.
Como buenos compatriotas	Like good countrymen
Y fieles americanos,	And faithful Americans
Libraremos de ese yugo	We will fight to lift the yoke
A los humildes cubanos. . . . [16]	From the suffering Cubans.]

With the advent of the railroad age came the missionary crusade. As early as 1879, Congregational, Presbyterian, and Methodist church ministries established rural mission schools in New Mexico for Hispanic, Indian, and Anglo children. Well-meaning Anglo-Protestant missionaries, imbued with the racial prejudices of their time, ventured west to "Americanize" and "Christianize" the Hispano-Catholic society that they perceived as foreign and heathen. Their project of social and religious education was placed in the capable hands of mission women and, between 1900 and 1914 alone, more than two hundred came to New Mexico and southern Colorado, according to Sarah Deutsch, in her book *No Separate Refuge: Culture, Class, and Gender on an Anglo-Hispanic Frontier in the American Southwest, 1880–1940*. In the larger communities of northern New Mexico, Hispanic men involved in commerce and trade came into contact with their Anglo counterparts, but in the smaller villages of the Hispanic heartland, the intercultural contact was between women. Missionary ladies felt their "calling" was to bring "brightness to these spots of darkness and superstition," and zealous to justify their own usefulness, they saw the otherness of Hispanic family life as morally degrading.[17] One Anglo woman who was more publicly outspoken and inflexible than most of her sister-workers was a certain Nellie Snyder, who wrote an article in the Las Vegas *Sunday Morning Review* on October 20, 1901, characterizing the Spanish-speaking population in typically disparaging and insulting terms. The following week a group of neomexicano citizens held a public protest and issued a statement, later published in the Hispano newspaper, *La Bandera Americana* (November 8, 1901), condemning Miss Snyder and saying she was unworthy of living in the community:

> ... después de disfrutar de la hospitalidad de nuestro bondadoso pueblo, nos ha pagado con infamias y repetidas injurias, y por esto proclamamos á la faz del mundo que deshonra el nombre de Señorita culta, bajo el cual quiere esconderse en contra de nuestra justa indignación.

> [... after enjoying the hospitality of our good people, she has repaid us with infamies and repeated insults, and thus we proclaim to the world at large that she dishonors the name of cultured Lady behind which she tries to hide from our just indignation.]

The unmistakable reference to gender in these words reflects the traditional Hispanic notion that a woman should be gracious, welcoming, and not publicly aggressive. To be insulted by a woman was particularly outrageous to the neomexicano male who looked with disapproval on the missionary effort to redefine Hispanic gender roles so as to "domesticate" the Hispanic female in Anglo terms.[18] Protestant mission ladies believed that neomexicano women were too involved in labor outside the home, too trusting of others to watch their children, and thus neglectful of their role as home builders and nurturers. Women like Nellie Snyder—many with more tolerance and civility than she exemplified—met with only limited success among Hispanic mothers, but with the next generation as their objective they established mission schools all around northern New Mexico. By 1902, fifteen hundred Spanish-speaking children were attending classes taught by women whose knowledge of the youngsters' language and culture was minimal, but whose impact on their education would be significant.[19]

With outside influences threatening the cultural pride of neomexicanos and marginalizing them as citizens, the local Spanish-language press launched a campaign to empower the Hispanic community to speak for itself and re-claim its embattled identity. The message it sent repeatedly to its readers was that a good education and the self-confidence it provided was the single big-gest factor that could turn the tide in their favor. A history of economic ne-cessity and poor schooling in New Mexico was the result of years of neglect on the part of Spanish, Mexican, and finally U.S. authorities, yet outside crit-ics insisted on citing high neomexicano illiteracy rates as evidence of an in-nate laziness and disregard for learning.[20] The enactment, after much debate, of a comprehensive public school bill in 1891 theoretically gave neomexicanos the means to achieve the desired objective.[21] However, the local press knew that parental reluctance to abandon Catholic parochial schools, coupled with the economic burdens of a recent recession, might keep children from at-tending the public schools. Furthermore, some of these schools were too far from the rural mountain villages to be easily accessible. The campaign to push public education precipitated some tough appraisals of patterns of life and thought that were amazingly forthright and often self-critical.

Articles promoting education were directed almost exclusively to the na-tive Hispanic public, not the outside world. A good education should be an equalizing social factor leading to the full enjoyment of rights, a sense of ethnic accomplishment, and, eventually, to statehood and political autonomy for New Mexico. The last lines of a poem called "Reflexión," signed by G. Morales and published in *El Monitor* of Taos on July 2, 1891, states the objec-tive with rhetorical flair:

La educación busca presto	[Seek out education quickly,
Ponla por mote en tu senda	Make it the motto of your life
Y verás cuan estupenda	And you will see how marvelous
Mostrará de manifiesta	It will turn out to be
Ser tuya la mejor prenda;	To have the best prize be yours;
Haz tus hijos educar	Have your children educated

Y aca les verás triunfar	And you will see them triumph
Del yugo del servilismo;	Over the yoke of servility;
Eso hace a todos lo mismo	This makes everyone equal
Y al tirano hace temblar.	And makes tyrants tremble.]

One of the best newspapers of the period, *El Independiente* of Las Vegas, whose editor for a number of years was Enrique H. Salazar, defined the role of the Hispanic press as never ceasing to impress upon its people the overwhelming necessity of a good education for both sexes.[22] The same newspaper published frequent articles in the 1890s about the benefits of education. One article of June 23, 1894, stressed the connection between education and reading newspapers:

cada quien posee el arbitrio, si así lo elige, de poder educarse asímismo por medio de tres factores que son: el cimiento colocado por medio de la escuela pública, la ilustración lograda por la lectura de libros útiles, y el conocimiento general adquerido por medio de la lectura del la prensa.

[each person has the means, if he so chooses, to educate himself in three ways which are: the foundation built by public schooling, the enlightenment gained by reading useful books, and the general knowledge acquired by reading newspapers.]

Newspaper editors like Salazar, who were looked up to as men of culture and sophistication in their communities, felt the moral obligation if not the financial necessity to encourage the habit of reading. For the average person with minimal reading skills, the daily paper could not only be a link to a wider world but also a vehicle for self-empowerment. Many editors expressed a sense of professional mission to bring the average neomexicano, richly endowed with a popular oral tradition, into the lettered world. This was the world of modernity that increasingly controlled New Mexican economic and political life, which had heretofore been based on personal, face-to-face relationships. Documents and deeds were now required in Anglo courts to defend one's property, and many illiterate neomexicanos were the hapless victims of unscrupulous speculators and their lawyers.

Written texts could also defend the historical property of a culture. An article in *El Independiente* of April 6, 1895, called for someone to write a true history of New Mexico, since all such efforts since 1846 "se reducen a enaltecer y referir los hechos de los conquistadores sin ocuparse en nada de los sucesos, vicisitudes, costumbres y vida íntima del verdadero pueblo de este territorio" [are reduced to exalting and referring the deeds of the conquerors without bothering at all with the accomplishments, vicissitudes, customs, and intimate life of the true people of the territory]. What was needed, it said, was someone capable of portraying "la constancia y arrojo de los hombres de raza española" [the steadfastness and courage of the people of the Spanish race], not just the Anglo-Saxon viewpoint.[23] The author concluded that without an educated populace, free of the inferiority complex bred by negative stereotyping, no such histories would be forthcoming.

Neomexicanos in the 1890s were conscious of having lost out economically to Anglos whose competitive business practices and drive to accumulate individual wealth were new to the Hispanic community. Many newspaper articles of the period urged the native people to acquire a practical education and to learn trades essential to the changing industrial landscape of the territory. The following excerpt is from an article entitled "Graves defectos que deben corregirse" [Grave defects that must be corrected], written by José Escobar, who places the burden of retooling themselves for the new economy squarely on the shoulders of neomexicanos:

> En épocas anteriores, por razones que á todos se les alcanza, los medios de educación eran más que dificiles, imposibles; pero hoy todo ha cambiado: Ya no hay que luchar con las bandadas de indios nómades azote constante de la civilización de otros tiempos: Nuestro territorio está lleno de escuelas y planteles de enseñanza en los que se educa convenientemente á nuestra niñez y juventud, y si tal es el caso, más censurable aún es esa indiferencia de los viejos nativos que quieren que sus hijos permanezcan en un estado de retroceso que no puede menos que causar vergüenza al mismo elemento hispano-americano medianamente instruido.[24]

> [In previous eras, for reasons known to all, the means of education were more than difficult, impossible; but today, everything has changed: now it is not necessary to struggle with bands of roving Indians, a constant affliction of the civilization of other times. Our territory is full of schools and nursery schools in which our infants and youth are well educated, and if such is the case, even more censurable is the indifference of the old native inhabitants who want their children to stay in a state of backwardness that can only cause shame to the average educated Hispanic American element.]

Neomexicanos, and especially the poor who were the most numerous, needed to be convinced that there were thousands of ways to earn an honorable living without having to raise small herds of cattle, cut wood, or grow grains that do not yield enough to live on, much less live in comfort. Educate the young people in practical trades, says Escobar, and the carpenter's chisel, blacksmith's anvil, weaver's loom, and tailor's scissors will produce four times the income of those traditional, unproductive labors.

Newspaper articles frequently exhorted neomexicanos to imitate the Anglo's practical way of life and use it to their own advantage.[25] The rhetoric of these articles was clearly in line with the liberal philosophy of positivism, which had developed a strong following among intellectuals on both sides of the border in the late nineteenth century. After the disastrous war with the United States, and then the French occupation of Mexico in the 1860s, the liberal intelligentsia under Benito Juárez—most of whom were journalists— defined the need for national reconstruction in terms of a new social order based on a practical, secular, and rational approach to life. According to Leopoldo Zea:

> It was thought that by means of a positivistic education a new
> type of man could eventually be created, free from all the defects
> he had inherited from the colony ruled by Spain, a man with a
> great practical mind such as had made the United States and
> England the great leaders of modern civilization.[26]

North of the border, in New Mexico, newspaper editors espoused the positivist objectives, but with the realization that the context of neomexicano society was different. What they saw as the major obstacle to the progress of their people was the disunity and debilitating self-doubt engendered by having been a "conquered people" who, despite being in the majority and still living in their homeland, found themselves at a cultural disadvantage in the American way of life that had invaded the Southwest. A front-page article— probably by E. H. Salazar—entitled "El porvenir de nuestro pueblo" [The future of our people], in *El Independiente* (November 9, 1899), analyzes the psychological dimensions of the problem facing neomexicanos but does not absolve them of the responsibility of doing something about it:

> Los cincuenta y tres años que han transcurrido desde la adquisi-
> ción de Nuevo México por los Estados Unidos no ha bastado
> para que se disipen enteramente la timidez y desaliento que
> recaen sobre todo pueblo conquistado, aún cuando sus conquis-
> tadores se muestren benévolos y no procuren abusar demasiado
> de sus derechos. Pero la conquista siempre es conquista y los
> vencidos por fuerza quedan por largo tiempo sumerjidos á los
> vencedores, mayormente cuando estos tienen la ventaja en
> conocimientos, civilización y ártes, que acrecentan la superioridad
> que poseen con el hecho de pertenecer á la nación conquistadora
> . . . . Nuestro pueblo no ha sabido aprovechar como debiera los

privilegios que le concediera el gobierno americano, y parece que
se ha desanimado, se ha achicado, desconfiando en tal manera en
sus propias fuerzas y capacidad que en todas las ocasiones posi-
bles ha dejado sus poderes á manos extrañas, con tal resultado
que la costumbre se ha convertido en ley no escrita, y no hay
ninguna singularidad en que nuestros protagonistas nos aprecien
en conformidad con el valor que nos damos. Dice un adagio, "Al
que se hace de miel, se lo comen las moscas," y esto es un evan-
gelio chico que retrata fielmente en muchos puntos la historia del
pueblo nativo de Nuevo México. Aún peor que eso, damos un
ejemplo de imprevisión y falta de perspectiva luchando unos con
otros, rebajándonos mútuamente y dando á conocer por medio
de nuestras discordias que nuestra ambición principal es que
todos permanezcamos en igual estado de insignificancia y opro-
bio. . . . Tenemos á la vista el espejo donde debemos mirarnos en
los actos y procederes de los inmigrantes que de otros estados
vienen á resentarse en nuestro medio, los cuales, sean lo que
fueren en otros respectos, son dignos de alabanza por su amor
acendrado al trabajo y por el esfuerzo constante que siempre
están haciendo para mejorar su suerte. Imitando sus virtudes é
ignorando sus defectos es como se abrirá para nosotros la senda
del adelanto y progreso que es tan indispensable para que no
seamos relegados á la categoria de séres inferiores, sin indepen-
dencia y sin iniciativa, con el sólo arbitrio de obedecer el man-
dato y recoger las migajas que caen de la mesa de los amos.

[The fifty-three years that have passed since the acquisition of
New Mexico by the United States have not sufficed to dissipate
entirely the timidity and discouragement that befall every conquered people, even when its conquerors are benevolent and try
not to abuse their rights too much. But conquest is always conquest, and the losers necessarily remain submerged for a long
time by the winners, especially when the latter have the advantage in knowledge, civilization and the arts which enhances the
superiority they possess by virtue of belonging to the conquering
nation. . . . Our people have not known how to take advantage, as
they should have, of the privileges the American government has
accorded them, and it seems that they have lost their spirit, their
stature, by distrusting their own strengths and ability, leaving
their power too often in foreign hands, with the result that the
custom has become an unwritten law, and it cannot be surprising
that our protagonists judge us in accordance with the value we
place on ourselves. An old adage says, "One who is made of
honey will be eaten by flies"; this is a simple proverb that faith-

fully portrays many aspects of the history of the native people of New Mexico. Even worse than this, we offer a regrettable example of lack of vision and perspective by fighting among ourselves and letting it be known through our discord that our principal ambition is that we all remain in the same insignificant and despised condition. . . . We have in front of us the mirror to see ourselves in the actions and conduct of the immigrants from other states who come to settle in our midst, who, whatever they may be in other ways, are worthy of praise for their pure love of work and the constant effort they always make to improve their luck. Imitating their virtues and ignoring their defects is the way to clear the path for us to improvement and progress which is so indispensable if we are not to be relegated to the category of inferior beings, without independence or initiative, with the sole option of obeying orders and picking up the crumbs that fall from the master's table.]

Salazar was calling for neomexicanos to look at their situation vis-à-vis that of the Anglos and to adjust their habits for their own benefit. Not to do so, in his opinion, would be to accept a marginal, inferior status for themselves in American life. Was he advocating a new identity for his people? I don't believe he was suggesting something that drastic; rather, he seems to interpret the reality of bicultural coexistence in a capitalistic society as necessitating a modified ethic—or a new set of civic virtues—on the part of Hispanics, so as to reap the full benefits of citizenship.[27] Salazar espoused the liberal intellectual perspective of his time and culture, claiming that individual freedom and constitutional rights enabled all citizens to improve their situation and that affiliation with the United States had, on the whole, made a manifest improvement in the well-being of most neomexicanos in contrast to what they had known before.[28] In Mexico, as Salazar and other intellectual neomexicanos knew, by the late 1880s the Díaz dictatorship had curtailed civil rights, closed down the free press, and undermined the positivist motto of "Liberty, Order and Progress" on which it had campaigned.[29] By force of historical and geographic circumstances, Salazar argued, Spanish-speaking New Mexicans now had the obligation to look at themselves in the mirror of the dominant "other", and not to disparage but to emulate what they saw in practical ways if they wanted to be protagonists of history. The objective was not assimilation or acculturation, but accommodation for the betterment of the native community.

Some of Salazar's compatriots, unmoved by positivistic idealism or pragmatic realism, were skeptical about any "new order" or accommodative effort in view of the unrelenting racist epithets they heard around them. In the early 1900s, New Mexico was still struggling for statehood and being manipulated by political factions who saw advantages in repeatedly blocking this initiative, or in pushing joint statehood with Arizona, or for a change in name for the new state in order to Americanize it more. All of these moves had some foundation in racial bias, and much of it came from the eastern New Mexico counties of Eddy, Chavez, and Roosevelt, where newer Anglo immigrants, many of them Texans with segregationist beliefs, had settled. Frequent newspaper articles in the Spanish-language press attest to the native population's outrage and disgust with maneuvers to deny Hispano voting rights. Between 1905 and 1907 many editorials in *El Independiente*, and in other newspapers as well, drew attention to the way that race was being injected into politics by a few segments of the Anglo population, allegedly from the Democratic party, who were claiming the superiority of "whites" and labeling the native population as Indians and Mexicans. An anonymous poem in the same newspaper, signed simply "Veritas," protests this situation and reads in part:

A los Democratas Anglo-Texanos de Eddy y Chavez

¿Porqué, con ódio implacable,
Persiguís á los nativos
Y os mostrais hoscos y esquivos
Sin achaque razonable?
Vuestra ruindad miserable
Que blasona de arrogancia,
Tiene algo de concordancia
Con los netos de esclavistas
Que fundaron sus conquistas
En hollar la tolerancia.

. . . .

Estos tan recien venidos
Demócratas rozagantes
Son malos ó intolerantes
Con fueros establecidos;
Por eso tan decididos
Se hallan en su necio plan
De procurar con afan
Y bajo ardides contrechos
La anulación de derechos
Que garantidos están.

[To the Anglo-Texan Democrats of Eddy and Chavez

Why, with implacable hatred,
Do you pursue the native people
And act sullen and scornful
Without reasonable pretext?
Your miserable malice
Which is boastfully arrogant,
Has something in common
With the tenets of slaveholders
Who founded their conquests
On contempt for tolerance.

. . . .

These recent arrivals
Pompous Democrats
Are ignorant or intolerant
Of established laws;
Thus they are very determined
In their foolish scheme
To try as hard as possible
And with dirty tricks
To annul rights
Guaranteed by law.]

El Independiente referred to these racial supremacists as "un cáncer interior" [an internal cancer] that was threatening to destroy the vital forces of native New Mexicans.[30] In fact, it had the beneficial effect of drawing the neomexicano community closer together in a renewed determination to guard and preserve the rights of *la raza* when statehood was imminent and it came time to negotiate a state constitution in 1910.

Elected delegates to the constitutional convention were more than two-thirds Republican, the dominant party in New Mexico since the latter part of the previous century. Of the one hundred delegates, thirty-two were Hispanics—all Republicans. Despite their low representation in proportion to their majority status in the population, the Spanish-speaking delegates were considered a "formidable force" at the convention where Hispanic voting and education rights were written into the constitution and made nearly impossible to amend.[31] Without the guarantees of the Treaty of Guadalupe Hidalgo behind them, and without their voting power as a group, which made the other delegates sensitive to compromise, measures to protect the cultural integrity of the Spanish-speaking community might not have been so fully incorporated into the constitution. This document would set New Mexico's future course and define it as the only legally bilingual state with particular responsibilities to its Hispanic citizens—at least in theory.

In the elections of 1911, however, neomexicano candidates in both parties lost to Anglo opponents because a significant percentage of Anglos voted race before party. This obvious slap in the face to neomexicanos awakened a new sense of ethnic consciousness and added further fuel to the argument that New Mexico Hispanics needed to stop bickering among themselves and unite across party lines to elect native sons if they wanted to defend their interests in the new state. An article in *El Combate* of Wagon Mound, on December 1, 1911, entitled "Abajo Mexicanos" [Down with Mexicans], commented sarcastically that Anglos had unilaterally co-opted the term *Americans* and voted against *Mexicans*, who would thus not have a representative voice in the state in which they were the majority population. "Los así llamados Americanos" [the so-called Americans] must realize that native New Mexicans may have ancestry in Mexico but "somos Americanos verdaderos en todo el sentido de la palabra" [we are true Americans in every sense of the word]. If we are to understand this statement today as it was meant in its original context, we must entertain the notion that, for native New Mexicans of Spanish-Mexican background, being American was not incompatible with or antithetical to retaining a Hispanic cultural identity—in other words, that nationality should not be confused with race.[32] It presupposed the possibility of being both authentically American on the basis of rights and citizenship, and ethnically and culturally Hispanic, without disloyalty to either side.

The issue of identity and appropriate nomenclature is a sensitive one for

Spanish-speaking Americans today just as it was a century ago. It is undoubt-edly exacerbated by misconceptions on the one hand and ideological per-spectives on the other. Hispanics themselves have adhered to mythologies of identity when it suited their needs. The ambivalence felt by middle- and up-per-class neomexicanos when large numbers of poor Mexican immigrants poured into the Southwest after the revolution led many of them to proclaim themselves *Spanish* Americans, denying they had any Indian blood or ances-tral roots in mestizo Mexico. They preferred to ally themselves with a mythic cultural identity that "glorified the region's Spanish heritage while ignoring or discriminating against living Mexicans."[33] The fact that the roots of the vigorous Hispanic folk traditions in the mountain villages of New Mexico could be traced to Spain made the case for a "Spanish New Mexico" more colorful but not really defensible. Another side of the mythical identity coin is the notion of Aztlán, an ethno-spiritual homeland dear to Chicano activ-ists who cleave to the embellished memory of their Indo-Hispanic ancestors. They have posited the formation of "a new man" in whom "Indio mysticism is merging with modern technology" to create a liberated future, free of the colonized past.[34] Narrative myths of the right and the left are equally subject to flights of fancy and cultural nationalism.

The major contribution of the Spanish-language press in the late nine-teenth and early twentieth centuries was its self-conscious stance vis-à-vis the collision of cultures in New Mexico and the way it articulated the issue of identity, examining it from so many angles. There was no unanimity among editors in the territorial period any more than there was uniformity within the neomexicano community. Nonetheless, certain collective concerns are evident and allow us to see that, at the end of the last century, the Hispano press began resisting and combating with the printed word the distortions and untruths that continue to be the target for today's Chicano writers. The theory of some scholars that Hispanics were victimized and rendered an in-visible minority by racist internal colonization needs to be modified in the light of the evidence in black and white newsprint in Spanish.[35]

Hispanics have not been a silent minority in this country, and if they were not heard it is because their contributions to American intellectual and liter-ary history have not been valued. Their perspective, after all, did not jibe with what was being said in mainstream historical discourse at the turn of the century about the American frontier. When Frederick Jackson Turner chided his fellow historians in 1893 for not realizing the significance of the frontier in American history, he meant that the Great West, as he called it, contains "the record of social evolution," that the frontier is "the outer edge of the wave—the meeting point between savagery and civilization" that in-evitably leads toward the great objective: Progress.[36] Turner was right in see-ing the frontier as a crossroads and a site of transformation that set Anglo westerners against easterners, but Turner's ethnocentrism caused him to de-value cultures that did not reflect his modernist view of human development, advancing ever forward, harnessing the power of industrial technology.

The Spanish-language press, as a bridge between tradition and modernity and as an advocate for its people in Hispanic New Mexico, served as a counter-discourse contesting the Anglo myth of the frontier and claiming a space for otherness in American society. In its pages one finds the multivocal reality of neomexicano cultural identity that resists any monolithic definition. As the voices of the Hispanic past join those of the present, it will become harder and harder to turn a deaf ear and allow stereotypes to survive.

6

Language and Cultural Erosion

An integral and reciprocal relationship exists between language, culture, and reality. Culture is embedded in language, language is based on and derived from a lived reality, and both language and culture create and mold that reality.[1] Thus, to take away any part of this intimate connection is to endanger the cultural community. According to Edward Sapir, language is the crucial element:

> Language is a great force of socialization, probably the greatest that exists. By this is meant not merely the obvious fact that significant social intercourse is hardly possible without language but that *the mere fact of a common speech serves as a peculiarly potent symbol of the social solidarity of those who speak the language.* The psychological significance of this goes far beyond the association of particular languages with nationalities, political entities, or smaller local groups. In between the recognized dialect or language as a whole and the individualized speech of a given individual lies a kind of linguistic unit which is not often discussed by the linguist but which is of the greatest importance to social psychology. This is the subform of a language which is current among a group of people who are held together by ties of common interest.[2] [Emphasis added]

As the vehicle for cultural accumulation and historical transmission, language defines a social group. Its codes of communication, or sign systems, relate to both "high" (elite) and "low" (popular) culture. By virtue of its social function, language is not static or monologic. The nature of human discourse, as Mikhail Bakhtin has theorized, is dialogic—shaped by the anticipation of a response from an "other"—and characterized by a constant multivocal struggle for interpretive power.[3] On the individual as well as the group level, the articulation of language is a dynamic, interactive process of self-definition that has political implications. If one segment of society tries to dominate and control discourse, the response of the other may be oppositional, contestatory, or subversive.

Alfred Arteaga, in a recent study of colonialism and the language of Mexican Americans, observes that the United States "espouses a single language ethos [and] it strives very actively to assert a monolingual identity," and thus, "being 'chicano' is a process of continual remaking, a discursive process that is always negotiated within the context of the circumscribing discursive practices of the United States."[4] Arteaga acknowledges his debt to the work of Rosaura Sánchez, who posits a direct connection between the ideology of the capitalist system and the subordination of minority languages: Latino immigrants, she says, buy into the myth of English-language acquisition, attend schools that promote the dominant ideology, and later find they are locked into low-paying jobs and an inferior social status.[5] I cannot subscribe to the Marxist orientation of her theory, but there is substantial historical evidence that linguicentrism is as deeply ingrained as ethnocentrism in the United States. The general disregard for foreign languages and for the benefits of retaining immigrant language facility through the proper implementation of bilingual education in American schools is as debilitating to the United States in the global economy as it is to the psyche of its non–English speaking immigrants whose native culture erodes with the loss of their native language. Hispanics in the United States have negotiated this linguistic bind more creatively and energetically than most groups, largely because of their proximity to and ongoing contact with their lands of origin. Spanish in the United States today is not just localized in a few ethnic enclaves, but is becoming an integral part of our national culture and is, ironically, being reinforced rather than excluded by the capitalist system. As Hispanics become the largest minority group in the country in the twenty-first century, their language of origin is becoming a market vehicle and an exploitable resource that may gain more profile and attention for its speakers than any political protest they mounted in the past.

The situation of neomexicanos in the nineteenth century operated inversely. They were the dominant culture, in the majority by population, but Anglos were pouring into the territory and increasing in number every day. It was the English language that was becoming commercially profitable. In that context and at that time, therefore, the politics of education and the relationship between language, culture, and reality were issues of crucial significance for neomexicanos. In the discourse of the Spanish-language press one finds a keen awareness of the power that English represented in the territory and a resistance to the myth of English acquisition if it meant the sacrifice of the Spanish language and neomexicano cultural heritage. But the issue of language and its power to shape culture actually goes farther back in the history of New Mexico and its Hispanic people.

The empire of Spain in the sixteenth century justified its conquest of the so-called New World not only on religious grounds, but also on the belief that the indigenous cultures were inferior in their dependence on orality and visual representation, rather than the use of the written word.[6] With Spanish colonization came the displacement of aboriginal cultures: Spanish, the language of European *logos*—of bureaucrats and evangelizing priests—imposed its cultural values over the *mythos* of Amerindian speech. Theoretically, the Laws of the Indies promulgated by the Spanish government in the mid-1500s guaranteed protection to the native peoples, but *encomendero* overlords exploited their charges and made a mockery of the law. The semiotic gap between theory and practice meant cultural exile for the conquered: their voices could not be heard, and if heard, they were not understood, except through the medium of interpreters whose motives and vision were rarely the same as the native speakers themselves. In the struggle for interpretive power and cultural identity, the weak were those who did not control, much less understand the language of the invading empire.

Before contact with Anglo-Americans, the Spanish-speaking community in New Mexico lived in isolated settlements, primarily in the mountains, high plateaus, and valleys within a fifty-mile radius of Santa Fe. If the myth of great wealth and edenic pastures lured the explorers, friars, and their attendant Indian-mestizo retinues to this region in the 1530s, the reality of harsh terrains and great distances separated them from the colonial cities to the south and left those who first settled New Mexico with Juan de Oñate in 1598 to fend off attack from marauding Indians and to survive by their own wits. They might have abandoned their remote outpost and endured the long journey back to Mexico City had not the Franciscan friars insisted on their obligation to stay.[7] Abuses and discontent suffered by the Indians sparked the indigenous revolt of 1680, driving the settlers south to seek refuge, but in late 1692 Diego de Vargas led a resettlement north once again. Like an island cut off from colonial centers of learning, cast adrift for another hundred years by a viceregal Spanish government that sent officials to govern on a rotating basis, the Hispanic settlers of northern New Mexico created a unique culture of both Spanish and Indian stock that occupied its own living space, near to but separate from the Pueblo peoples of the upper Rio Grande Valley. Retaining archaic modes of speech from the early colonial period, in addition to some local Indian and Mexican Indian words, these neomexicanos spoke a distinctive dialect of Spanish, similar to but not the same as Mexican Spanish.[8] They were forced by circumstances to be a self-sufficient and tightly knit community in terms of kinship and reciprocal obligations, and thus the traditional caste system of New Spain broke down as rich and poor alike lived in simple adobe extended-family dwellings around central patios and plazas for protection, with their own intricate protocols for sharing land and water rights. They also shared a oral, folk-based culture rooted in the land and the traditions of their ancestors in which song, verse, narratives, plays, and proverbs were the primary forms of entertainment and of passing along knowledge from one generation to the next.

These early neomexicano settlers did without the educational facilities standard in other less remote Spanish colonies. Printed books existed in New Mexico, but they belonged primarily to the clergy and to the short-term provincial governors; even prior to the Pueblo Revolt, well-known works by recent Spanish authors such as Cervantes, Quevedo, Saavedra Fajardo, and even Antonio de Nebrija's Spanish grammar circulated among educated friends who had private libraries. Trial records of the Holy Office of the Inquisition, for example, reveal that the wife of Bernardo López de Mendizábal, governor of New Mexico from 1659 to 1661, was accused of heretical beliefs because witnesses saw her reading a text "in an unknown tongue," which turned out to be *Orlando furioso* by the Italian author Ludovico Ariosto.[9] Local prelates did not tolerate kindly any texts that might undermine their proselytizing mission, and most neomexicanos had no access to such texts or knowledge of how to read them. Almost two centuries later, Pedro Bautisa Pino, representing his neomexicano homeland before the Spanish parliament in 1812, spoke of the "miserable condition" in which his people lived:

> The province of New Mexico does not have among its public
> institutions any of those found in other provinces of Spain. So
> backward is it in this matter that the names of such institutions
> are not even known. The benefit of primary letters is given only
> to the children of those who are able to contribute to the salary of
> the school teacher. Even in the capital it has been impossible to
> engage a teacher and to furnish education for everyone. Of
> course there are no colleges of any kind.[10]

When Padre Antonio José Martínez established a school in Taos in 1826, his biographer and former student Santiago Valdez tells us, he had trouble finding a teacher who could even spell properly.[11] There was no printing press in New Mexico until 1834, when one was brought from Mexico by Ramón Abréu and used in Santa Fe by Antonio Barreiro, a government official, to print the first, short-lived newspaper called *El Crepúsculo de la Libertad* [The Dawn of Liberty]; Padre Martínez bought the press in 1835 and took it to Taos to print school texts and his own writings.[12] For many years the padre's school prepared students to be seminarians and lawyers, and after New Mexico became part of the United States, he urged all his students to reap the benefits of learning English. Native historian Benjamin Read has credited the

Catholic church with the only sustained support of education in early New Mexico. He notes that right after the American invasion under Colonel Stephen W. Kearny, Governor Donaciano Vigil reported to the first legislature in 1847 that only one public school existed in the territory, supported by county funds, and only one teacher was employed; Vigil called for a law establishing a school "in every town, village and neighborhood," but it was not enacted.[13] After Archbishop Jean Baptiste Lamy arrived in Santa Fe, the first free church schools teaching English were begun, and later the Sisters of Loretto Catholic academy for girls (1853) and St. Michael's for boys (1859) were established. Protestant mission schools followed shortly thereafter. In 1860, 1863, 1872, and 1884 the territorial legislature passed public school bills, but there was no funding to implement them.[14]

When the New Mexico territory was ceded by Mexico to the United States under the Treaty of Guadalupe Hidalgo in 1848, the Spanish-speaking natives who chose to become United States citizens were promised the "enjoyment of all the rights of citizens," as defined in the U.S. Constitution, and the status of statehood for the territory "as soon as possible."[15] Some thirty years passed without the federal government taking any more interest than had its predecessors in the development, educationally or otherwise, of the territory, or in granting it the autonomy of statehood. It was not until the arrival of the railroad that the native population felt increasing pressure to "Americanize," which presented real and potential threats to their traditional culture and language. Paradoxically, these threats were directly correlated to the implementation of the rights they had been assured in 1848.

Patricia Nelson Limerick has pointed out a widespread pattern of betrayal in the Anglo-American tradition of "verbal activity" in the West arising from "the treachery of words"; the credulous fan of western history may be disquieted to read her caveat that "western history is virtually the P. T. Barnum of historical fields, providing opportunities galore for suckers to confuse literal fact with literary fact."[16] Limerick recognizes not only that "the West" meant something entirely different to those who called it home before Anglos arrived, but also that conflicts of all kinds were often compounded by the inability to find a common language—literally so—or even a translator who could communicate accurately and fairly between cultures. There were and are still all kinds of reasons to distrust what one reads because "the process of invasion, conquest, and colonization was the kind of activity that provoked shiftiness in verbal behavior."[17] Considering the way Spanish-speaking New Mexicans were insulted in Washington for decades after the invasion of their native land, maybe they believed too much in the text of a treaty signed by elected representatives of the same government. The Treaty of Guadalupe Hidalgo guaranteed that their lives, property, and religion would be protected; there was never any explicit mention of the right to preserve the language and culture that had defined their identity in the mountains, mesas, and valleys where they had lived for centuries. Yet how could the promised "enjoyment of all the rights of citizens of the United States" be contingent upon a denial of the basic elements of their self-definition? The newspapers in Spanish articulated this paradox with eloquence. But even the rhetoric of the newspapers must be read with an eye to possible subtexts.

In 1888 a minority report of the Committee on Territories of the House of Representatives singled out New Mexico, the oldest of five western territories being considered for statehood under an omnibus bill, as being unfit and unready, citing sources that were outdated and insulting to the native Hispanic population.[18] Politics and prejudice guided the thinking of the Republican committee members, but the report also noted the lack of a nonsectarian public education system in New Mexico, where schools were traditionally church-controlled and conducted in Spanish. The eventual outcome of congressional voting was that Montana, Wyoming, and the Dakotas gained statehood and New Mexico, having tried four times since 1850, was rejected again. When Democratic candidate Antonio Joseph ran for reelection as territorial delegate to Congress in 1888, he had the Republican minority report reprinted in Spanish and English and circulated to voters in the territory. According to his opponent, Thomas Catron, who was an adept politician in English and Spanish, it was "the only thing on earth" that elected Joseph.[19]

In 1889, when a bill was introduced in the territorial legislature that provided for nonsectarian public schools and tax levies to pay for them Anglos supported it, but it was defeated by the traditionally Catholic and tax-fearing neomexicano majority.[20] Again, a year later, the voters rejected two-to-one a proposed state constitution containing similar provisions for public education. Politicians in the U.S. Congress continued to exert pressure on New Mexico by discussing, among other threatening ethnocentric and lexocentric strategies, the proposal that English be a qualification for jury duty in the territories.[21]

Barely four months after the defeat of the constitution, another comprehensive school bill was introduced in the territorial legislature and this time the vote was favorable. Its passage has been attributed to pressure from Washington and the local Anglo press as well as disunity among the ranks of Hispanos, some of whom favored public education and statehood strongly enough to go against the recommendation of the Catholic church, swallow their dislike of taxes, and support the bill.[22] The outcome promised educational opportunities for Hispanics, but actually represented a setback for their culture since the medium of instruction would shift from Spanish to English. The new school bill of 1892 made no specific provision against Spanish but stipulated only that Spanish would be taught in some districts alongside English and that "in school districts where the only language spoken is Spanish, the teacher shall have a knowledge of both English and Spanish."[23] The ambiguity of the law with regard to the language of instruction and the level of the teacher's ability in both languages left the door open to much bending of its meaning in a variety of circumstances.

Once the school bill had passed, Anglo editors in the territory seemed satisfied and showed little interest in pursuing the issue of education in their papers.[24] In contrast, the Spanish-language press all over the territory continued to devote considerable attention to the issue, with the most vocal newspapers being Las Vegas's *La Voz del Pueblo* and *El Independiente*. Porter Stratton claims that Spanish-language editors were "moderate in their demands and often apologetic when questions of ethnic differences were raised."[25] Conveying a similar assessment of the neomexicano attitude toward the 1891 school bill, Ralph Twitchell, a leading New Mexican historian, wrote in 1911:

> No opposition has ever been encountered in any part of the territory in the matter of employment of English-speaking teachers in districts where, prior to the enactment of the law of 1891, only Spanish had been taught. In truth, the Spanish-speaking people have evinced an almost universal desire and purpose to have competent teachers, well-versed in the English language, employed and assigned to teach in isolated districts where, in times past, the only schools existing were those in which the Spanish language alone was used.[26]

What Twitchell says is not incorrect in that English was recognized as a practical asset, but he and Stratton played down the oppositional nature of what they read in the newspapers in their desire to smooth over the clash of cultures and make New Mexico's history less confrontational. In their will to endorse cultural assimilation, they wrote out of their interpretations of New Mexican history, the concern, belligerence, and open resentment frequently expressed in the Spanish-language press after 1891 regarding the language of instruction, classroom techniques, and teacher credentials in New Mexico's schools. All of this had a direct bearing on how the Spanish-speaking student would be educated and to what end.

In reply to both Stratton and Twitchell's statements, it must be acknowledged that (1) Spanish-language editors did not focus on the subject of ethnic difference unless provoked to their own defense; (2) they realized that better education was sorely needed to improve neomexicano economic status and protect their rights; and (3) they recognized the practical need to learn English, which they referred to as "the national language." One newspaper, *El Promotor Escolar* of Las Cruces, dedicated a large portion of its space in 1891–92 to printing English lessons following the Ollendorff system. However, the learning of English was promoted as a means to an end, which was ethnic self-preservation and advancement, not complete assimilation into the Anglo mainstream. This excerpt from an article in *El Independiente*, January 2, 1897, makes that point:

> No nos basta con saber el castellano aunque sea en todos respectos mas hermoso y mejor que el ingles, pues bajo tal pie, nuestro pueblo se encontrará siempre en una posición desventajosa y a merced de aventureros y caballeros de industria cuya única superioridad consiste en que hablan el idioma nacional. . . . Mientras no nos asimilemos e identifiquemos *en el asunto de idioma* con los demas ciudadanos de esta república, seremos contemplados como extranjeros que no merecen ningun privilegio ni acatamiento en el ejercicio de nuestros derechos. [Emphasis added]

> [It is not enough to know Spanish even though it is in every respect more beautiful and preferable to English. Following that route, our people will always find itself disadvantaged and at the mercy of adventurers and gentlemen of industry whose only superior trait consists of speaking the national language. . . . As long as we resist assimilating and identifying with other citizens of this republic *in the matter of language*, we will be looked upon as foreigners who do not deserve any privilege or consideration in the exercise of our rights.]

Neomexicanos understood that learning English would empower them politically and economically, but they also perceived that to lose their native language would have the converse effect of eviscerating them culturally. Their vitality as a people—the core of their self-identity—would be lost if the schools did not also teach Spanish to neomexicano youngsters, and it was these generations that they were mainly worried about. These future neomexicanos, more and more exposed to English, would become linguistic exiles in their own homeland and without Spanish, would lose the collective memory of their culture. Article after article in the Spanish-language press from the 1890s well into the 1920s (after the state constitution of 1910 guaranteed Hispanic children "perfect equality with other children in all public schools")[27] called for teaching Spanish in the classroom alongside English. The modern roots of the bilingual education movement in the United States can be found in this period in New Mexico.

It might be argued that the Spanish-language press came out as a strong advocate of teaching Spanish in the schools in order to assure its own survival. But Spanish speakers constituted the most numerous segment of New

Mexico's population in the early 1900s and would continue to be the majority until the 1930s. Spanish was still the primary language of communication in the neomexicano community, not a mixture of Spanish and English. Much more plausible is the explanation that Hispanic editors of the time had a heightened sense of ethnic awareness and a greater-than-average appreciation of the Spanish language as a cultural lifeline for their people. One writer, in *La Bandera Americana* (Albuquerque), August 31, 1901, was optimistic in thinking that Spanish would be preserved by use in the home and was concerned that the teachers in rural Hispanic districts were not proficient enough in English to teach that language well, but he concluded by saying "es sumamente necesario, para todos fines, que á la par que sabemos un idioma sepamos el otro, esto es el Español y el Inglés" [it is extremely necessary, for all purposes, that just as we know one language we should know the other, in other words Spanish and English].

The following excerpt from *La Voz del Pueblo*, July 7, 1894, presents the case in favor of teaching Spanish and learning to use it well from a perspective that is equally valid today. Its one obvious *anglicismo* echoes the Anglo slant on values and was probably stressed to bolster the author's argument in bicultural circles:

> Ahora, si los hispano-americanos insisten en que se enseñe en las escuelas públicas y privadas del Territorio, el idioma español igualmente con el inglés, es porque aman ese lenguage sonoro y musical que aprendieron de sus antepasados, y en honor á su memoria quieren conservarlo para siempre integro como el único idioma del hogar doméstico. Hay aun otras dos razones, muy poderosas, porqué el idioma de Cervantes debe de enseñarse igualmente con el inglés en las escuelas de Nuevo México. La experiencia nos ha hecho conocer, que para que un educando aprenda propiamente un idioma extrangero se hace necesario que conozca algo del suyo. Esta es la primera y muy poderosa á nuestro parecer. La otra es muy importante porque se reduce á los "business". Sabemos que por ferro-carril ya no nos separan mas que unos cuantos dias de camino de las populosas repúblicas sudamericanas, y de nuestra vecina república mexicana. El idioma que se habla en esos países es el español, y por consecuencia todos los negocios mercantiles se transan en ese idioma. Tambien sabemos que los Estados Unidos estan haciendo un gran esfuerzo para ensanchar sus relaciones negociales con esas naciones á fin de que los mercaderes hispano-americanos compren de los de esta nacion todos sus efectos de consumo que ellos no producen, y los nuestros en cambio compren de ellos lo que no se produce en nuestro suelo. Esto, en vista de las amistosas

relaciones que existen entre los citados gobiernos, tiene que realizarse en un dia no muy lejano. Para tener buen éxito en sus negociaciones, los comerciantes tendrán que aprender el idioma español—emplear á otros que lo sepan para que puedan conducirles sus negocios. En las ciudades del oriente se esta enseñando ya el castellano en anticipacion a este orden de cosas, y los mexicanos de México en cambio estan entregándose asiduamente al estudio del inglés.

En vista de esto, hay que extrañar,—mas bien podrá culpársenos á nosotros los neo-mexicanos porque anhelamos el estudio de ambos idiomas? Los "business" requieren que estudiemos ambos idiomas; y se hace necesario que en las escuelas públicas de Nuevo México se enseñe el español y el inglés. Lo único que ahora hay que lamentar, es que por causa de haber permanecido Nuevo México como territorio por tan largo tiempo, y por causa tambien de langostas que hemos tenido entre nosotros, que no han hecho mas que chuparnos la sangre, una gran parte de las masas del pueblo se ha quedado sin recibir una buena educacion.

De la educacion; esto es, una educacion sana, tanto en un idioma como en el otro, depende la completa prosperidad y desarrollo de Nuevo México.[28]

[Now, if Spanish-Americans insist that the Spanish language be taught along with English in the public and private schools of the Territory, it is because they love that sonorous and musical language they learned from their ancestors, and in honor of their memory they want to preserve it forever intact as the only language of the domestic hearth. There are still two other, very powerful reasons why the language of Cervantes should be taught along with English in the schools of New Mexico. Experience has taught us that in order to learn a foreign language well, a student must know something of his own language. This is the first and, in our opinion, most convincing reason. The other is very important because it has to do with "business." We know that with the railroad we are now separated only by a few days journey from the most populated South American countries and from our neighbor, Mexico. The language spoken in those countries is Spanish, and thus all commercial transactions take place in that language. We also know that the United States is making a great effort to expand its business relations with those nations so that the Hispanic American markets will buy from this nation all the consumer products they do not produce, and so that, in turn, our markets buy from them what is not produced on our soil. In view of the friendly relations between governments nowadays, this has to happen before too long. To be successful in their dealings, business people will have to learn Spanish or employ those who know it in order to do business. In the cities of the East, Spanish is being taught already in anticipation of this order of things, and the Mexicans are also assiduously devoting themselves to learning English.

In view of this, is it any wonder, or can we neomexicanos be blamed for wanting to study both languages? "Business" demands that we study both, and it is imperative that the public schools of New Mexico teach both Spanish and English. The only regrettable thing now is that, because New Mexico has been a territory for so long, and also because there are leeches among us who have continually sucked our blood, a large number of the masses of people have been left without a good education.

The entire prosperity and development of New Mexico depends on education—that is, on a sound education in Spanish as well as English.]

All of the arguments presented above—(1) the desire to preserve the Spanish cultural heritage, (2) the importance of knowing one's own language well in order to master another, and (3) the advantage of knowing Spanish for conducting international business—are adduced today in support of bilingual education programs. Yet some seventy-five years before the issue of bilingual education received widespread national attention and endorsement by the federal government, the Spanish-language newspapers were advocating it in New Mexico.

Articles also appeared regularly expressing concern with how Hispanic students were being taught in the schools, which indicated that there was a double standard of education evolving and a two-sided problem as a consequence. On the one hand, impoverished rural districts were served by Hispanic teachers who knew very little English and who had no professional training in pedagogy; on the other, many Anglo teachers in other areas were not proficient enough in Spanish to communicate with native Hispanic students who therefore did not learn their lessons and felt inferior in the classroom.[29] Spanish-speaking students were in a double-jeopardy situation that only promised to get worse with time. Lorin W. Brown, of Anglo–Hispanic background, grew up in Taos and later taught school in the remote mountain village of Cordova, New Mexico. Documenting Hispano folklife for the Federal Writers' Project in New Mexico in the 1930s, Brown interviewed old-timers to find out what early schools were like:

As in most of the settlements of New Mexico, the first school in Cordova was conducted in a room of a private home. The teacher was paid fifty cents per month for every child sent to him. Each child was required to carry a stick of wood to the school each day to be used in the corner fireplace that alone furnished heat. Backless *tarimas* ("benches") served them as seats and a square of well-scraped hide served as a slate or copybook. A piece of charcoal was the pencil. Instruction was in Spanish and embraced three subjects—reading, writing, and spelling, the last taught in the old manner. Each syllable of the word to be spelled was spelled separately and its pronunciation given immediately after; the next syllable was treated the same, and so on until the whole word was pronounced in its entirety. The entire process, repeated at top voice by a class in unison, made the schoolroom a veritable Babel. All studying was done aloud. It is not surprising that the school term lasted only four months out of the year.[30]

When Brown himself taught school in Cordova in the 1920s, classes were given entirely in English, with no Spanish allowed in the classroom. This language transition, within about thirty years time, is an indication of how schools were changing in New Mexico, but without addressing the learning needs of the Spanish-speaking population.

The sustained demand expressed in the neomexicano press for the teaching of Spanish by qualified teachers alongside the teaching of English, "the national language," is an example of cultural politics in action. It began in approximately 1894 and increased around 1906–8, coming to the fore once again in 1914–16; all of these were periods in which Hispano ethnicity was particularly vocal in conjunction with political issues that threatened its discursive legitimacy in the intercultural dialogue (for example, enabling acts with attendant eastern criticism, joint statehood, state electoral politics, and so forth). The Spanish-language press acted as a cultural mediator in what most editors seemed to perceive as a crucial negotiation to halt the imposition of English (and Anglo culture) on the Hispanic population.

Language, culture, and reality were all inextricably involved in this negotiation on the western frontier that Anglos sought to tame, occupy, and Americanize. By the 1890s the subject position of neomexicanos, or their sense of cultural identity, was already in a state of in-betweeness or hybridity as a result of living for half a century under U.S. law as a conquered but not a displaced people. The showdown over language, as Hispanic editors interpreted it, would not be a classic western duel-to-the-death, but it would negotiate a shared space of understanding by unmasking prejudice and exclusion on the part of Anglos who wanted to outlaw and exile Spanish in New Mexico, and it would demand equal treatment and equal respect.

Discursive power inevitably involves politics. In the case of language and the schools, the press called for legislation to redress the inequity with which

Hispanics, as citizens and taxpayers, were treated. It claimed that the rights of Spanish-speaking people were being "pisoteados y hollados bajo las plantas de la injusticia y opresíon con el hecho de verse prohibida la enseñanza de su idioma en las escuelas públicas—escuelas soportadas con las contribuciones de todo el pueblo en general, siendo el producto de las mismas destinado al beneficio de todos sin distinciones"[31] [stepped on and trampled under the feet of injustice and oppression by prohibiting the teaching of their language in the public schools—schools supported with the contributions of the people in general, created for the benefit of all without distinctions]. The ignorance of policymakers regarding the most effective methods of language teaching and learning significantly compounded a problem that originated in ethnic and racial bias. As the same article pointed out, the New Mexican territory was acquired by invading and conquering a people whose language had been Spanish for three centuries, and the Treaty of Guadalupe Hidalgo certainly did not stipulate that they had to speak English as a condition of enjoying the rights and privileges they were guaranteed.

Most editorials were not quite so belligerent. In fact, the Hispanic population seemed reasonably disposed to, if not enthusiastic about, learning English along with Spanish. In 1909, the territorial legislature responded to some of the complaints of this constituency by creating the Hispanic-American Normal School in El Rito (Rio Arriba County), whose mandate was to prepare Hispanic teachers with good skills in English for the hundred or more rural schools where the first language of the students was Spanish; these schools essentially would have a bilingual environment in which students could learn in English with guidance from teachers knowledgeable in the vernacular.[32] Sensitivity surrounding the literacy issue was also a factor in the Spanish-language press, which urged its readers to take care in responding to the census taker; many Hispanos had been identified as illiterate when, in fact, they were able to read and write Spanish. An editorial in *El Nuevo Mexicano* (Apr. 9, 1910) reminded its readers that "El Congreso y el mundo entero basarán sus ideas acerca de la población, riqueza, recursos y grandeza de Nuevo México, en mucha parte, sobre los retornos oficiales del censo...." [The Congress and the whole world will base its ideas about the population, wealth, resources and greatness of New Mexico largely on the official results of the census....]. Simultaneous with the ethnic self-awareness of the native-son movement, a bill was proposed in the state legislature in 1915 to require that all teachers of Spanish in the predominantly Hispanic school districts be tested for their accuracy and proficiency in the language; this bill was not approved, but it does exemplify another aspect of the concern to maintain some quality control over the use of Spanish in the schools.[33]

A certain portion of the press's message regarding language and cultural erosion was directed at neomexicanos themselves. Particularly in the border areas of southern New Mexico, where editors were frequently Mexican expatriates, the newspapers were very vocal in promoting the purity of Spanish, fearing its loss or misuse because of contact with Anglo culture. A newspaper in Las Cruces, for example, satirized the attitude of students who balked at studying Spanish grammar.[34] Another newspaper from the same city criticized incipient code-switching, or shifting from one language to another, for which there was no lexical need.[35] Still another paper, up in Las Vegas, published a humorous poem satirizing the affectation of those who used English only to impress others.[36]

One of the tragedies associated with the "acculturation syndrome" in the United States has been the inability to adapt to the dominant culture by those who have rejected their native cultural identity.[37] It was this kind of cultural limbo and social dislocation that neomexicano newspapers began to observe and lament in the 1890s. An essay signed by "Zig Zag" (José Escobar) and published in *El Nuevo Mundo* in Albuquerque (July 10, 1897) raises the specter of cultural erosion with specific reference to language, politics, and the neomexicano reality of the time. With the influence of ever-increasing numbers of Anglos, the dynamics of acculturation had already begun to destabilize neomexicano society, particularly among the urban middle- and upper-class youth who tended to become *agringados* [gringoized]. In real jeopardy lay a future that, in Escobar's opinion, only neomexicanos themselves could reshape. I reproduce below his entire essay in translation (and I also acknowledge the special irony of this linguistic "betrayal," committed for reasons of space):

Difference between the Past and the Present: Social Plagues

What a disagreeable surprise the former owners of this land would experience if they could rise from the tombs where they have slept for so long the deep and eternal dream of death!

Absolutely everything has changed in this land discovered by the Franciscan Fray Marcos de Niza, explored by Espejo and Coronado, colonized by Oñate, and reconquered by the celebrated don Diego de Vargas. The destructive appetite of the genius of progress has, in a very few years, completely demolished New Mexico's past. Civilization, with its triumphal chariot, the locomotive, has cut a path through the deserts previously inhabited by savages. Today our legends and national traditions preserve the deeds and ancient customs of our ancestors who may have lived in times of less culture, but they were times of greater prosperity and success for our people (*nuestra raza*).

The slow, heavy carts of our old wagon trains have been

replaced with the rapid steam engine. In the arid deserts of days past are now rising beautiful modern cities joined by telegraph and telephone wires. Commerce, mining, the arts, manufacturing, and agriculture have developed notably in our midst, and for the benefit of our children and young people, schools, academies, and institutes have opened in great numbers in almost all the towns of the territory.

And yet, amid all the progress and advancement, Spanish-American people have found only the source of their ruin and the foundation of their degradation in being reduced, politically and socially, to zero, or its equivalent—nothingness!

The youth of Latin background, born for the most part under the American flag, have had to adopt Anglo Saxon habits, which may be the only salvation of the legitimate owners of this soil. But among this youth, unfortunately, there is a certain element of "slick boys" and "crank girls" who, despite their "tanned" complexion, have gotten it into their heads that they are "true Americans" and they want nothing in the world to do with conversing in the lovely language of Valera and Nuñez de Arce. It is not unusual for "Miss Jacinta or Mister Mulehead" to make a slang or patois of the two languages which is more than a little difficult to understand.

In our customs, as in our language, the styles of the North have been imitated, and now we have "ladies" who smoke and ride bicycles, and naturally the number of marriages listed in the Civil Register has declined, because to marry a "modern" woman is the same as taking a rope and hanging oneself . . . quite simply.

If the "mamas" of these modern girls gave them the benefit of some sophistication in sewing and cooking they would do them much more good than by letting them spend their "pennies" on outlandish hats costing a king's ransom, which pleases the shopkeepers while the fathers and husbands "uncongratulate" each other.

The "slick" types are not outdone by these "crank girls"; by nature, they are idle, or rather, lazy. They care little that the "old folks," as they call their parents, have had to work hard to accumulate a modest or sizable fortune. These slick fellows take it upon themselves to squander it on all kinds of "sports," and the sad thing is that when they are left "without a cent" or any means of getting by, they then become ridiculous and degrading blemishes among their people, whose "scent" both the destitute and the rich pick up and ferociously pursue. Miserable guys!

With regard to learning, they are not too advantaged, shall we say. They "manage to speak" a little bit of English, and even less Spanish, but of course when the case arises—and particularly in political meetings—they speak with so much aplomb that one who does not know them might take them for modern Demosthenes or Ciceros.

If all the foregoing amounted to no more than a big joke for our people, we would not bother ourselves with this matter. But in those small and futile causes lie social problems of great consequence for the future of our people.

What will New Mexico be able to expect from men and women like these, who sooner or later will have to be the ones to educate those of our people who will follow us? What kind of future awaits the descendants of those men of the past, the honor and glory of New Mexico's history? Will those who follow us have to emigrate to another country, forced to leave behind in the hands of a horde of eager adventurers the homes where their parents were born and the sacrosanct graves of their grandparents?

People should think seriously about what we have only briefly sketched out here. And so should our public figures, who could better use the energy of their political resentments and personal hatreds. In the name of public interest, let everyone unite like one single man and, following the foreigner's example, work without distinction between political camps for the betterment of our people, which is more honorable and meritorious than tearing each other apart and reaping benefits for one who does not talk so constantly or decisively but works for his people without considering if they are Democrats, Republicans, or Populists.

If America is for Americans, then let us say: New Mexico for New Mexicans, without having this mean the exclusion of the good Anglo Saxon element that has invested its capital here and, in fact, is as much entitled to hold and benefit from public office as are its true sons from this part of the country.

If all this were accomplished and if some of the officeholders were to recognize that they are the servants and not the masters, our people would in a short time return to their flourishing condition, capturing at the same time the respect of the foreigner who until today has only had disdain for the Mexican element.

As in many other essays of the time dealing with neomexicano problems, the issue of ethnic unity is central to Escobar's thesis. His concluding remarks were blunter than most other editors and provoked criticism on that score; the oppositional way he drew the bicultural picture waved a red flag in the face of Anglos and some Hispanos who were more assimilation-minded. Considering Escobar's close ties to Mexico, it is not surprising that he would speak of Anglos as foreigners and anticipate that neomexicanos might soon have to emigrate if they had no future, no place for self-definition, in their own land. The mirror of reality, as he saw it, was not reflecting familiar images but, rather, masks and distortions, some imposed from without and others from within the neomexicano cultural matrix. Donning his own mask of "objectivity," the journalist "Zig Zag" looks at his community and sees disruption, dislocation, disunity, and disempowerment while all around there is talk of progress. Betrayal of the ancestors, linguistic denial, loss of public face. The scenario he evokes is discouraging—unless this essay is read alongside many others that convey different messages, less dire than his.

The breakdown of language cohesiveness among neomexicanos, not only with the influx of Anglos but also with that of Mexican immigrants after 1910, spelled change and a loss of the social solidarity that Sapir identified with the sharing of "a common speech." For some neomexicanos it meant a gradual loss of Spanish, for others a mixture of two languages, and for still others, in mountain villages, the retention of the old forms of communication in their isolation from modernity. One editorial noted that a new language, Anglicized Spanish, had developed among people who had been educated in English in the public schools: "Para nuestro pueblo se está haciendo tan natural que ya casi no se nota que se está hablando un idioma nuevo y no escrito"[38] [It is becoming so natural for our people that one almost does not notice that a new unwritten language is being spoken]. The editorial went on to say that this new language was appearing more and more in the newspapers, which, in turn, were reinforcing its legitimacy.

Were newspapers actually contributing to cultural erosion or combating it? Perhaps both; they were certainly not speaking with the forked tongue of strangers, but their role as cultural rangers on the horizon of the western frontier remains fraught with ambiguity at a hundred years' distance. As in all social discourse, the only hope is to try to hear the voices.

7

Mixed Messages:

Images of Women in the Press

From October 1893 to the following April, the Albuquerque newspaper *La Opinión Pública* advertised a *concurso de belleza* [beauty contest] open to *señoras y señoritas* from ages fourteen to thirty-five, residents of New Mexico, Arizona, and Texas. The lucky lady with the most votes would receive a gold watch and, if she wished, have her photograph published in a special edition of the newspaper. As an incentive, the newspaper offered potential voters the right to cast one hundred votes if their nomination was accompanied by the money owed on a current unpaid subscription along with payment for 1894 as well; a single new subscription would buy fifty votes. Needless to say, the winner would not necessarily be the most lovely candidate, but rather the one whose supporters were the most able salesmen. Either way, the fifty or so women whose names appeared weekly with the votes tallied "in their favor" were authentic objects of desire, valued for their beauty or profit-potential, depending on the eye of the beholder. By mid-January, Srta. Flora Santistéban of San Antonio, Texas, was in the lead with sixteen hundred votes. *La Opinión Pública* was evidently reaching more than a few readers outside New Mexico!

Neomexicano newspapers do not tell us what Flora or other women thought of such contests, although we know they continue to be popular in Hispanic communities today. Women's voices were rarely heard in the press at the turn of the century, and words written by their own hand were rarely published. Yet women's images in the newspapers are omnipresent in small and large ways in all types of contexts. When I first read the Spanish-language newspapers twenty years ago, I was looking for evidence of neomexicano women authors, and finding only reprinted examples of Mexican and Spanish women's writing, I discounted women's importance in and for the press—just as many readers have minimized the role women played in western history in general—simply because they did not speak for themselves. Going back more recently and reading with a heightened awareness of the way gender is culturally constructed and represented, I saw what I had missed: multiple images of Hispano women as readers, as consumers, as social subjects, and as sources of inspiration and of occasional vilification. Although denied a public voice, they were nonetheless important figures in the socioeconomic fabric of newsprint. Defined by a written language that was theirs only in a restricted sense, their images in the press offer a glimpse into the disjunction between daily life and the cultural ideology of their time.

The fact that newspapers depended for their survival on attracting as many readers as possible ensured that information of all sorts was reported if it was newsworthy or could stimulate a local reaction. Letters to the editor, legal announcements, government notices, and commercial advertisements supplemented the news gathered by a minimal staff. Of course, editors had their own ideological slants on the news, and given the unstable political and cultural environment of the territory, pigeonholing them now as liberals or conservatives can be misleading. Today's reader has to take into account the relationship between journalistic discourse and the sources of power and be sensitive to the ways in which newspaper texts—like any other media—can shape reader consciousness, especially in matters of gender representation. As Patricia Nelson Limerick reminds us, cultural mythologies are grounded in the power and complexity of language, and any discussion of social constructs in the realm of ideas and symbols in Western history can be notoriously slippery.[1]

Although images of women have been distorted in many cultures, the case of neomexicano women in the territorial period presents unique obstacles to understanding. Starting with the history of the American West, one must recognize gender mythology as a foundational fiction of the notion of the frontier itself. Frederick Jackson Turner's pivotal essay of 1893 on the significance of the frontier led one feminist historian to comment:

> Until recently, most western historians have not considered
> women a part of the frontier experience. Turner's frontiers were
> as devoid of women as the Great Plains were devoid of trees.
> Turner's pioneers were explorers, fur trappers, miners, ranchers,
> farmers—all of them male; and succeeding generations of west-
> ern historians continued to interpret the westering movement as
> primarily a male enterprise in which women played a largely
> invisible and subordinate role. After all, as T. A. Larson pointed
> out in a 1974 article, because women "did not lead expeditions,
> command troops, build railroads, drive cattle, ride Pony Express,
> find gold, amass great wealth, get elected to high public office,
> rob stages or lead lynch mobs," most writers assumed they did
> not play a significant role in the building of the West.[2]

Stereotypes of women on the western frontier were as unrealistic and yet as widely assimilated into American cultural iconography as the proverbial tobacco-store Indian. They served the cultural conventions of Anglo-American patriarchal society in the late nineteenth century, but even today the Anglocentric image of the frontier woman tends to obscure the lived experience of females, and particularly those of nonmainstream minorities.

A look at more contemporary scholarship can still mislead and blur distinctions between women of the West by the tendency to overgeneralize (by treating all Hispanic women in U.S. history as one group, or overlooking class differences) or to overspecialize (by focusing only on exceptional women or on a limited time period).[3] In the New Mexican territory, for example, neomexicano, Anglo-American, Native American, European, Mexican, and Asian women might have coexisted in the urban spaces of cities like Albuquerque, Las Vegas, Las Cruces, or Santa Fe. Also among Spanish-speaking women in New Mexico there were differences in terms of social class and family background, not to mention political awareness, educational experience, religious upbringing, national allegiance (some were recent Mexican immigrants), and, of course, qualities of character. It is unlikely that any of them conceived of the physical space they inhabited in New Mexico as being a "frontier" or that they shared Turner's view that the western frontier was "a new field of opportunity, a gate of escape from the bondage of the past."[4]

On the other hand, it would be quite reasonable to assume that Hispanic women were conscious of other, more troublesome border zones between themselves and women of other ethnicities or, even more significantly, between themselves and male members of their own and other cultures.[5] Whether they thought of themselves as a colonized group because they were female in a male-governed society is less likely than that they felt invaded by a foreign culture that threatened to change their way of life. Very few women of the territory in the late nineteenth century had any notion of feminism or the movement to claim equal rights; most of them passed on to their children the same social values and habits of life they had inherited from their parents.[6]

Both men and women in neomexicano society experienced the impact of Anglo-American conquest, but the fact that women had no right to vote or to express their will in public limited their voice in the dialogic community and their role in shaping its identity. We know very little about how Hispanic women felt about the increasing influence of Anglo culture or the contacts they had with Anglos in their midst, despite the fact that their experiences in southwestern history were unique to their culture. Racial intermarriage, for example, was an uncharted frontier that must have been as worrisome to a Spanish-speaking woman as an Anglo woman's pioneer trek.[7] The decisions neomexicano women made regarding marital or extramarital liaisons inevitably affected neomexicano men and the community at large, whether or not their actions challenged male authority and social tradition. For these and other reasons, the dynamics of gender must be sought out in texts of the time and factored into any discussion of affirmation and resistance between the cultures.

Although the lived experience of women in the Southwest in the period under discussion cannot be reduced to facile common denominators, the varied images of women in neomexicano newspapers are cultural artifacts that can help us deconstruct the mythologies of their time and reconstruct a clearer idea of the neomexicano female, for as Richard Griswold del Castillo has observed, "The ideals encompassed in the patriarchal tradition were often contradicted by the circumstances of day-to-day life."[8] The fundamental role played by the Catholic church in affirming patriarchal authority had its roots in Spanish colonial tradition, and this was later reinforced by the Napoleonic legal code of post-Independence Mexico. From studies of the earlier Mexican period, however, we know that neomexicano women on the remote northern frontier were more socially liberated than other Mexican women and their rights more protected by Hispanic civil law than their Anglo-American counterparts.[9] By the beginning of the American period, this had begun to change under the impact of Anglo gender attitudes and the Victorian cult of "true womanhood," which filtered into neomexicano society with the influx of Anglo settlers, and possibly also with more contact with mainstream Mexican culture. The simultaneous emergence of a secular reform movement in Mexico also had repercussions across the U.S. border, where liberal journalists sought refuge during the Díaz regime. Progressive Mexican thinkers, including the radical Flores Magón brothers, supported limited education for women and less church control at a time when the prevailing transnational wisdom regarding woman's role, both in traditional Hispanic cultures and in the United States, was that given her weaker constitution and maternal responsibility, woman's sphere was the home where she could nurture and mold the next generation.[10] Middle-class Mexican women who broke with tradition and actively supported the *magonista* movement by writing articles in liberal newspapers along the U.S.–Mexican border were censured for their lack of docility; exceptional women might enter the professions, but entering politics was taboo.[11]

The press was a natural conduit for the didactic objectives of both liberal and conservative journalists when it came to women's proper role in society. Given the exposure of most editors to intellectual currents beyond territorial borders, their discourse reflected controversial gender issues that connected New Mexico to larger forums of debate. Literate women, on the other hand, were voiceless readers for the most part, since the teacher–pupil rhetoric in the press only reinforced their subordination to a master discourse that effectively strengthened male hegemony. Frequent sermonizing about womanhood filled the pages of neomexicano newspapers, just as it did throughout the North and South American press in the Victorian era. Women were constantly admonished to be exemplary wives and mothers, as if no other destiny awaited them.

In New Mexico, prior to 1880, women followed traditional patterns of town and village life, which centered around their own culture and community in a self-contained, internally flexible system.[12] According to Frances Swadesh, writing about the late colonial period,

> The code regarding women in relation to men applied theoretically in New Mexico, but in practice it was often disregarded. This was due to frontier conditions and low population, which made it impossible to maintain the sexual division of labor that prevailed elsewhere in New Spain.[13]

With rapidly growing Anglo immigration after 1846 and the shift to an Anglo-dominated economic system, the lives of wealthy and poor Hispanos alike were affected by intercultural relations, and new adaptations were necessary for cultural survival. Recent studies of northern New Mexican village life at the turn of the century show that rural neomexicano women were not bound to the home, completely dependent on men, but rather performed labor outside the home that was integral to community well-being in an increasingly cash-based economy.[14] Abandonment by wayward husbands or desertion by male partners who left economically depressed villages to seek wage labor were frequent realities that women had to cope with on their own or with the support of kinfolk. Since domestic situations of this sort were not considered newsworthy, they went unremarked in the press unless they were accompanied by acts of brutal violence resulting in rape or murder. Likewise, neomexicano women of the middle and upper classes did not always live confined lives or conform to the one-dimensional stereotypes that Anglo novels of the Southwest liked to propagate.[15] They owned property, were often educated, were sometimes employed outside the home, and were accustomed to visiting friends and family in other cities, as was frequently noted in the social columns of the papers. Census records tell us that in Santa Fe about one in five households contained an unmarried woman over age thirty; many headed their own households, supported their families, and wrote wills, which "offered a measure of control over their circumstances."[16] Women across the social spectrum sustained the core of neomexicano family life and its cultural identity, but their lives involved many kinds of adaptation to changing circumstances in a multicultural context.

The rhetoric of socialization for Hispanic females in the late nineteenth century did not adapt accordingly, but continued to inculcate the notion that women were properly bound to the private, the domestic, and the morally superior domain of the home. The emphasis on women as consumers rather than producers, passive receptors rather than active agents in society, virtually obscures how their lives bridged private and public spheres, or how they subtly influenced the way cultural identity manifested itself in daily life. The impact of major socioeconomic changes on women was rarely mentioned in the press, or else was trivialized, as this refrain from a poem by H. V. González[17] in *El Independiente* (Las Vegas, June 13, 1896) shows:

Ya hoy no quieren las mujeres	[These days women don't want
Metate para moler	A grinding stone for corn,
Ahora ya quieren estufas	Now they want stoves
Y máquinas de coser.	And sewing machines.]

Writing about Mexican culture in *The Labyrinth of Solitude*, Octavio Paz has said, "Women are imprisoned in the image masculine society has imposed on them."[18] In the case of Hispanic women in territorial New Mexico, that symbolic prison is even more difficult to penetrate because of the cultural and linguistic differences between their experiences and those of Anglo and Native American women on the same so-called frontier. The textual evidence of Spanish-language newspapers is thus an important resource both for understanding neomexicano conceptualizations of gender and also for gathering some actual data about women's lives.[19]

A few examples gleaned from among many others will illustrate how neomexicano journalistic discourse simultaneously fostered and undermined patriarchal culture: in its function as a mirror of the dialogic community it both sustained the moralistic notion of womanhood that was the fictional ideal and also subverted it by documenting its quotidian unreality.

Woman as mother—poeticized, idealized, sanctified—is undoubtedly the most pervasive female image in the neomexicano newspapers. In editorials, poems, narratives, and folksy homilies, the mother figure is described as the moral and emotional foundation of the Hispanic social structure, with her behavior modeled on the image of the pure and ever-merciful Virgin Mother. To fulfill her chaste role to patriarchal satisfaction, the woman was supposed to practice self-abnegation and total dedication to the duty of nurturing her children and caring for the hearth. Raised to a mythic status and equated with the essence of the female gender itself, motherhood was both a proscriptive and prescriptive stereotype that disregarded woman's individual needs and sought to channel her destiny in society.[20] Among the many examples of newspaper pieces that reinforced gender polarization and a distinctly female ethic is an essay entitled "La madre" [The mother] in *La Opinión Pública* (Albuquerque, July 16, 1892). The language and rhetoric of the author is typically romantic in its exaltation of motherhood through religious imagery and excessive sentimentality. Placing the mother on a pedestal separates her from the impure world and rewards her self-denial with social sanctification. However, the net effect in the social context, as illustrated by this beginning excerpt, is to confine her influence to the emotional realm of the home and family:

> ¡Arrodillaos . . . !
> Hay un sér en esta tierra de martirio y expiación, de quien no es dado hablar sino con profundo respeto y veneración.
> ¿Sabéis cual es su nombre?
> "¡Madre!" ¡Madre! ¿verdad que nunca habéis oído nombre tan dulce? No; lo sé muy bien. No hay palabra, no puede haber sonido que conmueva tanto al corazón como el de madre. Es un canto del paraíso, es un himno de los cielos.

> [Everyone kneel down!
> There is a being on this earth of martyrdom and expiation who can only be spoken of with profound respect and veneration. Do you know her name?
> "Mother!" Mother! Have you ever heard a sweeter name? No, I know you haven't. There is no word, there can be no sound that moves the heart as much as that of Mother. It is a song of paradise, a hymn of the heavens.]

The author's rhetorical strategy of speaking not to the iconographic mother but to the rest of society (after all, even mothers have mothers) reinforces the gender socialization process that confers on the mother a status of moral superiority, but only in her defined space. Lest the lesson be missed, he reminds his readers that the mother is "mensajera de Dios en el hogar" [the messenger of God in the home].

The other side of the coin, the mother's responsibility for the moral upbringing of her offspring, is the lesson directed at women themselves in another typical essay found in *El Nuevo Mundo* [Albuquerque, July 27, 1899], "A las madres" [To mothers]. In this case, mothers are chided not to spoil their children by fostering "indisciplina" [lack of discipline], which can only lead to a life of vice and degradation. Here the operative exclamation is "¡Pobres madres! Hay para ellas algo peor que ver morir á sus hijos y es el verlos mal vivir" [Poor mothers! If there is something worse for them than seeing their children die, it is seeing them live badly]. Women can thus be cast as agents of God or the devil, a familiar dichotomy in biblical gender mythology.

If the Mary image is the ideal of patriarchal female stereotypes, then the Eve image is its obverse. An article entitled "La lengua" [The tongue], appearing about the same time in *El Nuevo Mundo* [May 18, 1899], begins with the traditional equation between moral character and probity of speech. The image of a "mala lengua" [evil tongue] is gender-related in this revealing passage:

> Un sabio que si acaso no era reputado como tal, trató de demostrar que la mujer no tenía alma, y se fundaba para ello, principalmente, en que su mala lengua acusaba la inferioridad de su ser.
> Los hombres valerosos no hablan mal de nadie pero los afeminados y cobardes se distinguen por su mala lengua.

> [A wise man who perhaps was not reputed as such tried to show that woman does not possess a soul, and he founded his argument for this primarily on the fact that her evil tongue revealed the inferiority of her being.
> Brave men do not speak badly of anyone but effeminate and cowardly men stand out by their evil tongue.]

Like the biblical Eve, women who talk too much are exiled from the earthly paradise devised by men. Paradoxically, it was culturally desirable for women to mold the child to be the future man, but not to use her persuasive powers in the public arena. The ancient patriarchal ambivalence regarding woman in the abstract is captured in a brief anonymous poem that appeared in *La Flor del Valle* (Las Cruces) on May 26, 1894. Both admired and mistrusted, woman is a mystery to man who sees her as "other," but not as an individual:

Pon el amor en mujer	[To place love in a woman
Es escribir en el agua;	Is to write on the water;
Guardar nieve en una fragua	To keep snow in a smithy's furnace
O en el mar un alfiler.	Or a needle in the sea.
Odiarlas! no puede ser;	To hate them! is not possible;
Amarlas! es un error;	To love them! is an error;
Así es que será mejor	So it would be better
Quererlas de cierto modo,	To love them in a certain way,
Que ni se quieran del todo	Neither loving them completely
Ni se dejen de querer.	Nor ceasing to love them.]

Many other examples in the newspapers reiterate the ideal qualities of womanhood, from poems and stories about daughters, mothers, and wives to obituaries praising their exemplary lives.[21] Neomexicano culture, like other traditional Hispano-Catholic cultures, was structured around a symbolic code of gender representation, and this system of signs was deeply inculcated by the socialization process of which journalistic discourse was a part. It was not less authentic for being transnational; however, because it shared so much with patriarchal cultures of similar roots, it is not necessary to give repeated examples here. Let us turn, instead, to other kinds of images of women in the neomexicano papers, images that call the gender mythos into question by documenting women's lived experience in other than the stereotypical roles.

Anecdotal evidence published in the newspapers that related to violent crime in the territory points time and again to the fact that neomexicana women were frequent victims of physical assault, rape, and murder. This is not necessarily unusual in a frontier society, but it calls into question the way in which justice functioned on their behalf and the kinds of risks they faced not only as women but as non-Anglos. Most of the violence against women, then as now, was domestic or within the immediate community, often involving allegedly adulterous relationships, unwanted attentions, or acts of revenge. Occasionally, newspaper editors interviewed male perpetrators awaiting punishment for their crimes; their testimony drew reader interest and often contradicted the findings of the law in such a way that the female victim was portrayed as bearing the blame for the violence. An example of this is found in *El Independiente* (Las Vegas), June 7, 1906, which reports the hanging in Raton, N.M., of convicted murderer David Argüello on May 25, 1906. The day before, Argüello had recounted to the editor, Segundino Romero, his version of the killing of his neighbor, Celia Dassart, a Hispanic woman married to a man of French descent. David had been found guilty of murdering Celia because she repeatedly rejected his advances; he was also seen leaving her house with a gun after the shots that killed her were fired. David told the editor, however, that he had paid someone else to murder Celia because she had poisoned him and refused to give him an antidote after their affair ended and he had returned to his wife. David escaped following the crime and was finally apprehended three years later. The front page of this issue of *El Independiente* shows a photo of David Argüello, with much more space allotted to his version of the crime than to the brief report of the court's findings. The same issue contains an anonymous poem about the hanging and another poem that Argüello had recited the night before in don Segundino's presence:[22]

Adios reina del cielo	Farewell, queen of heaven
Madre del Salvador,	Mother of the Savior,
Dulce prenda adorada	Sweet and adored treasure
De mi sincero amor.	Of my sincere love.
De tu divino rostro	As I must leave the beauty

La belleza al dejar,	Of your divine face,
Permiteme que vuelva	Allow me to kiss your feet
Tus plantas besar.	Yet one more time.
Más dejarte ¡oh María!	But to leave you, oh Mary,
No acierta el corazón,	Breaks my heart,
Te lo entrego, Señora,	So I offer it to you, dear Lady,
Dadme tú bendicion.	Give me your blessing.
Adios del cielo encanto	Farewell, delight of heaven,
Mi delicia y mi amor,	My joy and my beloved,
Adios, oh madre mía	Farewell, my own dear mother,
¡Adios, Adios, Adios.	Farewell, Farewell, Farewell!]

The cumulative effect of this reporting leaves the reader with quite a bit of sympathy for the convicted murderer and practically no information about the woman he murdered or what her role in the community may have been, other than the brief mention that she was under twenty, had lived in Colorado, and was "a pretty woman." In fact, Celia Dessart's moral character is called into question, along with the suggestion that she had witchlike powers, while her violent death is overshadowed completely by the detailed reporting of Argüello's last hours and his poetic contrition. Journalistic discourse, in this case and others like it, writes the woman out of the story and transforms the male protagonist into a fallen hero. Other examples, referred to earlier in this book, include the untold stories of Vicente Silva's wife, Telesfora Sandoval, murdered by her bandit-husband, and Rosita Durán, common-law wife of Germán Maestas. They and women like them who suffered at the hands of violent men were twice victimized: once in the flesh and again in the press.

Many neomexicanas did not have the ability to read or write and thus never realized how their gender was represented in the press or that women could, like any other citizen, use the newspaper as a public forum for grievances. A few women, however, were both literate and forthright enough to air their own complaints and seek justice in newsprint. They wrote to local editors to protest situations in which they or their loved ones had been dealt with unfairly in public or through the press. One such letter, dated November 6, 1899, came from Matilde Muñiz, a resident of Ranchos de Albuquerque, and was published three days later in *El Nuevo Mundo*. Her letter responds to another published earlier from her husband, Melchor Lucero, who warned potential creditors that he would not be responsible for her debts and claimed custody of their children. Maltilde's outrage is evident when she refers to her spouse as "Manchado" [dirty] Lucero and says he is trying to hoodwink the public, that he was rarely at home, never gave her enough from his pay to support the family, and when he did appear he would play cards with his friends and send her out for bottles of wine on credit. She is writing, she says, not at someone else's instigation but "de mi propia voluntad" [of my own free will], to tell the public what a fraud Lucero is and to declare that "seria yo una madre tirana si pusiera yo á mis pobres hijitos en manos de Lucero . . ." [I would be a tyrannical mother if I put my little children in Lucero's hands]. Matilde's voice is unequivocal in its denunciation of her husband's irresponsibility and hypocrisy.

Given situations like this, it is not surprising that civil divorce, initiated by both men and women, was more common than might be expected in a patriarchal Catholic society. Among other newspapers, *El Sol de Mayo*, a conservative weekly paper in Las Vegas, came out in favor of a divorce law in 1891, and by 1900 *El Nuevo Mexicano* of Santa Fe carried reports of many divorces in the surrounding area. Court proceedings and census records at the turn of the century show that "almost every village had at least one Hispanic divorced person, usually female, and there were frequently more."[23] Their strategies for economic survival, especially if they were left without property, are an aspect of social history that is not documented in the press, but it seems that divorced and unmarried women were generally accepted by the community. According to information found in censuses and wills, these women lived under harsh conditions and, as a result of the Anglo conquest, their increased dependency on paid employment as laundresses and seamstresses for immigrant men left them particularly vulnerable to rising inflation and exploitation.[24]

Prostitution was ubiquitous in the West and it impacted neomexicanos just as it did all segments of society. As one front-page article, simply entitled "Prostitución!," explained, it was reluctantly tolerated among other social evils because "sería un absurdo incalificable el querer extinguirles por completo" [because it would be a unqualified absurdity to try to eradicate it completely].[25] The entire thrust of the article was aimed at male readers, pointing out the physical and moral danger of frequenting houses of prostitution and the negative impression their actions left on the public:

> ¡Y estos son los hombres que pretenden entronizarse en el poder
> y continuar derrochando el Tesoro Público y dandose una vida
> regalada!
>
> [And these are the men who aspire to enthrone themselves in
> power and who continue to dissipate the Public Treasury living
> the high life!]

Prostitution, drinking, and gambling were social evils that the press railed against regularly, but with little or no mention of the ways in which women's lives were affected by them.

Politics, another male domain in New Mexico, bred corruption, violence, and disunity among Hispanos while generating endless quantities of newsprint. If the women of northern New Mexico were actively involved in territorial politics, as Mexican women were in the liberal movement that was active along the border prior to the 1910 Mexican Revolution, their names did not appear in the neomexicano press.[26] To my knowledge, there were no feminist periodicals edited by neomexicanas similar to those that proliferated in Mexico in the nineteenth century and gave women an entry into the public dialogue, although it is very likely that some well-educated women in the territory read Mexican periodicals for and by women.[27] While the rights of women were debated and promoted among liberal activist groups across the United States, in the New Mexican territory in the late nineteenth century the feminist agenda was not highly visible in the Spanish-language press. Women's suffrage, which won approval in the progressive Western states of Wyoming and Colorado, was not on the platform of the Populist party in New Mexico for fear that it would alienate Hispanic voters.[28] After statehood was achieved, women's role in politics would increase, but before that, Hispanic male voters did not sanction women's voices in their domain.

An occasional letter published in the press, such as the one sent by *La Opinión Pública* in March 1894 by Juliana V. Chaves, mother of the murdered mayor of Santa Fe, Francisco Chaves, draws the reader's attention by its candor and daring. Señora Chaves, along with many neomexicanos, believed that powerful political boss Thomas B. Catron was behind the murder of her son, who had been his opponent in local politics. When Catron spoke on behalf of the accused murderers, the Borrego brothers, during the public investigation and also accused Francisco Chaves of being an unfit mayor, Juliana Chaves added her voice to those who attacked Catron. In her long letter, she bluntly enumerated Catron's self-incriminating behavior in support of the Borrego brothers, and she challenged him again and again to come forth with any evidence showing that her son had harmed in any way the people had he served. Accusing him of defaming the good reputation of a dead man, she ended her letter with this statement:

> Soy pobre, anciana, y cargada de pesares, pero todavia corre por mis venas algo de aquella orgullosa sangre de mis antepasados y defenderé la memoria de mi hijo aunque me vea precisada el ir á verme con usted cara á cara y en persona.

> [I am poor, old, and burdened with worries, but some of the proud blood of my ancestors still runs through my veins and I will defend the memory of my son even if I am obliged to go confront you face to face and in person.]

The threat of an old Hispanic woman defending her son's honor may not have meant much to Catron, but her voice is simple and eloquent testimony to the strength of ethnic pride and maternal dignity in a situation where women were expected to remain silent.

Catron, and other Anglo men in New Mexico as far back as the early nineteenth century, developed close ties with the Spanish-speaking community, sometimes to gain economic and political power and other times out of simple personal need for human relationships. Much literature about the West has stereotyped the way Anglos connected with Hispanic women, either by demonizing or romanticizing these liaisons. Prior to the American invasion, non-Hispanic men of European stock came to New Mexico on the Santa Fe Trail and married neomexicano women. According to Rebecca Craver, 122 intermarriages and common-law relationships were recorded between 1821 and 1846, primarily around Taos—a strategic point on the trade route—and most of them involved Hispanic women of modest economic means; from these unions, at least 273 children were born who, potentially, would have reached maturity in the latter part of the century.[29] Darlis Miller has documented mixed marriages in the post–Civil War period in New Mexico, noting, for example, that in 1870 in Santa Fe 63 percent of the Anglo men residing there were married to Hispanic women.[30] Interethnic and intercultural families were thus already a fact in the territory by 1880, when Anglo immigration soared, and they provided a precedent of political, economic, and social interaction to build on. Anti-Mexican racial prejudice increased with the influx of Anglos, however, and neomexicano resentment and resistance to acculturation also became more pronounced. Some Spanish-speaking women were still attracted to and attractive to Anglo men, but this was now looked upon with more concern in the neomexicano community than in the earlier periods of the century. One front-page story in a newspaper called *La Verdad* (Las Cruces), on March 26, 1898, gives the first-person testimony of a local man rejected by the woman he loved. Calling her "la Diosa de los Neo-Mexicanos" [the goddess of New Mexicans], the author confesses his disillusionment and fear that his rival might be an Anglo. Imagining her future marriage, he says, "espero que no será con un Cara Blanca—ojos azules. . . . Las jovenes mexicanas se facinan de los ojos azules y la cara blanca les encanta, el pelo huero les simpatiza" [I hope it won't be to a White Face—blue eyes. . . . Young Mexican women are fascinated by blue eyes and delighted by a white face, and blond hair appeals to them].[31] More than ten years later, another neomexicano, Benjamin M. Read—himself of mixed parentage—wrote an article for a section called "Para Las Damas y El Hogar" [For the ladies and the home] in *La Revista de Taos*. Read's concern in 1911 was that young neomexicanas would be corrupted by the worst elements of the "elemento extranjero" [foreign element]—those who were not honorable and respected:

Con frecuencia se encuentran señoras y señoritas de lo más
selecto de nuestra sociedad en la compañía de personas de mala
vida y de ningún carácter reuniéndose con ellas en los teatros, en
los paseos, en las tertulias—reuniones familiares y aún, ¡triste es
admitirlo!, dice uno de los más ilustres prelados, en los bazares
promovidos para fines de caridad. ¡Cuántos crímenes se cometen
por medio de las malas amistades!

[Frequently, women and young ladies from the best of our
society are seen in the company of people of no character and ill
repute meeting in theaters, outings, social events, or family
gatherings, and even, sad to say, according to one of our well
known priests, in charity bazaars. How many crimes are committed because of bad friendships!][32]

Read made it clear that even the best families were shamelessly welcoming
"los advenedizos llamados 'Americanos'" [the immigrant so-called "Americans"] in situations in which "les niegan á los de igual vida de su propia raza"
[they would reject those of the same ilk of their own race]. Perhaps the double
standard women tolerated had something to do with their own desire to be
accorded more freedom, but it could also have been social climbing, or simply the euphoria of impending statehood and full incorporation into American citizenship.

Social news was a regular section of most neomexicano papers, found in
brief notes and in special sections called *gacetillas*, *crónicas* or *noticias locales*.
Only the middle and upper classes, however, are reflected in the reports of
baptisms, engagements, birthdays, marriages, deaths, and the various comings
and goings of the *buena sociedad* [high society]. Then as now, the papers
courted readers, and the illiterate were not potential subscribers; the social
elite, on the other hand, thrived on being noticed. Occasionally, reports of
social events could be rather lengthy, such as the article in *La Opinión Pública*
(July 21, 1906) describing a party in honor of a young lady's saint's day attended by the reporter/editor. The rhetoric of society reporting, as illustrated
in this case, is unmistakably geared to female readers, as evidenced by the
male author's chatty, ingratiating, and mock self-deprecatory tone of voice.
After an introductory description of the guest of honor, Carmen Garcia, whom
he praises effusively as "un modelo de nobleza" [a model of nobility], the rest
of the article recounts how the party evolved, what refreshments were served,
and the names of the guests who sang or played for the others. With musical
entertainments including a two-step, Mexican dances, and German songs
sung by young Aurelio Espinosa—then professor at the University of New
Mexico—the party was a multicultural potpourri highlighted by a selection
from a *zarzuela* performed by a Señorita Paz, who, in the author's words,

"estuvo más que graciosa y verdaderamente coqueta con su canastito en el brazo" [was more than amusing and truly coquettish with her little basket on her arm]. The entire article is a coded verbal performance aimed at pleasing the female audience of readers, but its rhetoric also effectively demarcates these frivolous social pastimes as part of a woman's world, different from that of men to whom serious news was directed.

Another example of a gender-segregated feature section is *El Defensor del Pueblo*'s "La semana al vuelo" [The week's overview], directly addressed to its "Lectoras" [Women Readers] and signed with the pseudonym, "Rubén." Carried on the front page of this paper in 1892 (and most likely the work of José Escobar), it described the week's social events in Albuquerque with a similar ingratiating tone, overabundance of detail, and romantic flourishes. One week's entries, for example, include Rubén's impressions of Mardi Gras celebrations and of a dance to inaugurate the Commercial Club's new building, where the introduction of electric lighting added to the glitter of an atmosphere "digno de los maravillosos palacios de las Mil y una Noche" [worthy of the marvelous palaces of the Thousand and One Nights]. There, amid heady perfumes and vaporous gowns, says Rubén, the waltzes began and

> mil lindas criaturas que llenas de dicha y de ilusiones mas blancas que las blondas de sus trajes y sus alabastrinos bustos, se olvidaban de la prosa de la existencia y reian y gozaban entregadas del todo á sus felices sueños.

> [a thousand pretty creatures, full of joy and illusions that were brighter than the whiteness of their dresses and their alabaster bosoms, forgot the prose of existence and laughingly enjoyed being swept up completely in their happy dreams.]

Rubén is a consummate aesthete, coy and given to sensual indulgences worthy of Manuel Gutiérrez Nájera, Mexico's preeminent modernist writer, much admired by the liberal intelligentsia in the late 1800s.[33] The woman reader, meant to identify with the lovely objects of his contemplation, also assimilates the message that women are desirable in proportion to their ability to evoke a world of purity and fantasy—in other words, not the real world. As woman, she is a potential commodity of enjoyment, and as reader, she is a potential consumer: an ideal combination for the male-dominated print media struggling to survive in New Mexico.

Appealing to the woman reader was thus a good business tactic for newspapers hard put to make ends meet. Although the number of women readers in a Spanish-speaking population of about 100,000 in 1890 may have been less than 5 percent, they could be a powerful force in promoting family reading habits and also in deciding which merchants to patronize.[34] Newspaper editors identified certain kinds of reading as "for the ladies," and it is not unreasonable to assume that many of the lighter reading selections, including literary works by women authors from Mexico and Spain, were targeted to female readers. Both sexes undoubtedly enjoyed reading matter that reflected traditional male/female gender roles with humorous, satirical, or ironic twists, and it was thus a staple of the time. Didactic prose, short stories, and poetry were deemed more appropriate for young female readers than novels; one editorial in *La Voz del Pueblo* (Las Vegas), March 5, 1892, warned that romantic novels could be a "monstruo destructor" [destructive monster] for impressionable and docile minds, "y más peligroso es esto en el caso de las hijas de Venus y señoras" [and this is more dangerous in the case of the daughters of Venus and married women].

A gradual increase in female literacy after the implementation of the 1891 school bill meant more potential readers for books as well as newspapers, and from the early 1890s on, several newspapers advertised lists of books in Spanish that could be bought through the press, with special requests available direct from Mexico City. One such list printed in *La Opinión Pública* (Albuquerque), in 1892, offered to ship prepaid from a variety of more than sixty books in Spanish, including the poetry of Mexican author Manuel Acuña ($0.25), a marriage manual ($2.00), *Don Quijote de la Mancha* ($2.00), a two-volume history of Mexico ($8.00), and the story of Our Lady of Guadalupe ($0.50). *El Hispano Americano* (Socorro), also in 1892, was offering more international selections, such as books by Victor Hugo, José Espronceda, Jorge Isaacs, Chateaubriand, Aesop, and a "profusely illustrated" manual on how to judge men by their appearance ($1.50). By 1910, the books on sale through *La Revista de Taos* had doubled to more than one hundred titles in Spanish, including translations of French, Spanish, Mexican, and English authors, as well as the memoirs of Padre Martínez ($0.50), and "how to" books on such topics as selecting a husband ($5.00), making a spouse love you ($4.00), breaking in horses ($1.00), growing alfalfa ($1.00), learning English ($1.00), and playing cards ($1.50). Still another indication of the level of public interest in reading was the proliferation in the 1890s of literary societies with philanthropic, social, and educational objectives. As Francisco Lomelí has pointed out, these societies may have been formed as much to encourage as to satisfy literary inclinations, but they were also intended to heighten ethnic pride and promote intellectual dialogue within the Spanish-speaking community.[35] Women took part in literary societies, as shown by announcements in *La Voz del Pueblo* (Las Vegas); one cultural evening planned by the Sociedad Protectora de la Educación in 1896 included various musical selections and a speech by O. A. Larrazolo, to which the public and "especialmente a las señoras y Sociedades Literarias de la ciudad" [especially the women and Literary Societies of the city] were invited.[36] The emergence of public libraries in the West was an initiative supported by the industrialist Andrew Carnegie, whose foundation contributed to the new library in Las Vegas. However, the women's auxiliary of Santa Fe's Commercial Club raised nearly ten thousand dollars locally, as reported by *El Nuevo Mexicano* (Feb. 8, 1908), to cover the costs of construction for a new library there. In the early part of the twentieth century, Hispanic women attended the new teachers' college in El Rito, founded in 1909, and by the time statehood was approved, young women like Aurora Lucero were winning awards for their oratorical skills and seeing their essays published in the local newspapers.[37] Whereas in the late 1890s only an occasional poem can be found signed by a woman, by 1917 such contributions are not unusual.[38]

Neomexicano women who read the newspapers were clearly moving toward more autonomous expression at the turn of the century. Although journalistic discourse continued to advocate a traditional role for women, there were signs in the more progressive segments of the press that gender expectations were beginning to change. In Latin America and the rest of the United States, women were joining the work force of newly industrialized societies, entering universities and the medical and legal professions, and agitating to be treated equally under the law. Similarly, since 1880 changes in New Mexico's socioeconomic conditions had brought many women out of their homes and into more active contact with the public sector. Old photographs from the turn of the century show women working in the offices of the Santa Fe *New Mexican,* but they cannot tell us how much of a voice they had in reporting or interpreting the news.[39] Attitudes were changing, but still New Mexico lagged behind other western states in granting women the right to vote; one article in the English-language press suggested, as late as 1917, that "the lack of a more general interest in the subject probably arises from the fact that most of the women [Anglo and Hispanic] feel that the time is not ripe for women's suffrage in New Mexico, and that there is much in the way of educational work among the men yet to be done before any satisfactory results could be accomplished."[40] In this era of transition in the territory, with male editors often more conservative in their social attitudes than their female readers, it is not surprising to find mixed messages in the Spanish-language press with regard to women's education. A particularly interesting contrast in perspectives can be seen in two series of essays, one running for five weeks in 1891 and the other for thirteen weeks in 1900.

The first, the more progressive viewpoint, was published in *El Defensor del Pueblo,* the Albuquerque newspaper owned and edited at the time by Juan José Herrera, the Knights of Labor organizer and Gorras Blancas agitator.[41] This series, running from October to December 1891, was a reprint of a long study in five parts by Soledad Acosta de Samper, the most famous Colombian woman author of the late 1800s, in which she commented on a French book, published in 1873 by Paul Leroy-Beaulieu and entitled (in Spanish translation), "La Educación de las Hijas del Pueblo" [The education of the people's daughters]. Soledad Acosta, educated in Colombia and Paris, was the daughter of an Englishwoman and a Colombian hero of the Independence period. She was the author of many books and articles at a time in Latin America when educated women were able to participate in the task of nation building only from the margins of journalistic discourse. In this study, Acosta de Samper argues for the need to offer a useful education to women, especially those of the underprivileged classes, an education that will prepare them to be independent, skilled workers with the ability to earn a decent wage. Acosta de Samper's concerns were directed at Colombian society, but they were equally valid for women on the western frontier:

> La mujer del pueblo (y aun la de las clases elevadas) debería aprender siempre un oficio lucrativo, útil y que pudiera en todo tiempo darla con qué subsistir, para que sepa que es libre y que no necesita absolutamente del trabajo del hombre. Ese es el bello ideal de la civilización cristiana, en la cual el deber es el que impera, y en donde la mujer es libre porque sabe trabajar con independencia, y hacerse respetar y honrar. Esa es la verdadera libertad, la verdadera independencia, la del alma, porque esa nadie nos la podrá quitar, ni las cadenas, ni el cautiverio, y esa es la mayor satisfacción que puede experimentar el ser pensador.

> [The woman of the people (and even of the upper classes) should always learn a lucrative and useful skill that she can subsist on at any time, so that she knows she is free and absolutely does not need to depend on man's work. That is the beautiful ideal of Christian civilization, in which duty reigns, and in which woman is free because she knows how to work independently and earn respect and honor. True liberty and true independence is that of the soul because no one can take it away from us, nor can chains or captivity. It is the greatest satisfaction that a thinking being can experience.]

Acosta de Samper, a feminist and a populist, was also deeply devoted to a Catholic tradition of social responsibility, and it was within this philosophical framework that she argued against "mujeres inútiles" [useless women] and for "la enseñanza profesional de la mujer" [the professional education of women]. In choosing to publish the work of this woman author, *El Defensor del Pueblo* was not only endorsing an enlightened view of women's role in modern society, but also drawing attention to the active role of woman as both reader *and* author.

The second example is found between May and September of 1900 on the front page of *El Nuevo Mundo*, a politically independent Albuquerque paper edited at that time by Mariano Armijo y Otero. The series, entitled "Cartas a Mi Hija" [Letters to my daughter] and signed by N. Chávez, may have run longer than eleven weeks, for the letters, one per week, do not seem to achieve closure when the surviving issues of the paper end in September 1900; the paper was known to have lasted until 1901.[42] I have not been able to identify N. Chávez, but Chávez is a very common surname in New Mexico, and some families can trace their genealogical roots back to the time of Juan de Oñate.[43] From the text of the letters, the author appears to have been a well-to-do neomexicano father. Although the letters do not contain specific cultural markers of the Rio Arriba area, they appear to be the work of an educated local individual. The language of the text shows verbal and cultural fluency, the letters themselves being modeled after well-known manuals of advice and similar to the widely read Spanish classic, Fray Luis de León's *La perfecta casada* [The Perfect Married Woman]. It is also remotely possible that, given the subject and its familiar mode of presentation, the author may have been a woman who intentionally disguised her maternal identity in a masculine voice so as to establish literary credibility and authority. Directed to "mi hijita" [my dear young daughter] and intended to set forth "nuestro propósito de que seas con el tiempo una mujer de provecho" [our plan for you to become in time a successful woman], the letters reflect a traditional vision of the female role in society. The writer advises his daughter, above all, to be virtuous and learn how to manage a household, since "la familia es el imperio de la mujer" [family is a woman's empire]. She should be friendly to all, but remember the importance of moderation and dignity in her dealings with young men who love to boast about female favors. Interspersing advice with illustrative anecdotes, the letters show great concern and affection; some personal references to the child's developing talents and those of other members of the family (a brother who draws well) add natural, authentic flavor to the father's wise, albeit very conservative, counsel. He advises the child to cultivate music, painting, gardening, sewing, and dancing—although he has some reservations about the latter. Most of the social arts are given detailed attention in the letters, with the obvious conclusion that a young woman's well-being depends on her public reputation; too much going out and about is frowned upon: "Nada hay que vulgarice mas á las jóvenes, que el encontrarlas á toda hora en la calle ... " [There is nothing more debasing to young women than to find them in the street all the time]. With regard to the education of her intellect, the fatherly advice is quite clear: a little will go a long way since "las mujeres no han nacido para gobernar Estados ni ilustrar las ciencias; pero sí para dirijir sus casas y gobernar sus familias, que no es poca cosa" [women are not born to rule Countries or illuminate the sciences, but rather to manage their homes and govern their families, which is no small thing]. Knowing that his daughter loves to read, he cautions against picking up any book without getting a competent adult's opinion first, and under no circumstances should she read novels:

> las jóvenes, que generalmente toman muy á lo serio todo lo que leen en tales libros, llenan su cabeza con mil ideas extravagantes, y se vuelven locas, ó románticas que es lo mismo, lo cual es una verdadera desgracia

> [young women, who generally take everything they read in such books very seriously, fill their heads with a thousand wild ideas and become crazy or romantic, which is the same thing and a real misfortune.]

With such a protective and cautious approach to raising a young woman, it is highly unlikely that Sr. Chávez's daughter would be allowed to read a local newspaper. The cult of true womanhood that motivates his letters represents a gender ideal of the late nineteenth century that the daily news in the year 1900 showed to be an ever more unrealistic anomaly in the territory. Not only was it an ethic imaginable only within an upper-class existence, but even within this class it was untenable in the face of increasing Americanization and modernization. And yet, in its basic contours of restricting women's influence to the home and exalting her role as a moral example, it remained the prevailing mode of teaching daughters their place in society.

Neomexicano women, like women all over the American West, entered the twentieth century in a conflicted subject position: on the one hand, their culture taught them to be content with traditional roles, yet, on the other, their environment was no longer the same as their parents had known. Beyond this, however, many neomexicanas had to cope with interethnic relationships and unfamiliar social customs, both in their private and public experiences. How women of Hispanic roots in New Mexico negotiated these obstacles to self-knowledge and self-realization, and how this affected their evolving cultural identity, is an aspect of neomexicano history that can be glimpsed in the newspapers, but remains to be told more fully from a variety of historical sources.

8

Felipe Maximiliano Chacón:

An American Author

In 1973, while browsing through the shelves of the Museum of New Mexico library in Santa Fe, I came across a small volume entitled *Obras de Felipe Maximiliano Chacón, El Cantor Neomexicano: Poesía y Prosa* [Works of Felipe Maximiliano Chacón, The New Mexican Bard: Poetry and Prose]. My experience with Spanish-language newspapers had convinced me that some creative literature by neomexicanos of the late territorial period must have been published independently, but until that moment I had not located any such works. The small volume I opened that day had a simple title page, 183 pages of poetry and prose in Spanish, and a photograph of the author—a middle-aged, well-dressed man with an affable gaze focused directly on the reader.[1] The book had apparently been published in a limited edition by its author in Albuquerque in 1924, and had remained in relative obscurity since then.

A check of the library files revealed that Chacón's book was part of the Benjamin Read Collection purchased by the Historical Society of New Mexico in 1936. On the inside cover was a handwritten inscription in English: "To my friend the Hon. B. M. Read. With the Compliments and Best Wishes of the Author, F. M. Chacón. Aug. 1st, 1924." The first printed page carries a very brief preface by the author begging indulgence for his work's imperfections and declaring his modest aim to make "una simple contribución a la Lectura Recreativa, para las masas populares de los pueblos, con debidas apologías a Teólogos, Filósofos, Retóricos y Lógicos" [a simple contribution to Recreational Reading, for the popular masses, with due apologies to Theologians, Philosophers, Rhetoricians, and Logicians]. All of the foregoing would not be particularly remarkable were it not for the paucity of extant publications by neomexicano authors of past decades. As one of a very few books that have come to light from the pre-Chicano period, Chacón's book merits consideration as evidence of a part of American literary history that has been denied mention in standard texts.[2]

We would know very little indeed about the author, Felipe Chacón, were it not for a ten-page prologue written by his friend, Benjamin M. Read (1853–1927). Read's reputation in his time as a respected New Mexican historian, attorney, legislator, and translator made him an ideal literary intermediary for the younger Chacón. Read was a family friend and probably his mentor. The prologue is both a biography and an appraisal of the author's work, anticipating the reader's need for an introduction and orientation. In this capacity, Read reports that Felipe Chacón was born in Santa Fe in 1873. He was the son of don Urbano Chacón, a respected newspaper publisher in various towns of northern New Mexico and southern Colorado and a former superintendent of schools in Santa Fe, and doña Lucia Ward de Chacón, who survived her husband and was living in Albuquerque when her son's book was published. Benjamin Read, both as a friend of Felipe's parents and as a historian, knew the genealogy of the locally prominent Chacón family into which Felipe was born. The oldest relative at the time of publication was Felipe's uncle and Urbano's older brother, Rafael Chacón (1833–1925), who had fought with Kit Carson against the Utes and Apaches in the 1850s and later as major in the Union army in Civil War battles in New Mexico. In his seventies, Rafael Chacón wrote his memoirs in Spanish and had three copies made before his death, perhaps hoping that they would be published. One of these copies was given by his widow after the funeral to Felipe Maximiliano, who had published his own book of prose and poetry the year before; it would be the only copy known to survive.[3] Rafael's son, Eusebio Chacón (1869–1948), was an attorney educated at Notre Dame University, a published author, and a frequent contributor to neomexicano newspapers, but he apparently did not see the literary or historical value of his father's autobiography.[4] Given this family heritage of educated and articulate men, it is not surprising that Felipe Chacón also felt literarily inclined.

Chacón's education was the customary one for sons of established Hispanic families in northern New Mexico: public primary school and then secondary studies at the private St. Michael's College, founded by the De La Salle Christian Brothers in 1859 and located next to the old adobe church of San Miguel, a few blocks from the Santa Fe plaza.[5] Once on his own, Chacón divided his professional life between business and his father's career of journalism. He was an editor for various Spanish-language papers between 1911 and 1918, in Las Vegas (*La Voz del Pueblo* and *El Independiente*), Bernalillo (*El Faro del Río Grande*), and Mora (*El Eco del Norte*). After leaving the newspaper field for four years to pursue commercial interests, he went to Albuquerque in 1922 to be the editor and general manager of *La Bandera Americana*. In all likelihood, it was the printing press of this newspaper that produced Chacón's book in 1924. After the linotype press eliminated hand spiking in the late 1880s in New Mexico, contract printing became a way to supplement income from ads and subscriptions that never seemed sufficient to meet newspaper publishing expenses; as a consequence, these presses produced some of the earliest works published in Spanish in the United States by authors who found a way to underwrite their own literary efforts.

According to Benjamin Read, Chacón never intended to publish a book of his creative writing, even though he had been composing poetry since the age of fourteen. Some of his earliest verses, Read says, "fueron extensamente celebrados en Nuevo México" [were widely celebrated in New Mexico] and occasionally appeared in local newspapers.[6] But modesty inhibited Chacón's ambitions as a writer, in Read's opinion, because "como todos los genios, no se sabe estimar a sí mismo" [like all geniuses, he does not know how to value himself]. Chacón's talent is particularly noteworthy, Read points out, because he writes in both English and Spanish with "íntimos conocimientos de ambos idiomas" [intimate knowledge of both languages].

Chacón's bilingualism can be explained as a function of the New Mexican bicultural circumstance and his education in English at St. Michael's, but it is not this aspect of his work that Read considers most significant. After all, many upper-class neomexicanos and quite a few Anglos learned to communicate in both languages as a matter of practical necessity for doing business or politics in the territory. What Read praises, above all, is Felipe Chacón's mastery of the Spanish language to the point that he could write with distinction and true literary expression—a rare accomplishment in New Mexico:

> Una prueba de lo bien que nuestro poeta ha sabido aprovechar su tiempo, es la manera en que ha alcanzado aprender y cultivar la lengua castellana, sin ninguna ayuda superior, en un país cuyo idioma es el inglés, y donde hay pocas o ningunas oportunidades de aprender el castellano con propiedad.

> [A proof of how well our poet has known how to use his time is the way in which he has succeeded in learning and cultivating the Castilian language, with no outside help, in a country whose language is English and where there are few or no opportunities to learn Spanish properly.]

Benjamin Read's personal experience of growing up in New Mexico and his knowledge of the history of education in the territory informed his perspective. He realized that Chacón's literary talent had to be assessed within his own cultural matrix in order to understand its value and importance. The chronic lack of proper schooling for Spanish-speaking children and the minimal opportunities for learning to write eloquently in their native language meant that indigenous literary works in Spanish were a rare commodity. For this reason, Read added,

las obras literarias de Felipe Maximiliano Chacón están desti-
nadas a dejar como huella una época distinta en la historia
literaria de los Estados Unidos de America. Digo una época
distinta por haber producido *un genio netamente americano*, el
primero que diera lustre a su Patria en el bello idioma de Cervantes. [Emphasis added]

[The literary works of Felipe Maximiliano Chacón are destined
to leave their mark as a unique era in the literary history of the
United States of America. I say a unique era by reason of having
produced *a genuinely American genius*, the first to honor his
Fatherland in the beautiful language of Cervantes.]

Read's observation is perceptive on two levels. Up to his time, and indeed
to our own, seventy years later, histories of American literature have traditionally included only authors who wrote in English, thereby essentially denying national authenticity to literature in other tongues. Read objected that
Spanish-speaking Americans were being left out of national literary and historiographic traditions. Beyond this, however, his use of the phrase *genuinely American genius* underscores the injustice behind the prevailing
definition of what constitutes being American. To say that being American
means speaking only English is not just exclusionary but historically inaccu-
rate. Neomexicanos, who were primarily a mixture of the Hispanic and Indian races and thus descended from ethnic groups that had occupied the
land now called America long before the Anglos arrived, were being treated
like foreigners because they spoke Spanish. But neomexicanos, in Read's opinion, were more genuinely American than Anglos. As Read rightfully points
out, Americans can be patriotic and sing the praise of their heroes in languages other than English:

El poeta Chacón no debe ninguna apología por haber escogido la
lengua castellana para dar forma a las brillantes producciones de
su talento. En sus 'Cantos Patrios' Chacón ha querido manifestar
que las alabanzas y loores de los héroes que ha producido el
pueblo americano, al cual él pertenece, no se limitan a nuestro
propio idioma, idioma que tanto amamos, el inglés, sino que lo
mismo se cantan, con lujo de belleza, en otros idiomas del mundo civilizado que los hijos de America han alcanzado a cultivar
en curso de sus numerosas conquistas.

[The poet Chacón owes no apology for having chosen the Spanish language to express the brilliant products of his talent. In his
"Patriotic Songs" Chacón has tried to show that the praise and
glory of the heroes produced by the American people, to which

he belongs, are not only sung in our language, the language we love so much, English, but also, and with great beauty, in other languages of the civilized world that the sons of America have been able to cultivate in the course of their numerous conquests.]

With a wiser and deeper appreciation of the value of our country's multiethnic heritage than many other historians who followed him, Benjamin Read closes his prologue with these words:

> En mi humilde concepto, el pueblo de los Estados Unidos debe sentirse orgulloso de haber producido uno de sus conciudadanos que diera lustre a su Patria con las producciones de su talento en la lengua de aquellos reyes, los reyes Católicos, que tan señalada-mente contribuyeron al descubrimiento de América, el conti-nente que habitamos.

> [In my humble opinion, the people of the United States ought to feel proud of having produced a citizen who has ennobled his Country with the productions of his talent in the language of those kings, the Catholic kings, who contributed so outstand-ingly to the discovery of America, the continent we inhabit.]

It is more than likely, considering his experience in publishing his own works, that Benjamin Read was the one who encouraged Felipe Chacón to bring out this book and that he helped him to do so. As a mentor and facili-tator, Read was the best support that another neomexicano bilingual writer could hope for. But Read's involvement with this project was not simply an expression of literary collegiality; it was an affirmation of neomexicano cul-tural identity and validity within the American literary tradition. In light of the fact that in 1924 Spanish-speaking New Mexicans were losing the struggle for interpretive power in a state that was becoming more and more Anglo-American, the publication of Chacón's literary works becomes a statement of the right to ethnic individuality and difference within American society.

The major portion of Chacón's volume offers a selection of fifty-six po-ems of his own composition and seven of his Spanish translations of poems by English and American authors, namely, Byron, Dryden, Bulwer Lytton, and Longfellow. The final portion of the book contains two short stories and a *novelita*, as the author calls it.

The poetry is divided into two parts: "Cantos patrios y misceláneos" [Patri-otic and miscellaneous songs] and "Cantos del hogar y traducciones" [Songs of home and translations]. Written over a period of some forty years, they reflect a wide range of themes, some universal (love, family, religious faith, youth, the seasons) and others of more topical interest (New Mexico, statehood, World War I, and local politics). Chacón used both the traditional folk meters and the more cultivated hendecasyllable, showing communal as well as individual inspiration. Like his educated contemporaries, when he chose to write in the post-romantic style, his literary models were well-known Mexican and European authors of the nineteenth century. In style and content, Chacón's poetry, in fact, bears comparison with the popular and learned poetry published in many Spanish-language newspapers in the late territorial period, reaffirming the impression that other neomexicanos could have published literary volumes as Chacón did, had they had a mentor like Read and the monetary ability to do so. The paucity of neomexicano literature published in Spanish therefore points to the lack of a support network, not the lack of talent.

Some of Chacón's "Cantos Patrios" are more interesting to us today than his other poetry for what they tell us about the attitudes of many turn-of-the-century Spanish-speaking neomexicanos like himself who were fervently patriotic citizens of the United States. Their heroes were Washington, Jefferson, and Adams, as well as Alvarado, Oñate, and Vargas, although not all of them by any means were affiliated with the Republican party or from the educated elite like Chacón. The following Independence Day poem was written against the backdrop of the First World War, in which many New Mexico Hispanics fought with honor. It is particularly interesting that Chacón, in his patriotic optimism, identifies "civic equality" as the star that guides his destiny:

A la Patria	[To the fatherland
Cuatro de Julio 1776–1918	*Fourth of July 1776–1918*
Permíteme pulsar ¡oh, Patria mía!	Permit me to play, oh my Fatherland!
Mi lira deficiente para darte	My deficient lyre in order to give you
De sus férvidas notas la armonía.	The harmony of its fervent notes
Y empuñando felice tu estandarte,	And happily clutching your banner,
Pletórico mi pecho de alegría,	My heart plethoric with joy,
Mi patrio amor solícito brindarte,	I wish to offer you my patriotic love,
Que resistir no puede ni el cinismo	As not even cynicism can resist
Las glorias sin igual de tu heroísmo	The unparalleled glories of your heroism.
Contemplo en tus anales esplendentes	I contemplate in your shining annals
De Napoleón bizarro la proeza	The prowess of a bizarre Napoleon
Que pudo conmover los continentes;	Which was able to move continents;
La contemplo teñida en la nobleza	I contemplate it bathed in the nobility

De las almas de aquellos insurgentes	Of the souls of those worthy insurgents
Altivos que fundaron tu grandeza,	Who founded your greatness
Y un templo libre alzaron para el hombre,	And who raised a free temple for man
Do cantara alabanzas en tu nombre.	Where he might sing praises in your name
Por el suelo rodó la tiranía	Tyranny was dashed to the ground
Al oír de John Adams la elocuencia	Upon hearing the eloquence of John Adams,
Precursora de aquel gloriosa día	Precursor of that glorious day
En que Jefferson, lleno de preciencia,	On which Jefferson, full of foresight,
Trazó de su inmortal sabiduría	Drafted with his immortal wisdom
La gran Declaración de Independencia,	The great Declaration of Independence,
¡Madre bendita de los patrios lares	Blessed Mother of the homeland
Donde hoy alza mi musa sus cantares!	Where today my muse lifts its songs!
Quisiera yo la esplendorosa lira	Would that I had the splendorous lyre
Que ha labrádole a Homero eterna gloria	With which Homer gained eternal glory
Para cantaros lo que al alma inspira	In order to sing what that bright glow
Ese nimbo brillante de tu historia;	Of your history inspires
Pintaros con el fuego del que admira,	And paint with the fire of one who admires
Los lauros que circundan tu memoria,	The laurels that surround your memory,
Y en una Iliada hermosa, proficiente,	And in a beautiful Iliad, proficiently
Darte en mi trova lo que mi alma siente.	Give you in my verse what my soul feels.
Mas al pensar bendigo yo la estrella	In so thinking I bless the star
Que dirige en la tierra mi destino,	That directs my destiny on this earth
Y que guia mis pasos con su huella	And that guides my steps along the path
De cívica igualdad por el camino	With its promise of civic equality
Bajo el pendón augusto que descuella	Under the august banner that waves
Sobre tu altar cual símbolo divino,	Over your altar like a divine symbol,
Do Wáshington trazó con letras de oro	Where Washington wrote with letters of gold
"La Libertad," el sin igual tesoro	"Liberty," the unequalled treasure.

Recibe, por lo tanto, Patria mía,	Receive, therefore, my Fatherland,
Las notas de mi ardiente patriotismo	The notes of my ardent patriotism
En este aniversario de aquel día	On this anniversary of that day
En que al suelo rodó el imperialismo,	When imperialism was dashed to the ground
Con su yugo fatal de tiranía	With its fatal yoke of tyranny
Y el mísero baldón de su cinismo,	And the miserable insult of its cynicism,
Y nació como el sol de la mañana	And there was born, like the morning sun,
¡La eterna Independencia Americana!	Eternal American Independence!]

Chacón's references to Britannic imperialism and tyranny suggest no parallel to Anglo-American colonialism on the western frontier. In fact, he even wrote a poem, "Al explorador del oeste" [To the western explorer], that praises the Anglo spirit of adventure without any mention of the negative impact of what the frontiersmen accomplished. Chacón, like many citizens then and now, can accept the foundational myth and the noble spirit it evokes without condoning the outcome on a specific level. His experience in New Mexico had taught him to make the distinction between noble ideals and ignoble actions.

In his preface, Read quotes Chacón as having said: "He sufrido rudos golpes de la suerte en varias distintas épocas de mi vida" [I have endured rude blows of fortune in many different periods of my life]. The disillusionment he expresses in the next poem shows a less upbeat side of his nature, and we can only speculate as to its origins:

Paradoja	**[Paradox**
Con frecuencia común y lamentada,	With common and lamented frequency,
Cuando tú hayas palpado de la vida	When you have touched the hard reality
La dura realidad en tu jornada,	Of life along the way,
Hallarás, en verdad que desagrada,	You will find as an unpleasant truth
La gratitud del hombre desmentida:	That man's gratitude is false.
Sin pensar en el perro agradecido,	Not thinking of the grateful dog,
Creerás hallar la gratitud, sin yerro,	You believe you have found honest gratitude
En el hombre que tú has favorecido,	In the man you have favored,

Pero hallarás tu error esclarecido:	But you will find your error clarified:
Humano más que el hombre lo es el perro.	The dog is more human than the man.]

Whether Chacón's disillusionment was related to his ethnic background or just the inclination of a romantic temperament is not clear. Several other poems convey a vivid sense of social and political justice, which reflected the neomexicano experience of being treated like aliens simply because they remained loyal to their cultural heritage, which, in turn, was constantly nourished by proximity to Mexico.[7] The increase in Mexican nationals living in the States after the Mexican Revolution added to the problem of making neomexicano cultural identity understood within the larger American community, given that distinctions between Spanish-speaking ethnic groups were rarely recognized.

When New Mexico was officially granted statehood after more than sixty years of anticipation, there was great rejoicing among its native population. Chacón's poem on this occasion voices the opinion of many New Mexicans that recognition has been unjustly delayed because of racial prejudice in Washington. I will quote it only in part:

A Nuevo México	**[To New Mexico**
En su admisión como Estado	*On Being Admitted as a State*
Por fin habéis logrado, suelo mío,	You have finally achieved, land of mine,
De lauros coronar tu altiva frente,	The laurels that crown your lofty forehead,
Alcanzando del cielo del estío Una estrella gloriosa y esplendente;	Plucking from the summer sky A glorious and shining star;
Estrella cuyos lampos matinales Os proclaman Estado soberano. Que brille de la Patria en los anales	A star whose morning light Proclaims you a sovereign State, May it shine in the annals of the Fatherland
¡Eterno en el pendón americano!	Forever on the American flag!
Honor para tus hijos, que han sufrido	An honor for your sons who have suffered
Contigo numerosos desengaños	With you numerous disappointments,

Y con ellos tan solo conseguido	And with them have only reaped
El injusto baldón de muchos años;	The unjust insult of many years;
No obstante la lealtad indisputable	In spite of the indisputable loyalty
Que a la Patria tus hijos ofrecieran,	That your sons offered to the Fatherland
Luchando con el indio ingobernable	Fighting against the ungovernable Indian
Y contra los del Sur que secedieran;	And against those from the South who seceded;
No obstante que valientes se lanzaran	In spite of valiantly enlisting
A batir a sus étnicos hermanos	To fight against their ethnic brothers
Y con sangre que en Cuba derramaran	Proving with their blood shed in Cuba
Probaran ser del todo americanos.	That they were complete Americans.

. . . .

Luchaste contra el hado endurecido	You struggled against hardened destiny,
Batiendo del Congreso la injusticia	Fighting the injustice of Congress
Y con ella el insulto proferido	And with it the insult proffered
Del prejuicio racial por la malicia.	Of racial prejudice through malice.

. . . .

Ahora yo quiero, mi querido suelo,	Now I want, dear land,
Que digno de esa gloria, tu gobierno	Your government, worthy of this glory,
Tienda sus alas por el ancho cielo	To spread its wings across the wide heavens
Y sepulte en el golfo de lo eterno	And bury in the gulf of eternity
Leyes injustas que tu nombre manchen;	Unjust laws that soil your name;
Quiero ver tus archivos relucientes	I want to see your archives shining
De datos limpios que tu nombre ensanchen	With clear facts that will spread your name
A traves de los siglos sucedentes;	Across the succeeding centuries;

Ver que el honor para tu historia escriba
Con luz de su pincel inmaculado.

Hechos que lleven la mirada arriba
Y te hagan de la Unión feliz dechado.

Entretanto, tus hijos hoy elevan
De yítores un coro entusiasmado.
Cuyos ecos de júbilo resuenan. . . .
"¡Que viva Nuevo México, el Estado!"

See that honor writes your story
With the light of its immaculate pen,

Deeds that lift our sight higher
And make you a fine example of the Union.

Meanwhile, your offspring raise today
An enthusiastic chorus of hurrahs
Whose echoes resound with joy. . . .
"Long live New Mexico, the State!"]

Chacón, like many of his generation, wrote poems to family members, including quite a few to his children, and also to fellow citizens he admired, such as Democrat Octaviano A. Larrazolo, running for territorial delegate to Congress in 1908, and Adelina Otero-Warren, who was running for Congress on the Republican ticket in 1922, two years after the nineteenth amendment granted the vote to women. One stanza of Chacón's poem to Larrazolo, who later turned Republican and was elected governor of New Mexico after statehood, praises the candidate's eloquence in Spanish and notes that such gifts were not recognized by Anglos who treated neomexicanos as inferiors:

Que el sol de junio al despuntar apenas
Sus rayos en el límpido horizonte,
En tú ha dado un Péricles, cual de Atenas,
Que al enemigo sin temor afronte;

Nos ha dado tu lógica elocuencia,

Bello don del "nativo" predilecto,
Para destruir la despreciable creencia

Del que tacha al latinoamericano
De inferior al sajón por intelecto.

Pues como el cóndor que arrogante sube
A la cúspide altiva de los Andes,

[The June sun that barely shows
Its rays on the clear horizon
Has in you a Pericles, as in Athens,
Who fearlessly confronts the enemy;

As a "native" son, your reasoned eloquence
Has been a valued gift
With which to destoy the despicable notion

That the Latin American
Is intellectually inferior to the Anglo.

Like the condor who willfully climbs
To the high peaks of the Andes,

Tú elevas al "nativo" hasta la nube
Con esos timbres de tu mente
   grandes.
Y hoy que fogosa la campaña avanza

Tienes al pueblo por tu fiel escudo,

Y la voz de ese pueblo en alabanza
Que te brinda su férvido saludo.

You lift the "native" to the heights
With those great timbres of your
   thoughts.
And today as the campaign
   energetically advances
You can count on the people as a
   faithful shield,
And their voice will praise you
With a fervent salute.]

Many of Chacón's shorter verses contain familiar homilies in consonance with his stated aim to produce "recreational literature" for the masses. The very choice of this term on his part suggests that there was a neomexicano reading public whose appetite for enjoyable literature was not satisfied by the Spanish-language press or by occasional imported books. However, Chacón also, like his fellow neomexicanos, may have suffered from an acute awareness of being an atypical American, constantly challenged to prove himself the intellectual equal of his English-speaking neighbors. This final example of his poetry is a type of verse very popular with Hispanic readers in the late nineteenth and early twentieth centuries, one which incorporates a bit of proverbial wisdom and even a possible double entendre:

Axiomas

Nunca de sabio te alabes:
Tén presente a todas horas,
Que aun si es mucho lo que sabes,
Es mucho más lo que ignoras.

No te infle lo que te viene
De mera casualidad;
Más vale lo que se obtiene
De fiel laboriosidad.

Se engaña en su propia vista
Quien, irrisorio a porrillo,
Se presume ser legista
Porque huele a tinterillo.

Ninguna gloria conquista
Quien a los grandes remeda,

[Axioms

Never boast of being wise:
Keep in mind at all times
that even if you know a great deal,
What you don't know is even
   greater.

Don't be puffed up
By what you gain by chance;
What you achieve by hard work
Is worth a lot more.

One who frequently criticizes,
Thinking he is a skilled lawmaker
Because he smells of ink,
Is only fooling himself.

One who mimics the great ones
Will never win glory,

Que "aunque la mona se vista   For "though the monkey may
                                                 dress in silk . . .

de seda . . . mona se queda."   he remains a monkey by ilk."

There are only three samples of Chacón's prose in this small volume, with two of them no more than four pages each, and one a thirty-page novella.[8] The two shorter pieces, "Un baile de caretas" [A masqued ball] and "Don Julio Berlanga," are superior in their convincing portrayals of apparently true events and characters of the time. The *novelita*, "Eustacio y Carlota," is a romanticized saga of a brother and sister who are orphaned and separated very young in life and later miraculously recognize each other by matching birthmarks just as they are about to consummate their marriage! The author claims that the story is a true one and that it was highly publicized in New Mexico and Colorado some years earlier.[9]

In my opinion, "Don Julio Berlanga," which I originally translated for publication in 1977, is the best example of Chacón's prose. In its New Mexican locale, picaresque flavor, and bittersweet ending, it captures the authentic atmosphere of the era, portraying the pitfalls of a romantic spirit and the tragicomic nature of the human condition. It also contradicts stereotypical notions of gender by showing that neomexicano women were not helpless creatures, nor were men devoid of frivolous vanities. Most notably, "Don Julio Berlanga" is a believable story about a common man's illusions and disappointment. Berlanga is a shepherd by trade, who travels north seasonally to graze the flocks. His brief moment of glory occurs in Las Vegas, New Mexico, and his comeuppance has an ironic bicultural twist. He narrates his story to a casual acquaintance, who passes it on to us. Is this acquaintance, the listening "I", Chacón? The reader assumes so; his role as witness frames and validates the narrative stance taken by don Julio—an if-contrary-to-fact subject position in which the feisty shepherd relives a memorable occasion through dialogic performance. Had Chacón told the story in the third person, it would have lost the vividness of its testimonial impact and the authenticity of the narrator's ability to put his romantic disillusionment behind him. The theme of self-representation, and therefore of cultural identity, is prominent here in many ways, not the least of which is don Julio's ultimate satisfaction of being a real *león*, of being able to do for once, however briefly, just as he pleases. Chacón leaves the reader with the same question pondered by Cervantes: which is the true identity—the life lived every day or the fantasy of one night?

The original Spanish version of the story is omitted here for reasons of space, but it can be found, along with the rest of Chacón's poetry and prose, in his small book on the shelves of the New Mexico State Archives in Santa Fe, where the Benjamin Read papers are now located.

Don Julio Berlanga

It was in August of 1918 when I had the honor of meeting don Berlanga, from . . . , in Las Vegas, New Mexico.

Don Julio was an industrious man of forty-eight, nearly six feet tall, erect in stature, muscularly built, with a swarthy complexion, prominent cheekbones, thick mustache, dark hair, and lively, though somewhat sunken, eyes. A man not given to jokes and pranks, though he knew how to appreciate this talent in others, he was always candid and serious in his conversation, even when dealing with trifles.

In spite of don Julio's good qualities of sobriety, laboriousness, and constancy in his occupations, he nonetheless showed a kind of innocent vanity which, in a person of his serious nature, was very amusing. To give a clearer idea of his inimitable character, I intend to relate, in his characteristic fashion, the description he himself gave me of the happiest day of his life.

We were both seated in the waiting room of the railroad station, conversing, when he said to me, "I'll never forget this place, Las Vegas, and do you know why?"

I gave him an inquisitive look and, after a brief pause, he continued: "Because here I spent, last year, the happiest day of my life. You see, I arrived here the afternoon of the third of July from Guayuma, Wyoming, where I had been working with the sheep for a year. I came intending to spend about two weeks of rest and recreation attracted by the famous cowboy roundup that was being celebrated on the third, fourth, and fifth of that same month.

"As soon as I arrived, I ate a meal; later, I went to the barber and took a bath, changed my clothes, did my hair and beard, and went directly to a store to buy myself some clothes. I bought an outfit that cost me fifty dollars, a hat that cost me ten, some shoes for twelve, silk socks, a violet-colored silk shirt with its own collar and a matching yellow tie. I spent ninety dollars there as if they were one, my friend. But with the three hundred more that I had brought with me and the other three hundred I had left in the bank in Rawlings, what did it matter? I went to my room and put on my new clothes from head to foot, and as I had with me the watch and fob that had cost me sixty dollars in Rawlings, I put them on too, my friend, and, don't blame me, but I really shone in that mirror. . . .

"Both in the barber shop and in the street, I had heard talk about a dance that was being given that same night in a hall called *La Favorita*. After dressing, I walked around both plazas of Las Vegas, and even though I didn't know anyone, you might say

I had a good time, since I went to the race grounds to see the horse and cattle roping events and bronco busting done by the cowboys, and I liked it all very much.

"Returning from the grounds, I got it in my head to show myself off at the dance at *La Favorita* because there are some occasions when you just get an urge to show yourself off. After dinner I went to a show, and it must have been about nine o'clock when I arrived at the dance. After I entered the hall which was full of people, everyone looked at me from head to toe, because I'll tell you frankly, friend, there wasn't a soul there who could approach me without being 'eclipsed,' so to speak, by the beauty of my clothes and the elegance of my person.

"I looked around at all the ladies who were there until I saw the most beautiful woman I have ever seen talking to another woman at the side of the hall opposite where I was. I saw that she was looking at me and whispering to her friend; then I went and invited her to dance, and at once she took my arm and we danced to the center of the hall. Everyone was looking at us and admiring us, my friend, and I was something to look at with that beautiful woman. Finally, I stopped and said: 'Friends, all who wish to accompany this humble gentleman, Julio Berlanga, start waltzing! All who want to can dance and I'll pay!'

"There were two or three who shouted. 'Long live Julio Berlanga!' And then a sea of voices, my friend, shouted deafening *vivas* for Julio Berlanga, and I was something to see with that beautiful woman . . .

"Finally the collector came around and said to me: 'Twenty-six have danced. Are you going to pay for all of them?' And I answered yes, giving him a couple of dollars. He gave me back sixty cents, but I said, 'Keep the change, my boy.' Needless to say, friend, that collector was mine. I repeated the same move three or four times, and that dance was my throne, friend; everyone toasted me with every attention and courtesy, and I did just as I pleased. Of the twenty or more numbers I danced that night, my partner for fifteen of them was that beautiful woman I told you about. Finally, she let me accompany her home after the dance. This woman was married, but her husband had left her nine months before and she was living with a sister of hers. I finally asked her to come with me to Guayuma, and she agreed. After three days I went to St. Louis to see my family, and three days after that I returned and we left.

"But that woman, friend, finally betrayed me. I put her in a house in Rawlings and left her well provided with money and food until I could return from the sheep: a six week absence.

Since my work was ambulatory, I almost didn't expect to receive a letter from her, but a week after my departure, I received one in which she told me she was well and loved me as much as ever and that she was waiting for me to return to Rawlings so I could marry her. I answered her that it would be fine with me, but when I got back after six weeks, I found other people living in the house. Later I learned that she had sold the furniture and everything and had run off with an Anglo. I was mad as a rabid dog! . . . and I have never seen her again. But I'll never forget the day that I met her, that day when I enjoyed myself fully, and that dance, my friend, because at that dance I was the king, a real *león* doing just as I pleased. . . ."

Was Chacón portraying through don Julio the neomexicano's familiar experience of losing out to Anglo competition, or was this simply a tale of an ordinary man's brief moment of glory? The reader must decide.

Poesía y Prosa, by Felipe Maximiliano Chacón, is a book whose importance is as much sociohistorical as literary. Forgotten for decades, its rediscovery confirms the existence of an early neomexicano literary tradition and makes the case for reexamining the multicultural roots of American literature, and what it can tell us about the American experience, even stronger.

9

Luis Tafoya:

Inscribing a Culture in Transition

Twenty years ago, when I first became interested in anonymous poetry in the Spanish-language press, I singled out the work of a poet who published frequently in Santa Fe's *El Nuevo Mexicano* between 1893 and 1900 and who signed his poems simply "X.X.X." His insistence on anonymity, on verse forms of the oral tradition, and on themes of contemporary interest to the neomexicano population led me to call him "the people's bard." Like the balladeer in medieval Spain or the troubadour singer of his own time, "X.X.X." submerged his identity in the vibrant poetic discourse of folk culture, yet he used the literate medium of the press as an outlet for his work. This conjunction of the popular and the learned forms of cultural expression in the Spanish-language territorial press illustrates a fundamental difference between Hispano and Anglo cultures in the Southwest.[1] Among Hispanos, in a society that traditionally valued oral expression and in which literacy in Spanish was not energetically nurtured, the newspapers became a site of encounter for the vivid blend of art and politics that Ramón Saldívar has called an organic part of Mexican American community development.[2]

In my earlier research I was able to verify that "X.X.X." was in fact a well-educated and well-connected man in local politics. Autobiographical clues in his verses revealed that his mother was Refugio Durán de Ortiz, who was married to Antonio Ortiz y Salazar, a prominent figure in Santa Fe civic and political circles.[3] A poem to his alma mater confirmed that "X.X.X." had attended Saint Michael's College where he evidently received a superior education. Various translations of English and French poets published under the same signature demonstrated that he had well-rounded literary tastes and that he might well have chosen to write poetry in the fashionable romantic or modernist styles favored by his contemporaries José Escobar or Felipe Maximiliano Chacón. That was the extent of my information about "X.X.X." at the time I first wrote about him, but I never ceased wondering who he was.

When I went back to New Mexico to do more research in 1991, I decided to focus on the period 1900–1912. As I was reading through *El Independiente*, known for its militant defense of neomexicano culture, I came across a 1903 poem signed "X.X.X." and then three more in 1908, sixteen in 1909, and seven in 1910. In both style and content, they were comparable to those I had found earlier in *El Nuevo Mexicano*. Here was the familiar voice again, writing in a Republican-affiliated paper founded in 1894 in Las Vegas by Enrique H. Salazar, who had also started *La Voz del Pueblo* in Santa Fe in 1888; in Porter A. Stratton's opinion, these were the two best Spanish-language journals of their time.[4] The contributions of "X.X.X." stopped when Salazar left *El Independiente* in 1910, so this, together with the coincidence of his professional and social background, made me suspect that Salazar was the author I was seeking. Then I happened upon a 1907 obituary for Josefita Salazar de Manderfield, in which Enrique H. Salazar was identified as her son, the stepson of W. H. Manderfield, a member of the Santa Fe Ring and the publisher of the Santa Fe *New Mexican*.

After this dead end, I came across the name of H. L. Ortiz, who had also graduated from Saint Michael's and had been the editor of several Spanish-language newspapers, including the *La Voz del Pueblo* with Salazar. This seemed promising until I found that Ortiz was a Chaves on his mother's side.

Trying another tack, I went out to Rosario cemetery, just north of downtown Santa Fe, hoping to locate the Ortiz y Salazar family plot and discover more information. Next to Refugio Durán de Ortiz's grave on one side was the grave of her husband Antonio Ortiz y Salazar (1831–1907). On the other side, I noticed a stone marked "Luis Tafoya (August 24, 1851–September 7, 1922)." It rang no bell, so I merely jotted it down and went back to the state library to read Ortiz y Salazar's obituary.[5] There I discovered that he and Refugio Durán had four daughters and one son, Celestino Ortiz, and that he also had a stepson named Luis Tafoya. I was surprised that Tafoya did not carry his mother's maiden or married name, but a subsequent check of archival records confirmed that he was Refugio Durán's son from an earlier marriage to José Dolores Tafoya, whose ancestors had been among the early Hispanic settlers in New Mexico in the 1690s.[6] My next bit of information was gleaned from Tafoya's obituary in *El Nuevo Mexicano* (Sept. 14, 1922), which read in part:

> El finado, quien vivió una vida muy quieta y solitaria, era conocido por sus amigos ser un ciudadano justo y caritativo. Era escritor y experto traductor. En un tiempo fue editor del Nuevo Mexicano y contribuyó en varias veces a los mas de los papeles españoles publicados en el estado, ambos en prosa y en verso.

> [The deceased, who lived a very quiet and solitary life, was known by his friends as a charitable and fair citizen. He was a

writer and an expert translator. At one time he was an editor of
El Nuevo Mexicano and he contributed often, both in prose and
verse, to the Spanish newspapers published in the state.]

I had established the identity of "X.X.X.," but possessed no other record
of his writing. What else had he published and where? As chance would have
it, the following day I began reading *La Revista de Taos*, and in the issue of
January 27, 1911, I found a prominently featured, seven-stanza poem entitled "A Nuevo México," signed by "Luis Tafoya, Santa Fe, N.M., enero de
1911." It was composed right after the signing of the state constitution that
made the long-awaited goal of statehood and the reaffirmation of rights guaranteed by the Treaty of Guadalupe Hidalgo a reality.[7] This poem in alexan-
drine quatrains celebrates the anticipated end to neomexicano isolation and
repression:

Levanta Nuevo México esa abatida frente	[New Mexico, raise the downcast brow
que enubla los encantos de tu serena fáz,	that clouds the charms of your serene countenance,
y alborozado acoje corona refulgente,	and excitedly receive the shining crown,
símbolo de gloria y de ventura y paz.	symbol of glory, good fortune, and peace.
Después de tantos años de lucha y de porfía	After so many years of struggle and perseverance
tu suerte se ha cambiado y ganas la victoria,	your luck has changed and you win the victory,
llegando á ver por fin el venturoso día	finally coming to see the great day,
que es colmo de tu dicha y fuente de tu gloria.	culmination of your happiness and source of your glory.
Has sido un gran imperio, colmado de riqueza	You have been a great empire, blessed with riches
y grandes contratiempos tuvistes que sufrir,	and were forced to suffer great setbacks,
mas ahora triunfo pleno alcanza tu entereza,	but now your fortitude achieves full triumph
y el premio á tu constancia pudiste conseguir.	and the desired prize for your constancy.
Tu pueblo por tres siglos aislado y solitario,	Your people, isolated and alone for three centuries,
de nadie tuvo ayuda, de nadie protección,	had neither help nor protection from anyone,

luchó por su existencia osado y temerario,	but fought for its existence with daring and courage,
sellando con su sangre dominio y posesión.	sealing with their blood both dominion and possession.
Tras tan heroico esfuerzo por fin has merecido	After such a heroic effort you finally obtain
el bien que procurabas con insistencia tanta,	the objective you sought with so much insistence,
de que en la Unión de Estados fueses admitido	that you be admitted to the Union of States
con la soberanía que al hombre libre encanta.	with the sovereignty that delights free men.
Obstáculos y estorbos del todo desaparecen,	Obstacles and hindrances now disappear,
y entrada libre tienes a la gloriosa Unión,	and you have free entry to the glorious Union,
en do los ciudadanos prosperan y florecen	in which citizens prosper and flourish
con tantas garantías y tanta protección.	with so many guarantees and protection.
Por tan pasmosa dicha el parabién te damos,	We congratulate you for this marvelous happiness,
á ti como á tus hijos, de honor tan señalado,	you and your children, who receive this honor,
y que en tu nueva esfera de veras esperamos	and may you in your new capacity
que a fuer de gran imperio serás un gran estado.	instead of a great empire be a great state.]

After reading this, I was disconcerted that my earlier characterization of "X.X.X" as a folk-style poet might be incorrect. Then, on second thought, what seemed an uncharacteristically learned poem struck me as quite natural in this situation for a talented writer of Tafoya's background. On this momentous occasion, he turns to a more formal, ennobling verse style to affirm a sense of collective pride and personal satisfaction after years of struggle for statehood.[8] By portraying this effort as part of a much longer history of neomexicano resistance to domination, Tafoya underscores the importance of sustained ethnic unity and cultural affirmation. In this and in many other contributions to *La Revista de Taos* through 1919, Luis Tafoya's writings show the varied nature of his involvement in the intellectual discourse of his time. They also constitute a paradigm of the way in which Spanish-language territorial newspapers inscribed neomexicano culture during this critical transition period.

What did Luis Tafoya write? Probably much more than I have been able to document. Like other newspaper editors, he must have written many pieces without signing his name. Nonetheless, I have been able to identify more than fifty poems and around twenty brief nonfiction prose pieces, most written under pseudonyms but some under his own name.[9] With few exceptions, the poems are in the traditional popular style associated with "X.X.X."; the prose is a combination of editorials, essays, mock dialogues, and sermons, often appearing weekly and sometimes several per issue. The topics he favored were among those that appear most frequently in the Spanish-language journals of his time: the importance of educating young neomexicanos, the need to preserve the Spanish language as well as to learn English, the injustice of denying statehood for so long to a predominantly Hispano-Catholic people, and the need to document neomexicano history for posterity.

In both his poetry and prose, Luis Tafoya's primary concern was not to create a literary corpus of his own, but rather to interpret for other neomexicanos the cultural dynamics of their time. The identity he defines and inscribes in most of his writing is not personal but collective, reflecting the communal spirit of his ancestors in the upper Rio Grande Valley.[10] But Tafoya was also a learned man with a keen sense of history. The anonymous persona he preferred to adopt was more than just a culturally appropriate response to changing times; it was a rhetorical strategy that enabled him to persuade neomexicano readers of the political importance of retaining their individuality as an ethnic group. Form and content are inextricably linked in Tafoya's writing and, as such, they illumine the cultural drama of his time. We could say, in fact, that they prefigure what Ramón Saldívar calls the "unique borderland quality" of modern Chicano narrative, which is a literature of resistance in dialectical response to the threat of historical devaluation and cultural domination by Anglo society.[11]

Tafoya's work reveals a sophisticated understanding of the neomexicano historical situation. He perceives the dialogic dimensions of a society in transition, in which two cultures interact and shape one another in a struggle for power. This is what Mikhail Bakhtin would later characterize as "social heteroglossia" or "the natural orientation of any living discourse."[12] In Bakhtinian terms, all discourse is multivoiced and constantly changing. From this dialogic perspective, essentialist concepts of truth are rejected, the potential for transformation is acknowledged, and subversion becomes a vital and necessary way of appropriating space.

In the 1911 state constitution neomexicanos managed to unite to ensure that it would explicitly ratify all the rights, privileges, and immunities that had been guaranteed *de jure* if not *de facto* by the Treaty of Guadalupe Hidalgo. By the time statehood arrived, however, decades of Anglo machine politics had essentially factionalized a formerly cohesive and numerically superior community. According to sociologist Carolyn Zeleny:

Party politics was . . . a factor accommodative to inter-ethnic
conflict. Through it party pride and loyalty was substituted for
ethnic-group pride and loyalty. The issues of political strife
tended to be party-political rather than concerned with the
welfare of either group, and the lines of political cleavage only
occasionally have coincided with those of ethnic cleavage. Party
politics has successfully submerged inter-ethnic conflict during
most of the history of political relationships in New Mexico.
Only occasionally have clear-cut ethnic issues stirred conflict in
the political field, although much conflict of a less overt kind
may be discerned beneath the surface of the confused political
history of the era.[13]

During a lifetime that spanned the territorial period, Luis Tafoya witnessed
this transformative shift in cultural dynamics. His writing not only shows
the organic relationship between politics and art, but also the way the consolidated voice of folk culture becomes polemicized and dialogized by the
struggle for political power in the early era of statehood.

In an article entitled "Los paisanos de Don Quijote: Lo bien que conocía
Cervantes la índole de sus compatriotas" [The countrymen of Don Quijote:
How well Cervantes knew the nature of his compatriots], published in *La
Revista de Taos* on July 21, 1911, Tafoya appeals for cultural unity and collective resistance to assimilation by drawing an analogy to a comparably threatening bicultural situation between Spain and France. His article focuses on
the symbolic value of the hapless knight's indomitable spirit:

Miguel de Cervantes al trazar la personalidad de Don Quijote en
su inmortal obra, quiso figurar uno de los rasgos más salientes
del carácter español que ha consistido *y consiste* en acometer
empresas temerarias y casi imposibles que ningún otro pueblo o
raza hubiera ni imaginado emprender." [Emphasis added]

[Miguel de Cervantes, in shaping the personality of Don Quijote
in his immortal work, wanted to include one of the most salient
traits of the Spanish character which has consisted *and consists* of
undertaking fearful and almost impossible tasks that no other
people or race would have ever imagined doing.]

Affirming this as his thesis and using the example of a legendary hero whose
own fictionality is cleverly subverted by Cervantes, Tafoya then points out
several examples from the annals of Hispanic history. One is the heroic resistance of the *madrileños* against the overwhelming force of Napoleonic invaders on May 2, 1808, in which, in Tafoya's words, "el populacho de Madrid,

cediendo al impulso temerario y quijotesco de defenderse y no dejarse pisotear por un enemigo extranjero, se sublevó contra los invasores lidiando casi sin armas" [the populace of Madrid, giving in to the fearful and quijotesque impulse to defend itself and not allow itself to be stepped on by a foreign enemy, rose up against the invaders battling almost without weapons.]. Another example he offers is the defense of Zaragoza a year later, which also ended in failure but at great expense to the French. Overall, these battles made the ultimate defeat of Napoleon possible: "los paisanos españoles, aunque muchas veces vencidos y derrotados, jamás fueron subyugados y siempre retornaban a la lid con renovado vigor y entusiasmo" [the Spanish countrymen, although often conquered and defeated, were never subjugated and always took up the fight again with renewed energy and enthusiasm]. Tafoya's praise of the quijotesque spirit is not just an uplifting lesson in history for his compatriots, but a call to resistance. As in his poem in celebration of impending statehood in New Mexico, his message here is implicit rather than explicit, but it would have been easily decoded by readers who were sensitive to their own precarious moment in history.

Editorial commentary printed in the next weekly issue and signed by "El Corresponsal" [The Correspondent (from Santa Fe)], makes Tafoya's assessment of the political situation and the meaning of the previous article unmistakable. The issue under discussion this time is the political manipulation that would determine who controlled state jobs. Certain passages from this commentary underscore the way Anglo politics had, over the course of a half-century, profoundly affected the old customs of precapitalist neomexicano culture:

> Al tomar cuenta de las influencias que entrarán en pugna para tratar de dominar el estado no se debe olvidar que la política de Nuevo México está compartida en dos agrupaciones; la una del dinero, y la otra de los votantes. La primera tiene forzosamente que hacer un gran papel, no por el hecho de que los ciudadanos de Nuevo México sean más débiles—menos independientes que los de otras localidades de la Unión, sino porque en la época en que vivimos el dinero se ha convertido en poder superior y avasallador en política y en todas cosas y de esto tenemos amplia experiencia.

> [When taking into account the influences that will be fighting to control the state one should not forget that politics in New Mexico is divided into two sectors; one those with money and the other the voters. The first necessarily plays a big role, not because the citizens of New Mexico are weaker or less independent than in other parts of the States but because today money

has become the supreme, enslaving power in politics and every-
where. Of this we have ample experience.]

In the same column, Tafoya predicts that moneyed politicians can be defeated if the voters reject their hypocritical claims to superiority "tan solo
porque han traído diploma de afuera y son favorecidos por asociaciones
peculiares" [just because they have a diploma from elsewhere and are favored by certain groups]. Referring again to Cervantes' classic, he says: "Los
Sancho Panzas que aspiran son muchos, pero la dificultad es encontrar uno
que tenga los sentimientos desinteresados que demostró en su gobierno el
famoso escudero" [The Sancho Panza candidates are many but the problem
will be to find one who has the selfless attitude that the famous squire showed
when he governed]. The column ends with an unequivocal call to his compatriots to join forces to defeat those who would deny them a place in the
new government:

> En esta primera elección de estado es donde los hijos de Nuevo
> México deben mostrar si son capaces de defender sus derechos y
> de exigir la parte que les corresponde en los empleos principales.
> Decimos esto porque los de la minoría muestran disposiciones de
> repartirse entre si los empleos y conformar á los de por acá con
> cualquier hueso, como lo han hecho durante el regimen territo-
> rial. Si en esta elección no obtienen justicia, muy presto vendrá la
> inmigración compuesta de hombres que no quieren que haya
> empleados del páis y que están dispuestos á arrebatar á los hispano-
> americanos sus derechos en la primera oportunidad que se
> presente.

> [In this first state election the sons of New Mexico must show
> whether they are capable of defending their rights and demand-
> ing the portion of important jobs that they are entitled to. We say
> this because those in the minority show their intention to parcel
> out the jobs among themselves and make the natives do with a
> bone or two, as they have during the territorial regime. If this
> election does not bring justice, very soon immigration will bring
> more men who will be against having any natives as employees
> and will be disposed to take away the rights of Hispanic-Ameri-
> cans at the first opportunity.]

The contrapuntal effect of the various modes of discourse practiced by
Tafoya in the newspapers shows how the fourth estate functioned as a mirror
of the time and was, particularly for neomexicano writers like him, the only
persuasive and accessible vehicle for literary expression. In a poem published
in *La Revista de Taos* (Dec. 3, 1915) and entitled "Himno del hispano" [The

Hispanic's hymn], written under another favorite pseudonym, "Pero Grullo" [Known by All],[14] Tafoya shows that neomexicanos were still subject to discrimination based on prejudice and fraud:

No queremos ley de raza,	[We do not want racial law,
No queremos la discordia.	We do not want discord.
Queremos la unión y paz	We want unity and peace
Con igual derecho y gloria.	With igual rights and rewards.
Queremos ser hombres libres	We want to be free men
Que de libertades gozan,	Who enjoy freedom,
Sin los grillos y cadenas	Without the shackles and chains
Que usurpaciones abonan.	That come with tyranny.
. . . .	. . . .
Queremos que las escuelas	We want the schools
De alta y baja graduación,	Both primary and secondary
No se usen como pajuelas	Not to be used like matches
Para avivar la exclusión.	To inflame exclusion.
Somos libres, y no intrusos,	We are free men, not intruders,
Nacimos en este suelo,	We were born on this land,
No para aguantar abusos	Not to endure abuses
Que claman tan alto al cielo.	That cry for almighty justice.]

From this and other writings, it seems clear that Tafoya was one of the vocal proponents of what has been called the *hijos del país* [native son] movement, launched by Octaviano A. Larrazolo in 1911 in an impassioned speech to the constitutional convention.[15] A disillusioned Democrat turned Republican, Larrazolo called for ethnic loyalty across party lines:

> The movement, which was both cultural and political, liberal and conservative, was partly a response to the relegation of Mexicans [neomexicanos] to a marginal and foreign status as voiced by members of the elite as well as by populist elements; and it emphasized cultural and political rights due to Hispanos as natives with historical claims.[16]

Larrazolo's appeal to neomexicanos gathered momentum with support from the Spanish-language press, and by the 1916 campaign the movement was sufficiently strong to elect an Hispanic governor and defeat the Anglo candidate in Larrazolo's own Republican party:

> The 1916 campaign which achieved these results was a particularly bitter one. Virulent vilifications of each party's candidates

were made, high crimes and misdemeanors of every conceivable variety were openly charged against the candidates of the opposite party by the newspapers of the state and by stump speakers. Underneath lay much inter-ethnic ill-feeling.[17]

The Democrat who was elected governor with this support, Ezequiel Cabeza de Baca, defeated a powerful Republican, Anglo politician Holm Bursum. However, C. de Baca served for less than two months before suddenly taking ill and dying in office.[18] As an indication of the divisiveness of New Mexican politics among the Hispanic ethnic community prior to the election, it is interesting to note that, as lieutenant governor in 1914, Baca himself had been arrested for physically assaulting a co-editor of *La Voz del Pueblo* in Las Vegas—none other than Felipe Maximiliano Chacón![19] According to the paper,

> Las fuerzas físicas del señor Chacón son bastante limitadas, mientras las del señor Baca son diez veces superiores, causando bastante sorpresa en todo el estado que el señor Baca olvidara su dignidad como teniente gobernador y brutalmente golpeara un compañero y empleado de la misma redacción.
>
> [The physical strength of Mr. Chacón is rather limited, while that of Mr. Baca is ten times greater, causing quite a bit of surprise statewide that Mr. Baca would lose his dignity as lieutenant governor and brutally strike a colleague and employee on the editorial board.]

Given the fact that Luis Tafoya was outspoken and provocative in his newspaper commentaries, it should not surprise us that he too was the victim of personal attacks in his later years. Nonetheless, the blatant nature of these assaults shocked me as I read about them, quite unexpectedly, on newspaper microfilm. The first mention of them appears in a long article, probably written by Tafoya himself, on the front page of *La Revista de Taos,* Nov. 23, 1917. Under the headline banner, "Tentativa de asesinato contra Luis Tafoya, nuestro corresponsal en Santa Fe" [Assassination attempt against Luis Tafoya, our correspondent in Santa Fe], the article describes in detail a foiled attempt to run an electrical voltage line into Tafoya's house one midnight in order to cause an explosion that would kill him. Indirect testimony in the article explains that Tafoya heard the intruders in time to escape physical injury and that he recognized the aggressors. Although he may have dramatized the narrative reconstructing the event, it evidently had some basis in fact:

> Lo extraño en este case fue que algunos de los conocidos y vecinos más antiguos del señor Tafoya andaban abiertamente co-

operando para darle muerte, sin motivo ni grande ni chico para
obrar de esa manera. Eso hace creer que hubo algo en el negocio
y que el impulso principal de los actos patrióticos de los asaltan-
tes fue algo que les dieron como inducimiento. Fue también
digno de nota que no se hiciera ningún arresto cuando treinta o
cuarenta malhechores andaban atropellando la propiedad agena
y tratando de quitar la vida a un ciudadano. Tampoco la prensa
supo nada del negocio ni publicó palabra acerca de lo sucedido,
pero esto no hizo falta porque no hubo hombre, mujer o niño en
Santa Fe que no tuviera noticia del sensacional atentado. Hacía
más de un mes que el plan de asesinato estaba urdido, y varias
personas sabían que el señor Tafoya era la víctima predestinada,
pues daban a las claras a conocer que algo había entre manos. . . .
La circunstancia de que el señor Tafoya tiene 67 años de edad, y
está enfermo y debilitado por el reumatismo y por otras dolen-
cias, entre las cuales figura el mal estado de su vista, no son
suficientes para mitigar el odio feroz que le tienen sus enemigos.
Este odio es alimentado por la envidia que tienen muchos contra
cualquiera persona que no se humilla ante ellos y los adula.
Tambien sus escritos como corresponsal de La Revista de Taos
han contribuido a aumentar el aborrecimiento que le tienen
sujetos que leen el periódico sin pagar nunca la suscrición.
Naturalmente, los lectores de gorra son de instintos feroces e
inhumanos y quieren que todo se haga a su gusto. Por más de
cuatro meses el señor Tafoya ha sido objeto de una persecución
sorda e incesante que da a entender que tiene enemigos poder-
osos que buscan su ruina, cosa que no es difícil, pues él es pobre
y no tiene valimiento y está sujeto al azote de todos los vientos
que corren en contra suya. Se sabe mucho sobre la historia de
este negocio, pero todo debe quedar en reserva para hacer frente
a otros incidentes de la misma naturaleza que puedan desarro-
llarse en lo futuro. Mientras tanto el señor Tafoya no desespera
y tiene gran confianza de que Dios estará de su parte mientras
obre bien.

[The strange thing in this case was that some of the acquaintan-
ces and neighbors of Mr. Tafoya were openly cooperating in the
murder attempt, without having any known motive for doing so.
That makes one think that something else was involved and that
the primary impulse of the assailants' patriotic acts was some
other inducement. It was also worthy of note that no arrest was
made although thirty or forty perpetrators were trespassing on
someone else's property and trying to take a citizen's life. Nor did
the press learn about it or publish a word about what happened,
but this was not necessary because every man, woman, and child

in Santa Fe heard about the sensational crime. The assassination plot had been hatched a month earlier, and various people knew that Mr. Tafoya was the designated victim since it was widely remarked that something was being planned. . . . The fact that Mr. Tafoya is sixty-seven years old, unwell, and weakened by rheumatism and other maladies, among them poor eyesight, is not enough to mitigate the fierce hatred that his enemies have for him. This hatred is fed by the envy that many feel against anyone who will not bow down before them and adulate them. Also, his writings as a correspondent for La Revista de Taos have contributed to increasing the hatred felt by those who read the paper without ever paying for a subscription. Naturally, these parasitic readers have ferocious and inhuman instincts and they want everything done their way. For more than four months Mr. Tafoya has been the object of relentless persecution, which indicates that he has powerful enemies who seek to ruin him, which would not be difficult since he is poor and helpless and subject to whatever winds may blow against him. A great deal is known about the history of all this, but it will be kept in reserve in case there are other incidents of the same kind in the future. Meanwhile, Mr. Tafoya has not lost hope and he is confident that God will be on his side as long as he does the right thing.]

Political journalism was risky business even after the rough-and-ready frontier days had passed.[20] For a Hispanic editor, the liability was both internal and external, as his profession involved him directly in the double-voiced discourse of a bicultural power struggle. Another article published originally in *La Bandera Americana* in Albuquerque, and reprinted in *La Revista de Taos* (Dec. 14, 1917), tells us more about Tafoya, who consistently camouflaged his own voice and discussed the situation in the third person:

Don Luis Tafoya es hombre de edad ya avanzada pues cuenta 67 años y por muchos años en la casa solariega de sus padres ha vivido caso solo, alguna que otra vez acompañándole, por temporadas, alguna de sus hermanas. Su vida diaria en cuanto se ha podido observar, por muchos años, ha sido estudiar profundamente libros y autores y leer y mantenerse informado por la prensa contemporánea, conversar con sus amigos y vecinos y no hacer mal a nadie. Esta ha sido la vida del ilustre Luis Tafoya, vástago de una de las primeras y más prominentes familias de Nuevo México. Apacible, bueno y servidor.

[Don Luis Tafoya is a man of advanced age at sixty-seven and for many years he has lived alone in the house that belonged to his

parents, although from time to time one of his sisters may stay
with him. His daily life for many years, as far as can be observed,
has been to study books and authors in detail and to read and
stay informed through the contemporary press, also to converse
with friends and neighbors, not causing harm to anyone. This
has been the life of the illustrious Luis Tafoya, descendant of one
of the first and most prominent families of New Mexico. Peaceful, good, and attentive.]

If Tafoya knew who his assailants were, his unwillingness to press charges
seems to indicate a fear of further retribution or a doubt that justice would
be rendered through normal channels of authority. Were they Anglo, Hispano,
or both in political collusion? Was ethnic political bonding driving the opposition to take desperate steps to combat the verbal power of a low-profile
journalist? Tafoya did not point a finger at anyone in print, but he certainly
was not reluctant to express his outrage in a regular column in the Taos paper called "Chispas eléctricas" [Electric sparks], in which he strung together
many critical epigrams and verses, such as the following:

La calumnia es propagada	[Calumny is propagated
Por los hombres de malicia	By malicious men
Y no vale la justicia	And justice is worthless
Ni en el campo ni en posada	In both countryside and town
Porque reina la avaricia.	Because avarice reigns.]

Three months later, another attempt was made on his life, this time using
chloroform to try to drug him and kidnap him. Again, Tafoya foiled his at-
tackers and reported in the Taos paper that this had merely been the latest of
several unsuccessful attacks on his person. The report ends with these words:
"Esperando que algun día la ley recobre su fuerza en esta antigua ciudad y
tenga el ciudadano la protección a que está derechoso bajo la constitución y
las leyes ponemos fin a nuestros comentarios sobre la materia" [Hoping that
some day the law will recover its force in this old city and that the citizen may
have the protection to which he is entitled under the laws and constitution,
we put an end to our remarks on the matter].[21] The fact is that he continued
to write about the attacks off and on for another six months.

One of his favorite forms of social satire and political commentary was
the fictional dialogue, a literary device inherited from classical and medieval
rhetoric and popularized in the Mexican press of the time. The didactic quality
of these often humorous conversations between imaginary or historical figures shows how the dialogue effectively educates as well as entertains the
reader. Although they deal with contemporary issues on a local, national,
and international scale (such as the war against Germany, a national food

shortage, or the Mexican Revolution),[22] the dialogues have a literary structure that brings intertextual resonance to the polemic. One of them, echoing a dialogic novella by Cervantes, is entitled "Diálogo entre el curioso impertinente y el periodista" [Dialogue between the curious impertinent man and the journalist];[23] the journalist in this instance deplores the kind of readers who criticize what he writes without subscribing to the paper. In a second dialogue between the same interlocutors, the topic turns to New Mexican politics and the racial question in the light of a defamatory anti-Hispanic article published in the *North American Review*. "El chismoso" [The gossiper] says that the article was promoted by some malicious New Mexicans, "hombres de prominencia y de sustancia" [men of prominence and means] . . . "con el declarado objeto de levantar cuestión de raza y de vilificar a la gente nativa" [with the declared objective of raising the issue of race and of vilifying the native people]. "El entrometido" [The intrusive one] agrees but points out that not only Anglos were behind this:

> en ellos fueron cómplices y cooperantes muchos hijos del país que se asociaron a la conspiración por razones de venalidad y adulación. De modo que la alegación de que hubo cuestión de raza no puede tener mucho efecto porque tanto peca el que mata la vaca como el que sostiene la pata

> [many native sons were complicit and took part in the conspiracy for venal and vain reasons. As a result the allegation that race issues were involved cannot have much effect because the one who kills the cow is as guilty as the one who brings him to slaughter].

Was the lure of profit and power causing *hijos del país* to side with Anglos who opposed the native son movement? "El chismoso" seems to confirm this when he concludes: "Debemos . . . demostrar con nuestros actos que no somos traidores ni rebeldes a nuestro gobierno y que no nos une ningún lazo de amistad ni alianza con los enemigos de nuestra patria" [We should . . . demonstrate by our deeds that we are not traitors or rebels against our government and that we are not bound by friendship or alliance with the enemies of our country]. To support ethnic representation over party interests does not result from a lack of patriotism but, rather, displays an expression of resistance to cultural assimilation. This key point was misunderstood by those who opposed ethnic diversity, and it remains a problem today.

For those studying the origins of Chicano intellectual history, the specifics of these political conflicts that indicate the transformation in neomexicano society will be difficult to document. Tafoya himself may have been the prescient author of an editorial, in *La Revista de Taos* (Mar. 8, 1918), addressing precisely this problem; its lengthy title was "La historia de los partidos y de los partidarios que han figurado en nuestros anales formarán algún día un tema muy interesante para aquellos que la lean en algun tiempo futuro" [The history of the parties and party affiliates who have figured in our annals will one day make a very interesting study for those who read it at some future time]. Its lead sentence was the following:

> Aunque la mayoría de los políticos de experiencia que han muerto nunca tuvieron oportunidad de impartir los frutos de su información y experiencia a aquellos de sus contemporáneos con quienes estaban relacionados y asociados, y por esa causa se perdieron muchos datos preciosos que podrían ser de gran interés en nuestra historia política, sin embargo, todavía queda suficiente material para llenar varios tomos que contengan mucha información sobre nuestro pasado.

> [Although the majority of experienced politicians now deceased never had the opportunity to impart the fruits of their knowledge and experience to those of their contemporaries with whom they were related and associated, and as a result much valuable data was lost that could have been of great interest to our political history, nonetheless there is still sufficient material left to fill several volumes that could be very informative about our past.]

Calling for neomexicanos to be their own knowledgeable historians, the article makes the point that this history is still to be written:

> . . . la historia de Nuevo México cuando está bien escrita y no es un fárrago de colecciones inconexas copiadas de otros autores, es y debe ser el monumento principal que da honor y renombre a la presente y futuras generaciones, porque coloca a nuestro pueblo en la condición de una comunidad que estuvo al tanto de sus circunstancias en los tiempos críticos en que estaba sin guía ni dirección que le enseñase el rumbo que debía seguir. Ninguno de los historiadores que hemos tenido aquí ha escrito cosa alguna sobre las contiendas políticas que han amenazado el curso regular de los acontecimientos públicos, y aunque nadie niega el mérito que han demostrado al escribir sobre asuntos generales de nuestra historia, sin embargo, han dejado al campo vacío que se refiere al asunto más interesante que es el de dar relación sucinta y exacta de los principales incidentes de nuestras luchas políticas. Esta omisión es muy lamentable porque deja fuera muchos eventos de importancia y de gran interés dramático para todos los ciudadanos de este estado.

[... the history of New Mexico, when it is well written and not a confused mass copied from other authors, is and should be the principal monument giving honor and fame to present and future generations, because it situates our people as a community that was aware of its circumstance in critical times when it was without guide or directions to show it the way to go. None of the historians whom we have had here have written anything about the political battles that have threatened the regular course of public events, and although no one denies the merit they have demonstrated in writing about general topics of our history, still they have left the field open when it comes to the most interesting matter which is that of narrating succinctly and exactly the principal incidents of our political struggles. This omission is very lamentable because it leaves out many events of importance and great dramatic interest for all the citizens of this state.]

We will probably never know the full story of the writer Luis Tafoya and the political enemies who tried to silence him, but thanks to Tafoya and others like him in the Spanish-language press, we have a clearer picture of the internal dynamics of neomexicano culture during the late territorial period. The foundations of Chicano resistance literature in the 1960s and 1970s can be found in these newspapers as much as in the *corridos* sung along the Rio Grande border. Indeed, according to Ian Watt's theory, the intellectual climate that produces the essay is also conducive to the rise of the novel in that a traditional unified world view is replaced by a focus on "a developing but unplanned aggregate of individuals having particular experiences at particular times and at particular places."[24] Still, the Chicano novel would take another half-century to find its authentic voice.

At about the time when Tafoya died (1922) neomexicanos were soon to be outnumbered and overshadowed by the increasingly dominant Anglo population.[25] The travel business and the artistic community also began to refashion and romanticize Santa Fe and its native peoples. In the words of David J. Weber,

> writers, artists, the Santa Fe Railroad, and Fred Harvey appropriated and marketed the refurbished symbols of a once-reviled people. In their hands, the tarnished Spanish past gained respectability. Santa Fe, once regarded as a miserable collection of mud hovels, came to be regarded as "the only picturesque spot in America yet undiscovered by the jaded globe trotter."[26]

Even Hispanic writers of fiction and autobiography in the 1930s and 1940s were caught up in this "historical masquerade," as Genaro Padilla calls it, and "participated in their own submission in ways that they didn't clearly understand given their ambiguous relations with the dominant Anglo-American culture."[27] The turbulent history inscribed by neomexicano journalists like Luis Tafoya was conveniently forgotten and ignored, written out of the new mythos.

Contemporary Chicano scholarship is now recuperating much of this buried history. Luis Tafoya is one of a growing number of newly discovered early writers whose work helps us rewrite Hispanic intellectual history. His voice is both paradigmatic and unique in that it cautions us not to assume unity where there was divisiveness, and certainly not to forget that the anonymous journalists who inscribed their native culture were often individuals of powerful intellect and literary presence.

10

History and Identity:

Benjamin M. Read and His Neomexicano Precursors

In an open letter to territorial constituents on January 28, 1902, New Mexico's delegate to Congress, B. S. Rodey, asked their opinion regarding a proposed change of name for the anticipated new state, possibly to Columbus, Montezuma, McKinley, or Roosevelt. His letter, published on the front page of *La Bandera Americana* (Albuquerque), was accompanied by a vehement response from the editor who objected to the "sacrilege" of changing the name of a land and thereby also a native population who had inhabited it for more than three centuries: "El arrebatarnos este precioso nombre sería, como ya dicho, un sacrilegio, queriendo con ello sepultar para siempre nuestra historia y tradiciones"[1] [Taking away this precious name would be, as we have said, a sacrilege and an effort to bury forever our history and traditions]. Eastern Anglos rarely understood that those who called themselves neo (or nuevo) mexicanos felt that their identity was inextricably tied to their southwestern homeland. Noting efforts that had been made in other states to preserve the names of indigenous people, such as in the naming of Mississippi, Dakota, Wyoming, and Tennessee, the newspaper editor asked: "se nos ofrece á nosotros, los de la raza hispana, menos consideración que á las tribus de indios errantes que habitaban estos países?" [are we, those of the Hispanic race, being offered less consideration than the wandering Indian tribes who lived in these lands?]

Evidently the answer was yes. Four years after the defeat of this bill an attempt was made by Congress to offer joint statehood to Arizona and New Mexico, providing that the new state's name be Arizona. Ironically, the Arizona territory had been carved out of New Mexico in 1863, in recognition of its distinctive features and interests; now, in 1906, Arizona's predominantly Anglo population expressed disdain for consolidation with their Hispanic-majority neighbor.[2] This, however, was not the issue in an editorial in *El Independiente* (Las Vegas) on July 19, 1906, urging opposition to consolidated statehood. What this editorial wanted to convey to Hispanic readers was the legitimacy of neomexicano history and the cultural legacy it had sustained for centuries in the face of isolation, neglect, and constant threats from hostile Indians and greedy Anglos:

> Por más que en la actualidad sea moda entre personajes más ó menos eminentes tratar con cierta lijereza y desvío el nombre y antecedentes de la comunidad que más de tres siglos ha llevado el nombre de Nuevo México, es cosa evidente á toda persona sensata y bien informada que la historia de nuestro territorio es de las más dramáticas é interesantes entre los países de la América Septentrional.

> [Although it is currently fashionable among some more or less eminent people to treat the name and antecedents of the community that for more than three centuries has been known as New Mexico with a certain flippancy and indifference, it is evident to any sensible and well-informed person that the history of our territory is among the most dramatic and interesting countries of North America.]

A sudden, politically motivated change in the name of their homeland would deny the historical validity of neomexicanos; to erase the signifier, one might say, would be to negate the identity of the cultural community it signified. The voters of both territories were charged with deciding the fate of joint statehood in a referendum on November 6, 1906; a rejection by the majority of either one would doom the proposal.

When the results of the referendum were tallied, Arizonans voted it down by more than five to one and thus the proposal met defeat. New Mexicans, on the other hand, approved it by a margin of almost two to one despite the fact that five heavily Hispanic counties in the upper Rio Grande Valley recorded majorities against it.[3] The willingness to accept this change in New Mexico's name raised a red flag for those who shared the view of most of the neomexicano press and many prominent members of the educated Hispanic leadership that the ethnic pride of the Spanish-speaking community was highly vulnerable to the forces of change. In this referendum it appeared that the political and economic considerations of surviving in the present worried many neomexicanos more than preserving the heritage of the past. As the numbers of Anglos increased in the territory, intercultural contacts were gradually changing the contours of Hispanic identity and threatening its historical "memory," except to the extent that folklore and the popular arts kept it alive within the community itself.

The topic of history—or the retelling of earlier phases of neomexicano history—was not a common feature of neomexicano newspapers in the territorial period, when newspapers themselves were often as ephemeral as the political candidates they promoted. Newspapers were then and are now, however, historical texts. Their perceived value as artifacts depends on the recognition accorded to the society they serve, and within the greater United States, Spanish-language newspapers have only recently drawn academic attention.[4] As the testimony of editors, reporters, and various contributors whose views were often divergent, their content differs in quality and interest, but collectively they offer multiple insights into the history of Hispanic New Mexico. As ongoing ethnographic narratives they can help us reconstruct the cultural dynamics of the society they served if we as readers— quite different today from those for whom they were written—can decipher their intent and meaning. As a contemporary scholar has put it, "Just like the archaeological record, the historical record constitutes a many-layered cake of the customs of mankind, and the further the layer from the 'surface' of the present, the more effort we require to understand it."[5] The recognition that neomexicano newspapers both made and recorded history without necessarily *writing about* history is important considering that neomexicanos were being *written out of* U.S. southwestern history at the time.

Evidence of History in Territorial Newspapers

Between 1850 and 1900, the first decades of New Mexico's American phase of history, one finds only sporadic written evidence of a Hispanic historiographic tradition, a tradition which began in New Mexico with Cabeza de Vaca's *Relación* in 1542. Popular custom in the territorial period dictated that events be memorialized in verse and shared orally; only rarely were they written down or published as history or historical testimony. Personal memoirs of life in the territorial period, with a few exceptions, have been lost or may still await discovery.[6] In the print media, journalists felt their role was to voice the concerns of their Spanish-speaking constituents in contemporary matters such as education, crime, party politics, land grant controversies, and other issues that they knew would stimulate readership. Only a few instances can be found in the 1890s in which the subject of history and/or a historical consciousness surfaced in the press. Their appearance at this late date suggests the emergence of a more educated readership and a heightened concern with cultural erosion in the Hispanic community. If we compare this early period with the past three decades of Chicano literature (1965–1995), we can see that the nascent historical consciousness of the territorial period has grown into an obsession among today's writers, for whom, according to Chicano critic Bruce-Novoa, "this pilgrimage into the past" has become a staple of literature.[7]

One example of historical writing in the Spanish-language press had obvious political and didactic motives. It appeared in Las Vegas shortly after the worst period of fence-cutting and intimidation carried out by the secret society of night riders known as the Gorras Blancas, or White Caps. Beginning on February 18, 1892, and continuing for four weekly installments, *El Sol de Mayo* published a detailed historical narrative called "Noches tenebrosas" [Dark nights], accompanied by a large and ominous photograph of the white-hooded night riders. The series was unsigned but undoubtedly came from the pen of Manuel C. de Baca, who later wrote *Historia de Vicente Silva y sus cuarenta bandidos* [1896; *Vicente Silva and his Forty Bandits*, 1947] to chronicle similar elements of the same violent period in Las Vegas history. "Noches tenebrosas" reads like a docu-drama, but Baca called it "la verdadera historia" [the true history], claiming to have based it entirely on historical events of the years 1889–91. He had a flair for writing suspenseful narrative as well as evident zeal for discrediting the White Cap organization, whose lawlessness he characterized not as authentic popular protest but as politically manipulated terrorism in which he also implicated the Caballeros de Labor. Highlighting the evil of the perpetrators and the helplessness of their victims, among them women who were allegedly beaten and raped by gang members, Baca portrayed the mutual society founded by himself and Eugenio Romero as the only true defender of public interest, and he blamed Lorenzo López, who was also the local sheriff, for inciting violence behind the scenes. There is no question that Baca was writing from a partisan viewpoint, but his reporting of the facts here, as in his book on Silva, has been accepted as fair and corroborated by popular folklore.[8] His law-and-order message probably reflected the sentiments of a significant portion of the Hispanic community in San Miguel County who in the early 1890s were fed up with excessive acts of terrorism. As a cultural document "Noches tenebrosas" shows that neomexicano citizens were on both sides of the fence-cutting issue and that journalists used the power of the media not only to influence public sentiment, but also to construct a historical record supporting their viewpoint.[9] As popular history with literary pretensions, Baca's series deserves the same consideration as his more well-known portrait of the notorious Vicente Silva. Evidence that it succeeded in aggravating the opposition is a front-page denunciation of it in *El Defensor del Pueblo* (Mar. 12, 1892), the newspaper owned and edited by Juan José Herrera, who supported the Gorras Blancas.

In April 1894, *La Opinión Pública* in Albuquerque began publishing a biweekly series entitled "Nuevo México y sus hombres ilustres (1530–1894)" [New Mexico and its famous men] which was sold separately by subscription and advertised in newspapers around the territory as "sumamente barato, y toda persona amante de conocer la historia de su patria nativa debe pedirla inmediatamente" [extremely inexpensive and anyone desiring to know the history of his native country ought to order it immediately].[10] Structured around biographical portraits of noteworthy figures, it was the work of José Escobar, a friend and colleague of the *Opinión*'s editor, Pedro García de la Lama, who also backed the project. Escobar's interest in New Mexican history deserves notice, given that he was a Mexican national. Did his own marginal status within the community make him more sensitive to the historical roots of ethnic identity? Or was he simply moved by his impulse to write and sell newspapers? Advertised as the first and only Spanish-language history of New Mexico, with illustrations included, it was available to subscribers for six dollars a year. Other newspapers praised the endeavor, and from comments in *La Voz de Nuevo México* (Albuquerque) and *El Independiente* (Las Vegas) we know that Escobar was still publishing his history through the end of the year, although no issues appear to have survived.[11]

Two years later, on January 8, 1896, *El Amigo del Pueblo*, in the northeastern town of Ratón, published part of a series called "Historia popular de Nuevo Mexico, su pueblo, sus tradiciones y costumbres, 1534–1894" [Popular history of New Mexico, its people, its traditions and customs], also by José Escobar who was then one of the editors of that paper. The segment in this issue begins with the year 1493, describing Columbus's departure from Borinquen (now Puerto Rico), and ends in 1500, with the Catholic kings' investigation of accusations against the navigator. "Continuará" [To be continued], said the last line, but this is the only issue I have found to date.

At approximately the same time, *La Voz del Pueblo* in Las Vegas began publishing a series of lengthy historical articles under the title "América antes del descubrimiento" [America before the discovery]. In the four consecutive issues I have recovered (March 7–28), no author's name is mentioned. Stylistically, the writing demonstrates a depth of learning and capacity for dramatic, lucid prose that surpasses that of an amateur historian. The texts themselves deal with the possible origins of the indigenous peoples of the Americas and then describe the various tribes of Mexico, concentrating in depth on Aztec culture and religion. Since the narrator speaks directly to his audience from time to time, these articles may have originated in public lectures that were commonly sponsored by literary societies active in Las Vegas at the time.

Another instance of historical writing occurs in 1896, shortly after the founding of another mutual society in Las Vegas to support improved educational facilities and to subsidize the expenses of needy children in parochial or public schools. It was called "Sociedad Protectora de la Educación," and among its founding members and officers were Ezequiel C. de Baca and Otaviano A. Larrazolo, both of whom would become governors of New

Mexico following statehood. The society held cultural programs to enlighten the Hispanic community and to raise funds; in the spring of 1896 Larrazolo, who had recently moved to Las Vegas from El Paso, presented a series of talks entitled "Descubrimiento y conquista de América," which were later published in *La Voz del Pueblo*. Announcements for the presentations were published in the newspaper, and a special appeal was made to women and the local literary societies to attend (Mar. 14, 1896). Larrazolo's reputation as a gifted orator drew much attention, and his speeches transcribed in the paper testify to his depth of knowledge and rhetorical skills. Judging by his style, however, it does not appear that he was the author of the historical series published earlier in the same paper.

Attempts to write a history of New Mexico from the Hispanic perspective surfaced many times in the newspapers of 1896. Eusebio Chacón, a respected attorney and orator with literary aspirations, was known to have collected old historical documents and expressed the intention of writing a history of New Mexico. Brief biographies of him have noted a series of articles in *Las Dos Repúblicas* (Denver)—from March 7 to May 23, 1896—entitled "Descubrimiento y conquista de Nuevo México en 1540 por los españoles"[12] [Discovery and conquest of New Mexico in 1540 by the Spanish]. The similarity of this series to others mentioned above leads one to deduce that among neomexicano intellectuals in 1896 there was a definite push to get a history published. Was it because Anglo historians had taken the lead in writing about New Mexican history and the Hispanic perspective was being left out? Was a concern with Anglo historiographic hegemony compounded by an internal jockeying for position to see who could be the first neomexicano to accomplish this objective? Was so much emphasis being placed on the early periods of New Mexican Hispanic history because little had been done systematically to research and document the period after the Anglo-American invasion? Or was this simply evidence of some kind of collective identity crisis brought on by an awareness of greater political dissension within the Hispanic community?

While Escobar, Larrazolo, and Chacón were publishing their fragments in the territorial newspapers, a small book in Spanish was published in 1896, by the American Book Company in New York, entitled *Historia popular de Nuevo Mexico desde su descubrimiento hasta la actualidad* [Popular History of New Mexico from Its Discovery to the Present]. Its author was Francisco de Thoma, not a particularly well-known journalist.[13] In his introduction, Thoma acknowledged the backing of the Catholic clergy and the state superintendent of schools, who evidently intended to use his book in Spanish-language New Mexican classrooms. Thoma claimed that his principal objective was

recordar á los neo-méxicanos las glorias alcanzadas y las penali-
dades sufridas por sus antepasados heroícos; alimentar en sus
corazones aquel sentimiento altivo que nobles hijos siempre
deben tener en nobles padres; sacar del olvido en que injusta-
mente yacen los grandes beneficios conferidos sobre este suelo
por aquellos santos varones, los primeros misioneros; y, avivar en
sus almas el orgullo justo de formar parte de una de las razas más
hidalgas, generosas y valientes del universo, la ESPANOLA.[14]

[to remind neomexicanos of the glories accomplished and the
penalties suffered by their heroic ancestors; to nourish in their
hearts that proud feeling that noble sons should always have of
noble parents; to rescue from the oblivion in which they unjustly
remain the great benefits conferred on this soil by those holy
gentlemen, the first missionaries; and, to stir in souls a just pride
in forming part of one of the most noble, generous and valiant
races in the universe, the SPANISH.]

Thoma also boasted that his was the first "obra de este género" [work of this
type] to be published in Spanish, an accurate but misleading statement.
Thoma's history was, by his own admission, not original research but a compilation and condensation of material found in Hubert Howe Bancroft's *History of Arizona and New Mexico, 1530–1888)*, published in 1889. Moreover, it
was exceedingly brief (less than two hundred pages), superficial, and stylistically pedestrian. If Thoma intended it to inspire pride in neomexicano students, his treatment of the period 1871–1895 is shocking in its dismissal of
neomexicanos as active historical participants:

estos últimos veinticinco años no tíenen hechos sorprendentes,
actos de heroismo militar, ni grandes batallas, ni gloriosas conquistas, el pueblo había abandonado la espada y el fusil, y se
dedicó únicamente á cultivar sus campos, á fomentar sus indus-
trias. Las costumbres de antaño van alejándose, otras y nuevas
ídeas se introducen, y pasa el territorio por un cambio, que sin
embargo de ser lento, es completo.[15]

[the last twenty-five years have held no surprises, acts of military
heroism, great battles, or glorious conquests; the people have put
down swords and rifles and dedicated themselves solely to cultivating their fields, building their businesses. The customs of the
past are fading away, new and different ideas are being introduced, and the territory is passing through a change which,
though slow, is complete.]

Thoma was right about it being a period of change, but he romanticizes the pastoral life of neomexicano sheep ranchers and glorifies the contributions of Spanish explorers and missionaries to the extent that he denies the historical value of the dynamics of change itself. According to Russell S. Saxton, Thoma "is not writing history so much as he is reasserting a basic Hispano-Catholic myth in order to counter the Angloamerican myth of Protestant progress."[16] A thorough and accurate neomexicano history was yet to be written.

In 1897, José Escobar was again in Albuquerque, editing *El Nuevo Mundo* and writing passionate articles under the pseudonym "Zig-Zag," exhorting neomexicanos to wake up to the dangers of political divisiveness and the casual imitation of Anglo culture while their own historical identity was being forgotten.[17] In October of that year he was forced or was paid to leave *El Nuevo Mundo,* and his replacement at the paper was none other than Francisco de Thoma. Thereafter the quality of the paper declined and articles openly supporting "la raza hispano-americana" ceased. Escobar's departure may in fact have been precipitated by accusations from influential Anglos that he was fostering racism in his "Zig-Zag" editorials, or so Escobar alluded in one of his last articles in which he denied that he was promoting divisiveness (Aug. 14, 1897):

> No creemos justo de ninguna manera levantar cuestion de razas, pues que de hecho en este territorio no hay mas que americanos, pero sí creemos obligación nuestra defender los intereses de nuestros hermanos los latinos de preferencia á los de cualquier otra raza . . . ¿Acáso la prensa anglo-americana no está haciendo lo mismo . . . ?

> [We do not believe it in any way fair to raise the question of races since in this territory there are only Americans, but we do believe it is our obligation to defend the interests of our Latin brothers in preference to any other race . . . Doesn't the Anglo-American press do the same . . . ?]

Clearly, for Escobar, defending *la raza* did not constitute racism. The notion of *la raza,* then as now, referred to a collective historical legacy and cultural identity that the English word "race" does not convey. The fact that journalists used the Spanish term freely when promoting neomexicano interests may have occasioned some intercultural tensions, but for the most part it went unremarked by Anglos.

Contrary to the belief of some early Anglo scholars in the Southwest, the region was not "a place without a remembered or recorded history."[18] Ignoring evidence from the Spanish and Mexican periods, William Watts Hart

Davis, author of *El Gringo; or, New Mexico and Her People* (1857), and others who wrote their impressions of New Mexico, were often so blinded by cultural and racial prejudice that they saw only inferior "otherness" in the Hispanic era. Even those who wrote from the pro-Spanish romantic perspective of Charles F. Lummis or with the professional academic rigor of H. H. Bancroft (and his staff of co-writers) were not able to interpret New Mexican history without some ambivalence toward its cultural past.[19]

Neomexicano responses in the press to Anglo distortions of history were sustained and unequivocally forthright, and they made their readers aware of the injustices they were subject to as an ethnic group in the United States. But what of the need to respond by reconstructing a professionally respectable and "true history" of New Mexico—a comprehensive documentation told from the Hispanic perspective? This job would finally fall to a man of learning who published frequently in the neomexicano newspapers of the turn of the century and whose Anglo name belies his mixed cultural background.

Benjamin Read, Neomexicano Historian

Benjamin Maurice Read was born in Las Cruces, N.M., on September 20, 1853, the son of Benjamin Franklin Read and Ignacia Cano.[20] His father— from a prominent Baltimore family and a descendant of George Read, one of the signers of the Declaration of Independence—had come to New Mexico as a government agent with Kearny's forces in 1846. Three years later he married the daughter of Mexican-born Ignacio Cano. In 1828, decades before the rush to California, Cano had discovered with Antonio Ortiz the famed "El Real de Dolores" gold mine in Santa Fe County, later referred to as the Ortiz Mine Grant. How this marriage was viewed by the bride's family is not known. However, according to historian Juan Gómez-Quiñones, "Intermarriage often resulted from the availability of wealthy Mexican women and the lack of Anglo women," and in those cases it generally entailed some form of economic and political advantage on both sides; we also know that many Anglos married neomexicanas of more modest circumstances for a variety of less venal motives and that most Hispanic families did not resist these unions.[21]

Read was the second of three sons, none of whom ever really knew their father very well because he died in 1856. Doña Ignacia had a difficult time raising her sons without a husband and without financial means because her father's title to the Ortiz Mine Grant was tied up in litigation for years. All three sons eventually received an excellent education and became respected members of the community—all three were attorneys—but not without considerable sacrifice on their mother's part. Read later spoke of his debt to her and to Archbishop Jean Baptiste Lamy, who noticed the boy's intellectual promise and arranged for the purchase of schoolbooks for young Benjamin when his mother was too poor to afford them.[22] In his teens Read went to work for the Kansas Pacific Railroad in Colorado, starting as a section hand and advancing to conductor. When he was twenty he was hired as a translator for the territorial governor, Marsh Giddings, and from 1875 to 1878 he was an instructor at his alma mater, St. Michael's. From 1878 to 1880 he served as superintendent of schools in Santa Fe, then as private secretary to Governor Lionel Sheldon, and also as a translator in the legislative assembly. During those years, he became actively involved in the Republican party. In 1885 Read was admitted to the New Mexico Bar and became a successful Santa Fe attorney. According to a contemporary source, this was the result of winning his first three cases, "the first being a murder case, the second a perjury and the third an election law case . . . since which time his practice has steadily increased, and he now has numerous land and pension cases with the Government."[23] Read was more politically and socially connected than most neomexicanos, yet he also took time to help secure military pension benefits for widows and orphans.

Read's prominence in the Santa Fe community was confirmed by his election to several terms in the territorial legislature on the Republican ticket. The esteem in which he was held, even by his political opponents, is confirmed by a lengthy front-page endorsement by the opposition Democratic paper, *La Opinión Pública*, when he was running for representative in 1893. According to its editor, García de la Lama:

> Cuando un hombre es íntegro é imparcial, y desempeña el cumplimiento de su deber, como acto de nobleza el primero que debe elojiarlo es el enemigo por la razón que este sirve de ejemplo á nuestros propios amigos, pues tan buenos y malos hay en Republicanos como en los Demócratas, negar esto sería tanto como decir que el sol no alumbra en el día—que no comemos con la boca—que Santa Fé no pertenece á N.M. . . . Lo bueno debe ser imitado no importa de quien, y dichoso el pais que tiene entre sus hijos a hombres del calibre de Read.[24]

> [When a man is honest and impartial, and he does his job well, as an act of nobility the first to praise him should be his enemy because this serves as an example to our friends, since good and bad exist equally among Republicans and Democrats. To deny this would be like saying the sun doesn't shine by day or that we don't use our mouths to eat or that Santa Fe isn't in N.M. . . . Good examples should be imitated, no matter who it is, and any country who can count men of the caliber of Read among its sons is fortunate.]

In 1901 Read served as Speaker of the House, an honor in territorial govern-ment which he proudly accepted. The fact that he never missed a territorial convention from 1876 on points to his belief in politics as a solution and not as an obstacle to social development.

Read was a devout Catholic, but not an obsessive anti-Protestant, as one scholar has suggested.[25] He was an ideological conservative in many areas, but he despised bigotry in any guise and took pride in the antislavery stance of Hispanic New Mexico during the Civil War.[26] In matters relating to women's place in society, he held traditional views of gender roles, although he recog-nized the political rights women gained at the beginning of the century and supported them.[27] His mother's example undoubtedly influenced his more progressive stance in these matters. In 1876 he married Asensión Silva, who died two years later; Read then married her sister, Magdalena, with whom he had seven children. After Magdalena's death in 1893, he married Onofre Ortiz, daughter of a highly regarded neomexicano family and, according to con-temporary accounts, "one of the best educated and most refined ladies of Santa Fe."[28] She died in 1904, leaving Read with three surviving daughters from his second marriage. It was after this that Read turned his attention more fully to his avocation: the reading and reconstruction of neomexicano history, which would consume the final two decades of his life.

Although he was completely bilingual, his personal and professional life was conducted largely in Spanish, the language in which he spent most of his early years, surrounded by his mother's relatives. Read himself preferred to write in Spanish and he felt very strongly about the teaching of Spanish in New Mexico's schools, remarking with notable foresight:

> Es una verdadera lástima que, ya que el inglés y el castellano
> están destinados a ser, quizás por siglos, las lenguas dominantes
> en América, sean tan pocos los que de nuestra raza aprenden el
> inglés, como los de habla inglesa que hablan nuestra lengua.[29]
>
> [It is a pity, given that English and Spanish are destined perhaps
> for centuries to be the dominant languages in America, that so
> few of our race learn English and so few who speak English learn
> our language.]

Read's concern with language may, ironically, have worked against him. Sev-eral of his own works were translated into English at his expense in order to reach a wider reading public, but one of his contemporaries noted:

> The fact that he thought and wrote in Spanish and insisted upon
> a literal translation, robbed his English work of much of the

spirit and smoothness of his Spanish diction. This also made it difficult for him to find a publisher and he was compelled to finance his own publications with but meager financial returns to himself. The more praiseworthy was his loyalty to his Muse.[30]

An accomplished orator in Spanish, Read was often invited to deliver public addresses on ceremonial occasions, such as the welcoming of a new bishop to Santa Fe or the fiftieth anniversary of St. Michael's College. In the state legislature and at civic events, the eloquence of Spanish orators like Read and his contemporaries Isidoro Armijo and Otaviano Larrazolo was recognized in both the Anglo and Hispanic communities. When Benjamin Read died on September 15, 1927, *El Nuevo Mexicano* wrote that "su muerte remueve a uno de los ciudadanos más prominentes de Santa Fe: un historiador eminente, un hombre activo y enérgico, una figura distinguida" [his death takes away one of Santa Fe's most prominent citizens: an eminent historian, an active and energetic man, a distinguished figure].

History was Benjamin Read's lifelong passion. It may have started with an early love of reading and an awareness of his bicultural past, but it was largely inspired by his job of translating old documents from Spanish into English for the territorial legislature. In the lawmaking environment, the importance of historical documents and the damage that their mistranslation could cause took on new significance for him. With increasing interest, Read set about collecting books and original documents related to the history of the Hispanic southwest, eventually amassing a personal library and a wealth of knowledge that brought him into contact with others in the English and Spanish-speaking communities who shared his avocation. As a lawyer, jurist, and bibliophile, Read believed in the authority of written texts. He could not have overlooked the fact that the disproportionate influence of the Anglo community in territorial society was based on its control of law, commerce, and banking—all defined by a technical knowledge of regulations and documents—which was changing the informal, community-based patterns of life in New Mexico. Certainly, the Spanish colonial empire had been sustained by elaborate bureaucratic paperwork, but the isolated rural existence on its northern frontier did not entail much need for book-learning in the early days. Benjamin Read, raised to be bilingual and to absorb book knowledge, came to understand early on the advantages of knowing two languages, two cultures, and having the skills to mediate between them.

Comparative readings of Anglo and Hispanic texts convinced Read that the accurate transmission of history was critical to ensuring a stable and productive future for New Mexico. At a crossroads between Hispanic tradition and Anglo modernity in the late nineteenth century, New Mexico's cultural identity as a future state was still in flux as statehood approached. If the increasingly influential Anglo historians were allowed to determine how the story of New Mexico's past was to be told to coming generations, then the prospect for neomexicano cultural integrity would be undermined from the start. Seeing his role as a cultural liaison between the Anglo and Hispano communities, Read was determined to repossess crucial aspects of the telling of New Mexico's history that had been incorrectly incorporated into the building of a master discourse of American history.

Read knew that his rebuttal had to be accomplished in the most tactful and scholarly manner or it would not be taken seriously by Anglo scholar-historians who were, at the time, very preoccupied with professionalization in their ranks and dedicated to a "posture of objectivity."[31] His identification with the neomexicano community might call his impartiality into question unless he buttressed his opinions with abundant evidence. Read knew that written documents would be persuasive in scholarly historical circles in a way that the traditional New Mexican oral folklore, the vehicle of much popular history, would not. Nonetheless, he would occasionally seek out the *viejos* and ask them to share their recollections, carefully making notations of their testimony and quoting them by name in his works.[32] His primary strategy, however, would be to use original documents of New Mexican history, gleaned from archives in Spain, Mexico, and all over the territory itself.[33]

The more Read studied history and understood the way errors could be transmitted and perpetuated, the more he became a stickler for detail. On the subject of historical accuracy, he was absolutely unwavering and notorious among his colleagues, who testified that his "literal-mindedness had no patience with romanticism when it came to historical statements."[34] His search for authentic, original materials on both continents cost him much time, effort, and money, which he pointed out to his readers lest they assume he was borrowing from other authors' works, as had many Anglo and Hispano historians before him.[35]

There is reason to believe that Read began his historical research as early as the 1870s, when, in his twenties, he learned more about the role of Padre Antonio José Martínez in New Mexico's history. It just so happened that, in 1877, Benjamin's older brother Larkin married Teodora Martínez, daughter of Santiago Martínez (Valdez), who was the padre's foster son and one of his first biographers.[36] Through his brother, Benjamin must have met Teodora's father and listened to his stories about the outspoken Taos priest who had defended the interests of neomexicanos in the Mexican and early territorial periods, but who was later to be vilified by those who criticized his lifestyle and ecclesiastical modus operandi. At some later date, Read acquired the manuscript-biography that Santiago Valdez wrote shortly after the padre's death. A note found with it, among the Read papers in the New Mexico State Archives, indicates that Read intended to revise, annotate, and expand the

Valdez biography; he went to the trouble of translating it into English from a copy made by his brother, but he never published it.[37] It was apparently his intention to do so, for he was well aware of the need to preserve important documents that testified to the neomexicano experience in history; portions of this original document remain among his papers today. As he said years later, in a letter to the editor of *La Revista de Taos* (Sept. 24, 1909):

> Hubiera querido ya que alguno de los hombres públicos de los tiempos del Padre Martinez—y los hubo en gran número— hubieran escrito la historia de nuestro Territorio hasta la época del cambio de banderas, pero como desafortunadamente no lo hicieron, nos incumbe á nosotros, sus hijos y descendientes corregir esa gran falta y debemos excudriñar la historia y los escritos históricos é inéditos de aquellos revoltosos tiempos á fin de vindicar la memoria, reputación y buen nombre de nuestros antecesores.

> [I wish that some of the well-known men of Padre Martínez's time—and there were many—had written the history of our Territory up to the time of the changing of flags, but as unfortunately they did not, it is incumbent upon us, their sons and descendants, to correct that lack. We must scrutinize history and unpublished written documents of those turbulent times, in order to vindicate the memory, reputation and good name of our ancestors.]

Read, who was on the verge of publishing his two major historical works, anticipated that the use of original documents in Spanish, which had been unknown or overlooked, would set in motion a revisionist view of southwestern history. The zeal he devoted to pursuing historical justice was proportionate to the amount of misinformation that he knew to be already circulating. One hears his indignation in these words:

> puedo asegurar á Ud. que cuando se den á la estampa los resultados de mis estudios muchos de los llamados pro-hombres tan alto y falsamente elogiados quedarán relgados á oprobioso lugar en la historia y muchos de los ignorados aparecerán como los verdaderos caracteres dignos de ocupar honrosas páginas en la historia del suelo que los viera nacer. . . . Cuando se publiquen esos datos históricos se correrá el misterioso velo que ha, por tantos años, ocultado los verdaderos hechos, y ¡cuantos, y cuan amargos, desengaños habrá! ¡Cuantos y cuan injustas decepciones serán aclaradas!

[I can assure you that when the results of my studies are published many of the so-called great men, so highly and wrongly praised, will be relegated to a shameful place in history and many of those overlooked will turn out to be the ones truly worthy of honor in the history pages of the land of their birth. . . . When these facts are published, the mysterious veil that for so many years has hidden the true deeds will be removed, and how many bitter disillusionments there will be! How many unjust deceptions will be revealed!]

The two books that Read had been working on for some years would appear on the eve of New Mexico's long-awaited statehood. Since 1902, when Rodey sent his letter to constituents, and even long before that, the neomexicano press had deluged its readers with weekly progress reports on the struggle for statehood and had endlessly repudiated spurious statements from eastern newspapers and congressmen alleging that New Mexico was unfit to be a state because of the size and nature of its Spanish-speaking, Catholic population. In one of his essays in 1909, Read lambasted the bias of an investigative committee chaired by Senator Albert J. Beveridge from Indiana that had recommended against statehood.[38]

Nuesta gente ha sido tratada tan vilmente desde que el territorio fué incorporado á la nación americana, que desde entonces hemos estado nosotros y los que nos precedieron constantemente ocupados en refutar asaltos inmotivados, injustos, crueles y cobardes. *La prueba de la buena ciudadanía se halla en el verdadero patriotismo. ¿Ha dado el pueblo nativo esa prueba? Que responda la historia.*[39] [Emphasis added]

[Our people have been so vilely treated since the territory became part of the American nation that since that time we and those who preceded us have been constantly busy refuting unmotivated, unjust, cruel and cowardly attacks. *The proof of good citizenship is found in true patriotism. Has the native population given that proof? Let history answer.*]

Read intended his own publications to provide that answer before posterity rendered its decision.

His first book of history from the neomexicano perspective was published in Spanish in 1910 and entitled *Guerra México-Americana* [Mexican American War].[40] It was dedicated to his three daughters, which may point to Read's identification with this period as the symbolic juncture that gave birth to a new generation of bicultural families. As he clarifies in his prologue, he is not so much interested in the military aspects of the war itself as in the causes and consequences of it. Other Anglo and Mexican historians who analyzed the war in earlier works, says Read, have not traced the origins back far enough; his book will show that U.S. expansionism has its origins in the early years of the republic and that, out of the ethnic hatred it precipitated, "la historia se repite" [history repeats itself].[41] Of seventeen chapters, Read devoted five to the pre-1820 era, nine to the immediate causes of the war, and three final chapters to the special history of New Mexico before and after Kearny's troops arrived. In his final chapters, Read contests interpretations of New Mexican history by H.H. Bancroft and Ralph Emerson Twitchell. The latter had just published a book on the military occupation of New Mexico[42] and Read knew him as a colleague in Santa Fe; nonetheless, he took exception to Twitchell's characterization of Padre Martínez and his role in the Taos uprising. According to Read, the popular priest had been a hero:

> El Padre Martinez ha sido injustamente censurado por algunos escritores, valiéndose muchos de ellos de meras conjeturas para ofuscar la honorabilísima memoria de quien, se puede, sin temor de contradiccion afirmar, fué en el mundo cívico una de las figuras más brillantes de su época.[...] Todo lo sacrificó por amor al terruño que lo viera nacer, para poder así contribuir en mayor escala con su experiencia y saber al más rápido desenvolvimiento, material é intelectual, de sus compatriotas que ya empezaban á sentir los beneficios y las ventajas de la nueva civilizacion.[43]

> [Padre Martinez has been unjustly censured by some writers who based their opinions on mere conjectures in order to obfuscate the most honorable memory of one who, one can say without fear of contradiction, was in the world of his community one of the most brilliant figures of his era.[...] He sacrificed everything out of love for the land of his birth, to be able to contribute more with his experience and knowledge to the rapid material and intellectual development of his compatriots who were already beginning to feel the benefits and advantages of the new civilization.]

Read frequently found himself in the delicate position of having to contradict prevailing interpretations of history and simultaneously insist on his impartiality and objectivity, as if anticipating that his ethnicity and critical posture would alienate the goodwill of Anglo historical circles. But he did not hide his pride in being one of a generation of *new* New Mexicans and the author of "la primera obra de historia escrita por un hijo nativo de Nuevo

México, descendiente de ambas dos razas, la anglosajona y la latina" [the first work of history written by a native son of New Mexico, descendant of both races, Anglo-Saxon and Latin]. Above all, he hoped it would "aclarar la verdad en pro de la justicia histórica de que hayan sido privados los descendientes de los bizarros conquistadores" [clarify the truth and do historical justice to those deprived of it, the descendants of the brave conquistadors].[44] His tone, both in the prologue and the body of this work, is straightforward but not apologetic; he goes to the heart of the matter in the first chapter when he warns that he will pursue the origins of U.S. expansionism "a la raíz para demostrar, hasta la evidencia,—la supina ignorancia— la maliciosa preocupacion de algunos de los escritores Anglo-Americanos que han, sin intentarlo quizá, ofuscado la verdad"[45] [to its roots to show, as far as evidence permits, that the abject ignorance or the malicious intent of some Anglo-American writers, perhaps without meaning to, has obfuscated the truth].

Essentially, Read had a positive view of the impact of American rule on New Mexico insofar as it brought the advantages of democracy and freedom. His major objection was not to the American form of government, but to the ethnocentrism of Protestant Anglo-Saxon culture. New Mexicans in the Mexican period, said Read, had been left by the Mexican Republic to fend for themselves "dando por resultado la frialdad de los habitantes del territorio hácia su madre patria, y en último resultado, su anexion voluntaria á la Union Americana"[46] [resulting in the coldness the inhabitants of the territory felt toward their mother country and, as a result, their voluntary annexation to the United States]. It was not Read's habit as a historian only to criticize; he gave credit where it was due and prominently indicated points of agreement with Bancroft, Twitchell, and others. *Guerra México-Americana*'s reception in the neomexicano press was enthusiastic, with *El Neomexicano* (July 30, 1910) urging its translation into English and adding: "debería ocupar un lugar en toda coleccion histórica de libros y en toda familia hispano-americana del Sudoeste" [it should have a place in every historical collection and in every Spanish American family in the Southwest]. The translation never appeared.

On May 5, 1910, a long poem in rhymed quatrains was published in *El Independiente* (Las Vegas), entitled "A Don Benjamin M. Read," in anticipation of his next book of New Mexican history. It was signed by none other than "X.X.X." (Luis Tafoya) and read in part:

Este camino está llano	[This road is open
Para el hombre de talento	For the man of talent
Que ose estudiar el arcano	Who dares to study the past
Con empeño y ardimiento	With diligence and passion

Y que sea historiador	And who is a historian
De los hechos solamente	Of only the facts
Y con verdad defensor	And the true defender
De su país y de su gente.	Of his country and his people.
Aunque sabios los extraños	Although foreigners are wise
A fondo no entienden nada	They really understand nothing
Dando fé á muchos engaños	Believing many falsehoods
De ficción disparatada.	Of outrageous fiction.

Luis Tafoya and Benjamin Read, who lived only a few blocks from each other south of the plaza in Santa Fe, often published their work in the same issues of *La Revista de Taos*, owned by their friend, a native of Spain, José Montaner. The two Santa Fe authors had much in common intellectually and shared many a conversation, as well as front pages of the *Revista*, talking about local and national politics; they were both pro-statehood Republicans but were not particularly well-to-do or *agringados* [Anglicized], as was Miguel Antonio Otero, Jr., the former governor and prototype of the neomexicano elite of their generation. Both Tafoya and Read favored accommodation, not assimilation, as evidenced in their own more traditional ways of living and expressing their neomexicano cultural identity.

The very next year, 1911, saw the publication of Read's second and much more ambitious historical work *Historia ilustrada de Nuevo México* [Illustrated History of New Mexico]. Read dedicated this volume to his mother, Ignacia Cano, whose photograph and brief biography appear at the beginning of the book.[47] Divided into four parts, the volume runs 616 pages, with extensive footnotes, biographical sketches, and photos of notable territorial figures—a structure comparable to Twitchell's *Leading Facts of New Mexican History*, which began publication in the same year and which Read must have anticipated as a kind of master discourse to which he would partially respond. To ensure that his voice was heard among Anglos, Read hired a translator for an English edition that was published in 1912. Like Twitchell and Bancroft before him, Read researched and documented his work in scrupulous detail,[48] but unlike his Anglo counterparts, Read was aware of writing from the margins and contesting the dominant interpretations of history in a politically charged environment.

This time, perhaps in the spirit of cultural accommodation, Read explained the need for his new work in terms of linguistic, not racial, injustice. His experience as a translator, litigator, and legislator had convinced him of the susceptibility to error of those who trans-late [carry across] or inter-pret [explain value] between cultural communities. In reading history texts, he had noted "that remarkable differences and striking contradictions exist among some of the English speaking authors in their respective narratives of historical events" whenever they deal with Hispanic history.[49] A closer examination of the original texts they cited showed that this was due largely to the fact that "no two of them agree in their translations whence a great deal of confusion arises in their exposition of historical events and incidents."[50] Language was the critical element in the historiographic equation, he said. Without a precise reading of original Spanish documents, historical writing was bound to be flawed:

> It is thus seen how easy it is for the ablest of historians to fall into error when they are not thoroughly familiar with the language the original authorities are written in, having, necessarily to depend upon former authors who, for the reasons stated, were just as much in error, and who it is evident, never saw the source of their information, and had to depend on translation, tradition or hearsay evidence.[51]

By misreading and mistranslation, neomexicano history had been detached from its truth and lost in translation.

Benjamin Read was ahead of his time in warning readers of the special power of language both to transform and to be transformed. If, as Roberto González Echevarría has noted vis-à-vis Latin American literature, "culture is memory, and memory is rooted in language,"[52] then the subversive nature of language itself creates the potential for misinterpretation even before the process of translation is attempted. The impulse to mythologize, according to Lévi-Strauss, is intrinsic to language.[53] (The Spanish word *historia* recognizes the slippage between history and imagination as it means both *history* and *story*, depending on its context.) A historical text claiming objectivity and truthfulness, in fact, has a rhetorical subtext in which the narrator, consciously or unconsciously, conveys a message about the quality of the subject. According to Hayden White, in *Tropics of Discourse*: "the very use of language itself implies or entails a specific posture before the world which is ethical, ideological, or more generally political: not only all interpretation, but also all language is politically contaminated."[54] To translate language or carry-over meaning from one culture to another is a both a decoding and recoding process fraught with danger to the original text: the process of translation and then the way the translation is situated within another text constitutes a double-jeopardy situation. Crossing the border between languages and cultures thus signaled to Read not only a potential abuse of "author-ity" but also an expropriation of meaning that could distort truth and deny neomexicano identity. In seeking to turn the historiographic tables through a focus on language, Read hoped to transform a monologue of cultural suppression into a communicative dialogue.

Read's *Illustrated History*, then, was an attempt to rescue and retell the history of New Mexico at a time when the larger community was embarking on the transition from territory to statehood. The preservation of Hispanic culture, its historical memory, and its verbal artifacts was of central concern to forward-thinking neomexicano citizens in the legislature, the press, and the public-at-large. The unique provisions of the state constitution that was negotiated in 1910, and which Read heartily endorsed, attest to the effective influence of this awareness.[55] Under the New Mexico constitution, the guarantees specified by the Treaty of Guadalupe Hidalgo were reaffirmed and the voting and education rights of all Spanish-speaking citizens, regardless of their ability to speak English, were ratified.[56] With these guarantees, the composite identity of the new state would have a good chance of reflecting the dialectic of cultures that so concerned Benjamin Read.

During his lifetime, however, this process of state identity-formation was in its infant stage. Read wanted to ensure its healthy maturation, so he continued his research and writing. Education was one of his favorite topics; Read wanted it known that Hispanos in territorial New Mexico had struggled to establish the first schools and had maintained them despite neglect from the federal government.[57] He adamantly supported the need for a competent bilingual method in the schools, stating that it "was the surest and the safest one to accomplish the desired results."[58] He also defended the role of the Catholic church in New Mexican history and wrote that New Mexico owed much of its cultural vitality to the commitment of the early friars and to later benefactors, like Archbishop Lamy, who enriched educational opportunities for both Anglos and Hispanics. Read was a prohibitionist and traditional in his understanding of gender roles, but unlike many of his culture and class he favored women's suffrage and female access to the highest state offices after suffrage was granted. History, Read said, proved that

> notables damas figuraron en todos los departamentos del saber humano y en las grandes guerras que registra la historia—no se diga, pues, que entre las señoras de Nuevo México no hay mujeres que merezcan ser elevadas a tales distinciones. Competentes, y de acendrado patriotismo, las tenemos en abundancia.[59]

> [notable women have figured in all areas of human knowledge and in the great wars recorded in history—don't say, then, that New Mexico does not have women deserving of being appointed to high positions. We have competent and truly patriotic women in abundance.]

Writing history continued to be Read's passion even in his sixties and seventies, the more so as he noticed the perpetuation of many untruths. In 1919, he published *A Treatise on the Disputed Points of the History of New Mexico*, an eighteen-page pamphlet he sold for "50 cents delivered." The points that Read addressed included the origin of the name "Nuevo México" and the exact location of the first colony established there by the Spaniards. Each point is corroborated by quotations from documents original to the period and discussed in the sort of detail that only a specialist could love. Whether to bolster his credibility or invite further discourse—which he probably relished—Read concludes with an offer to show "cheerfully" to any interested party the documents in his possession that proved his points.

In his own northern New Mexican milieu in the decade or so following statehood, Benjamin Read was a well-known public figure, but he found it no easier to get his works published. To this day, two book-length manuscripts languish in typescript among his papers: one, in English, is entitled "Hernán Cortés and his Conquest of Mexico," copyrighted in 1914 by the author when he apparently had the intention of publishing it in Boston.[60] It offers a very favorable historical portrait of Cortés and of his native female interpreter, La Malinche, whom Read saw as "a heroic figure in the world's history."[61] The other manuscript is in Spanish, with the title "Nuevo México en las guerras de la Unión Americana, 1855–1919" [New Mexico in the Wars of America, 1855–1919], and deals with neomexicano participation in U.S. wars after the 1846 invasion. It includes a section of eleven chapters on World War One from Read's later revisions to the *Illustrated History* (English edition), translated into Spanish by his friend and protegé, Felipe Maximiliano Chacón. It also carries a laudatory and flowery introduction in Spanish written by the then-governor of New Mexico, Otaviano A. Larrazolo.[62] Both books focus on Hispanics as protagonists in history—not on the margins but courageously at the center of action. Here, as before, in his profiles of Hispanic heroism, Read insists on his ability to maintain an impartial stance in the writing of "the true facts in the simplest form."[63]

In the final analysis, Benjamin Read protested too much for us to discount the personal motives that fueled his writing. History is the discourse of cultural memory, the inscription of an identity, an affirmation of difference, both collective and individual. Read represented his writing as "truthful history" in dialectical response to Anglo versions of the truth. Equipped with the irrefutable proof of original documents, he believed he represented all neomexicanos whose cultural dignity had been diminished by the influence of "foreign" texts and an alien mythology. His affirmation of his mother's culture—its language, religion, and historical past—made him a spokesman for his people, whose interpretation of neomexicano history incorporated a demand for historical justice and Hispanic cultural identity on a national scale.

However, there was also another, more subjective side to his mission as a historian. Benjamin Read carried both Anglo and Hispanic blood in his veins, and although raised by his mother, he bore his father's name with an honest pride that surfaced on numerous occasions when he spoke of "these glorious United States" and the good fortune of New Mexicans to have become "citizens of this the greatest and the most powerful nation in the world."[64] He sincerely admired the principles of democratic government and the civil liberties it promised, and he felt patriotic pride for the heroes of American history who had lived up to those ideals. Despite the ethnocentrism of many Americans past and present, Read believed in the possibility of a multicultural United States where neomexicanos would be empowered by democracy to fulfill their promise as citizens. History had convinced Read that the governments of both Spain and Mexico had disdained and neglected New Mexico and that only the sacrifices of courageous individuals, both Catholic and non-Catholic, had raised the level of civilization over the centuries in these remote borderlands.[65]

Read may have seen in New Mexico's history a kind of orphanhood similar to his own fatherless experience as a child; his effort to rise above poverty through education, encouraged by his mother and her Catholic neomexicano culture, is mirrored in New Mexico's six decades of struggle to achieve autonomy as a state. On the eve of statehood, he wrote an article in which he said:

> Después de una buena educación solo la ambición de ser buenos ciudadanos es tan importante para los hijos de Nuevo México, y no pueden ser buenos ciudadanos si no toman parte activa en la política y en el gobierno del estado.[66]

> [After a good education only the ambition to be good citizens is as important for the children of New Mexico, and they cannot be good citizens if they do not take an active part in politics and state government.]

Under statehood neomexicanos were guaranteed the right to use Spanish in schools and in the state legislature; thus, in theory, they would have the opportunity to express their cultural identity and transcend the orphanhood of their past.

A few years later, in 1917, an unsigned article published in *El Nuevo Mexicano* and *La Revista de Taos* seemed to bear out Read's view of the neomexicano's adoption of and by the stars and stripes. "El amor a la patria" or love of country, as the title suggested, was for neomexicanos viscerally linked to a love of "el suelo que los vio nacer," the land of their birth:

> Los habitantes de Nuevo México hemos vivido durante seten-
> ta y un años bajo la sombra del pabellón estrellado, y tenemos

sobrada razón para estar conformes con nuestra suerte y para sentir un afecto verdadero a la nación que nos cobija con su protección. Aunque muchos de nosotros somos de distinta procedencia a la mayoría de los habitantes, no por eso nos quedamos atrás en nuestro afecto y lealtad hacia la patria común de todos. . . . No deseamos otra patria que ésta, ni tenemos razón alguna para deplorar la feliz suerte que nos colocara bajo la autoridad de este gobierno.

[We who reside in New Mexico have lived for seventy-one years under the shadow of the star-covered flag, and we have plenty of reasons to be content with our situation and to feel true affection for the nation that shelters us with its protection. Although many of us are of different background from the majority of citizens, this does not diminish our love and affection for our common fatherland. . . . We want no other country than this one, nor do we have any reason to lament the fate that placed us under the authority of this government.]

Benjamin Read's story was one of many in the New Mexican Hispanic American community. He was a man of greater than average learning, with a broader than common awareness of how history had evolved in the borderlands of the Rio Grande. Like others before and after him, he wanted to explain that history to his own people, lest they forget their past, and to Anglo-Americans, lest they deny a part of their national legacy that had evolved for over three hundred years. Read's passion for accuracy and historical justice might not seem well served by some of today's crowd-pleasing celebrations of Hispanic culture in New Mexico. However, he himself recognized the wide appeal of pageantry and was not above taking history somewhat lightly on occasions that brought Santa Fe residents and visitors together: two days before his death at the age of seventy-three he donned a regal costume and rode the float as King Ferdinand in the annual Santa Fe Fiesta parade. Cultural identity is also reflected in the multi-faceted mirror of a community's imagination.

11

Conclusion:

The Language of the Press

To a limited degree, Read's hopes for neomexicanos have been realized. His-panic history and culture form an integral part of the state's identity—more so than any of its southwestern neighbors—even though Hispanics now con-stitute only 38 percent of New Mexico's population. This is the highest pro-portion in the fifty states, and according to recent statistics,[1] New Mexico is the only state where Latinos have surpassed parity representation in state and local government. Hispanics also have greater income equality in New Mexico than their counterparts in Texas or Arizona, but because the New Mexico per capita income is low the actual poverty level for Latinos there is worse. New Mexico ranks first in Hispanic-owned businesses, and yet the rate of unemployment for Hispanics (9.3 percent) is several points higher than the state average. In education, New Mexico ranks fifth in school-age population and first in average daily attendance, but below the national norm in state and local expenditure per pupil in public elementary and secondary schools.

When other states with substantial Latino populations voted English-Only amendments to their constitutions in the late 1980s (California, Florida, Colorado, and Arizona), New Mexico—an officially bilingual state—did not. The state capital, Santa Fe, boasts a popular bilingual radio station and a well-received magazine called *La Herencia del Norte* [The Heritage of the North] that uses both English and Spanish to draw awareness to the rich cultural legacy of neomexicano ancestors, but there are no politically influ-ential Spanish-language newspapers that can compare with those of the turn of the century. Hispanics and their culture are valued in New Mexico, as are Native Americans, but their numbers have not necessarily worked to their advantage in the formation of public policy. Latinos are still among the poor-est, most unempowered segments of the population.

The vexing contrasts that work against the greater success of its otherwise high-profile Hispanic population can be explained in part by the diversity of socioeconomic status and individual perspective among Hispanics in New Mexico. This diversity is even more problematic than it was in the late nineteenth century, when Spanish speakers were in the majority. Today, there are Hispanic families of all income levels whose roots in the region go back to the seventeenth century, while others crossed the border much more recently, seeking refuge from political or economic devastation in Mexico and Central America. Most Hispanics in the state do not define themselves as "Mexican," nearly two thirds preferring to refer to themselves as "Other Spanish," according to a 1988 survey.[2] Despite this insistence on Old World roots, New Mexico can still be defined as a cultural borderland area between Latin America and the United States, where past and present, self and other meet in a strongly Hispanic regional community marked by both continuity and change. Today, just as a hundred years ago, the Spanish-speaking people who call New Mexico home are best defined, to use Stuart Hall's words, "not by essence or purity, but by the recognition of a necessary heterogeneity and diversity; by a conception of 'identity' which lives with and through, not despite difference; by *hybridity*."[3]

Earlier in this century, Russian linguist Mikhail Bakhtin put forth his theory of the heteroglot nature of discourse. Bakhtin observed the coexistence of many socio-ideological "languages" in all forms of discourse, the way in which they intersect and vie for dialogic dominance. In the past several decades, the Jamaican-born scholar Stuart Hall and others working in the interdisciplinary field of cultural studies have built on this idea and pointed out the centrality of language in the struggles of social history. By this they do not mean language in the sense of English, Spanish, German, and other languages, but rather that all forms of communication (written, oral, visual and otherwise) are systems of signs or languages encoded with a power-based agenda that enable the hegemony of some cultures to exploit, colonize, or debase others. It seems evident today that a "politics of language" underlies the conflictive history of cultures around the globe and that embedded in it are issues of race, class, gender, and multiple other indicators of difference in society.

Contemporary scholars dissect ways in which language historically has been at the heart of struggles for interpretive power in all the fundamental institutions of society. As Henry Giroux has put it, "Language makes possible both the subject positions that people use to negotiate their sense of self and the ideologies and social practices that give meaning and legitimacy to institutions that form the basis of a given society."[4] The contemporary press and mass media are prime examples of the politics of language in action on the eve of the twenty-first century, shaping a global public consciousness with more persuasion than ever. Equally dedicated to a language of politics nowadays is the gamut of historically oppressed groups with a newly raised consciousness and a commitment to "talk back" in order to take back their right to self-definition.[5]

In New Mexico, from 1880 to 1920, the Spanish-language press was of central importance in the power struggles that increased in intensity as the political and economic stakes rose with each decade. At the heart of this multilayered conflict—not neatly defined by either race, class, or political affiliation—was a clash of cultures and languages that was unique in the history of the United States, and even in the Hispanic Southwest, by virtue of New Mexico's particular evolution as a cultural region. If, as Giroux says, culture is "a site of multiple and heterogeneous borders where different histories, languages, experiences, and voices intermingle amidst diverse relations of power and privilege,"[6] then the role of the neomexicano press in the years in question is particularly rich in significance for understanding the politics of identity in our nation's history.

Not only did the Spanish-language press enable those who had the advantages of education and verbal literacy to sustain a discursive dialogue both within the Hispanic community (north and south of the border) and across cultural borders (with the Anglo power structure in the United States); it also gave representation and voice to those who were ex-centric to the traditional power structure within Hispanic society. Enjoyed by many and financially supported by a few, neomexicano newspapers were a far cry from the established cultural industries of mass media today. They were products of their turbulent era, appearing and disappearing with the regularity of the political seasons. Timeliness was their main objective and obsolescence their eternal threat. Despite this vulnerability, some neomexicano papers endured long enough to command respect and influence. As the bulletin boards of public opinion, they served the powerful and even the weak, those in authority and at least some of those who railed against it. Bringing neomexicanos into this typically American public dialogue, the Spanish-language newspapers became, as Francisco Lomelí has noted, a middle ground for oral and literary traditions that mingled there without dichotomizing and formed a chronicle of living history in the making.[7]

The Spanish-language press survived in the New Mexico borderlands long enough and with sufficient strength to affirm the cultural identity and political clout of an indigenous Hispanic community that was undergoing a transformation more dramatic than it had known since the beginning of its long history in the Southwest. As a discursive force in a multicultural society, the press shaped and was shaped by the cultural context in which it evolved over the better part of a century. Its value should not be judged in the commercial terms of today's corporate-driven media, but rather in the cultural matrix of a community affirming its right to be heard. Within this affirmation and the many discursive challenges to self-expression that it entailed, was embedded change for the Spanish-speaking community. The press gave voice to the people, but it also transformed their consciousness and thus transcended the realm of the spoken word by which they had lived in the past. By the time its influence waned in the 1920s, the Spanish-language press had left its mark in many ways, not the least being the enhanced value of literacy in a society that had hitherto been primarily oral. The popularity and image of authority associated with the press—if not its financial success—underscored the power of the printed word and inevitably downgraded the impact of oral culture. As a tool of modernity, the emerging industrial society, and the globalization of knowledge, the neomexicano press may have actually undermined the traditions of the neomexicano past. Yet without their own newspapers, Hispanic New Mexicans would never have had the same leverage in the struggle against Anglo domination, nor would we now have the detailed record of Hispanic cultural identity inscribed in their pages.

The cultural technology of the press transformed all of American society, but its impact on the regional community of Spanish-speaking New Mexico in the late nineteenth and early twentieth centuries was especially potent. Benjamin Read acknowledged this in his *Illustrated History of New Mexico* when he wrote of "the great power of the press to diffuse civilization, to destroy ignorance, by making itself the voice bearer of the ideas which implant the spirit of true liberty and civicism in the inhabitants of a nation."[8] Many of the neomexicano editors of Read's day saw the potential of the free press primarily as a vehicle for improving society. As *La Voz del Pueblo* put it on January 4, 1896, eight years after its first issue: "Ahora por medio de la prensa hasta los niños que apenas pueden decifrar el significado de las letras, saben hoy, lo que de importancia pasó en Europa ayer" [Today, thanks to the press even the children who barely know how to decipher the meaning of words know what events of importance took place in Europe yesterday]. The language of the neomexicano press was extraordinarily self-conscious and self-reflexive, showing its editors' awareness of the power of the printed word to influence cultural evolution as well as to promote social cohesion. As a professional group they accepted a need for accommodation between the two major cultures and directed their efforts toward the integration of neomexicanos into the American democratic system—but in a way that would ensure the preservation of neomexicano cultural integrity.

Editors were more aware than most neomexicanos of the long-range consequences of finding themselves "foreigners in their native land." As individuals who negotiated the terrain between languages, cultures, political factions, and commercial pressures, their lives and professional roles deserve more study. There is room for further analysis of the relationship between the neomexicano press and other Spanish-language periodicals in the border states and Mexico. It would also be helpful to have more information about how neomexicano newspapers were important to Hispanic women and to readers who identified themselves as Anglos or as Indians, but who lived within a Spanish-language culture. More research could be done with regard to the rhetoric of the press, and certainly more Hispanic social history might be gleaned from its detailed reportage of all kinds of daily news. Editors of the time were not only less objective in their documentation of news, but they were not above giving even the most unsavory newsmakers (whose words could sell newspapers) more of a personal voice in their columns. The anonymous contributions of those who composed popular poetry or who sent letters to their local newspapers draw us closer to the lived experience of ordinary neomexicanos. When complemented by archival research, their voices and their narratives are rescued from oblivion.

More than anything, I hope this book has shown that we cannot take language for granted as a determining factor in American cultural history. By this, I mean that we need to be knowledgeable about the different languages in which people have expressed their most intimate and authentic identity in this country as well as about the languages of the institutions of power that might have prevented them from doing so. The history of the American West at the turn of the century owes a great deal to the Spanish-language press not because it represented all of Hispanic society—many voices were left out— but because it offered a discursive space in which different voices could speak for themselves without fear of being branded un-American. When English-Only advocates today speak of the need for an official language as a means of establishing a common bond between diverse peoples in our country, I think of Benjamin Read and other neomexicanos who knew that the only meaningful common bond is responsible citizenship, not language. By empowering through their own language those who faced an erosion of their past as well as a threat to their future as American citizens, neomexicano newspapers recorded the evolving cultural identity of a long-established Hispanic American community during a significant era of its history.

Appendix:

Profiles of Neomexicano Editors

The following biographical sketches are offered to supplement the information about Hispanic editors found in the main section of this book. Although these profiles are brief and limited by available information, they will give an idea of the backgrounds and careers of a few members of the neomexicano community who were active in the Spanish-language press during the late territorial period.

Isidoro Armijo was born in 1871 in Las Cruces, New Mexico, where his father, Jacinto Armijo, was a well-known public figure, state legislator, and land-owner. As the eldest son who often accompanied his father on campaign trips through the region, Isidoro Armijo took an early and active interest in politics in Doña Ana County. He attended local public schools and the College of Agriculture and Mechanical Arts in Mesilla Park. After a short stint working in Puebla, Mexico, Armijo returned to Las Cruces, where he became a court interpreter and ran on the Republican ticket for county clerk, receiving the largest number of recorded votes for any county candidate. In 1900 he was elected probate clerk of Doña Ana County and then county delegate to the state constitutional convention in Santa Fe in 1910. He worked for a time as editor of *El Progreso*, in Trinidad, Colorado, and as editor of *La Flor del Valle* and *El Eco del Valle* in Las Cruces. Armijo was widely admired as a skilled orator and poet in both Spanish and English; one clipping of the time notes with typical partisan exuberance: "He writes poetry like Keats, his prose is classic as that of Addison and in humor he is a Josh Billings and a Mark Twain combined." Married to Jennie Archuleta, Armijo had a reputation for serving the needs of his Hispanic constituency: "he is very popular in his home county and many citizens, especially of the native class, come to him for advice and consultation which are always freely given without charge." [Source: *El Nuevo Mexicano*, Oct. 1, 1910; Benjamin M. Read, *Historia*

Ilustrada de Nuevo México; assorted newspaper clippings in the L. Bradford Prince Papers.]

Félix Martínez was born in Taos County in 1857, a direct descendant of don Félix Martínez, captain general and governor of the province of New Mexico in 1715. His early education was in the hands of private tutors and thereafter he went to St. Mary's College in Mora and then to a business school in Denver, Colorado, where his parents had moved. Starting out as a salesman with a Denver firm, Martínez opened his own general store in El Moro, Colorado, in 1877. In 1879 he moved to Las Vegas, New Mexico, where he owned a store, traded livestock, and got involved in real estate ventures. In 1880 he married Virginia Buster and they were the parents of six children. He entered politics as a member of the Democratic party in San Miguel County in 1884 and was narrowly defeated in the race for county treasurer despite running in a heavily Republican district. In 1886, Martínez was elected to the office of county assessor. He became an active supporter of the Partido del Pueblo Unido and two years later he won a seat in the territorial assembly; in 1892 he was made chairman of the New Mexico delegation to the national Democratic convention. Martínez was well known in Las Vegas as both a political figure and publisher of *La Voz del Pueblo*, which actively supported the Democratic ticket, was sympathetic to the Gorras Blancas, and opposed the influence of the Santa Fe Ring. He later was involved in other newspapers in New Mexico and Texas. In 1897 Martínez moved to El Paso, where he opened a real estate office and became involved in negotiating a water supply agreement between New Mexico, Texas, and Mexico, which resulted in an accord between Presidents Taft and Díaz and the formation of the El Paso Valley Water Users' Association, which regulated the division of waters of the Rio Grande. In El Paso, Felix Martínez was also a director of the First National Bank and officer of several investment companies. He also was president of the Martínez Publishing Company of Las Vegas. In 1913 he was appointed by President Wilson to lead a diplomatic pan-American commission to South America, an indication of the high esteem in which he was held by his state and country. [Source: Ralph Twitchell, *The Leading Facts of New Mexican History*; Mario T. García, *Desert Immigrants: The Mexicans of El Paso, 1880–1920*; *La Unión del Pueblo* (Clayton), Sept. 13, 1913; Benjamin M. Read, *Illustrated History of New Mexico*.]

José Montaner was born in 1877 in Barcelona, Spain, where he received a liberal education. In 1898 he emigrated to the United States and lived briefly in Tampa, Florida, where he filed naturalization papers. Thereafter, he moved to Trinidad, Colorado, and published a newspaper there called *El Tipográfico*. In 1901 he went to Taos, New Mexico, where he began publishing *La Revista de Taos,* which eventually had as many as five thousand subscribers. In 1909 he founded an English-language paper, the *Taos Valley News.* He was affiliated with the Republican party and first ran for public office in 1904 and, after many years of public service, was elected to the state senate in 1924. In addition to a successful career in journalism, he acquired considerable real estate and commercial properties in Taos. Montaner was the secretary-treasurer of the Teachers' College in El Rito, and in 1912 he was appointed county school superintendent; he was responsible for the building of forty new schools in Taos County and established the first high school in Taos. He was married in 1906 to Mariquita Valdéz, daughter of Santiago Valdéz y Martínez of Taos, a local legislator and author of a biography of Padre Martínez. Montaner was thus a brother-in-law of Larkin Read who, in turn, was the brother of Benjamin Read. [Source: Charles H. Coan, *A History of New Mexico*; Read, *Historia Ilustrada de Nuevo México.*]

Nestor Montoya, editor of *La Bandera Americana,* was born in Old Albuquerque in 1858, into one of the oldest families in New Mexico. He was graduated in 1874 from St. Michael's College and was appointed assistant postmaster in Santa Fe, where he worked for six years. In 1884 he was appointed court interpreter, and in 1888 he founded *La Voz del Pueblo* with E. H. Salazar. In 1890 Montoya sold his share, but stayed on as editor under the leadership of Félix Martínez, during which time the paper moved to Las Vegas. In 1894 Montoya moved to Albuquerque, where he was deputy assessor of Bernalillo County and also worked as a court interpreter, a job he held for more than twenty years. In 1901 he founded *La Bandera Americana* in his hometown of Albuquerque. Montoya was a member of the Republican party. He was elected to the state legislature in both San Miguel and Bernalillo counties and was also elected a delegate to the 1910 constitutional convention. In 1920, when the tide was turning against Republican domination in New Mexico, he was elected on that platform to the U.S. Congress. A public servant with an outstanding record of service over many years, Montoya was also a member of the Alianza Hispano-Americana, the Knights of Columbus, and the Mutual Protective Association of Old Albuquerque. He was married in 1893 to Florence Maes and was the father of five children. Montoya died in 1923. [Source: Twitchell, *Leading Facts of New Mexican History*; Read, *Illustrated History of New Mexico.*]

Victor L. Ochoa was a Mexican citizen who went into exile to foment revolution against the regime of Porfirio Díaz. His career as editor and publisher in New Mexico apparently began in El Paso, where he was associated with *El Bravo del Valle* and *El Latino-Americano.* In 1891 he became the editor-owner of *El Hispano Americano* in Socorro, New Mexico, and in early 1892 the paper moved with Ochoa to Las Vegas. At the same time Ochoa promoted the formation of an Hispanic American Press Association, which held its first meeting in March 1892 and elected Ochoa as its first president. He led the association until 1893, when his activities against Díaz led to his arrest by U.S. officials in El Paso. Ochoa was accused of employing and supplying arms to insurgents and sending them into Mexico to fight federal forces. Later acquitted of these charges, Ochoa was put under surveillance by U.S. and Mexican agents who suspected his ongoing subversive activities. He was eventually captured again by Texas Rangers southeast of El Paso and charged with organizing an armed invasionary force on American land. When he was tried, Mexicans in El Paso celebrated him as a hero; a federal judge, however, found him guilty of violating neutrality laws and sentenced him to three years in prison in 1894. [Source: García, *Desert Immigrants*.]

Hilario L. Ortiz was born around 1861 and raised in Santa Fe, where he attended St. Michael's College. He began his career as a bookstore owner in 1881. He later became a teacher at St. Michael's and worked there until 1884, when he went to Socorro to teach at and direct the Christian Brothers' academy there. In Socorro he acquired a printing press and began to publish *La Estrella de Socorro*, a Democratic paper, also owned by Juan José Baca. In 1886 Ortiz went back to Santa Fe because he was in ill health and had family property to oversee. After 1886, Ortiz switched to the Republican party, which was the most influential party at the time. He was elected superintendent of schools for Santa Fe County and also began the study of law. In 1888 he joined E. H. Salazar in founding *La Voz del Pueblo* in Santa Fe, and in 1890 he edited *La Estrella Mexicana*, an Albuquerque newspaper. Ortiz was admitted to the New Mexico Bar in 1893 and served as city attorney of Santa Fe for two terms. Fluent in both Spanish and English, he was known as an able public speaker. He also owned an extensive personal library, particularly of books of law; his special field was criminal law, and he prosecuted and defended many cases in his time. Ortiz was descended from an illustrious neomexicano family that traced its roots back to the early Spanish settlements; he was the great-grandson of José Chaves, a governor of New Mexico in the Mexican period, and he was also related to the Spanish explorer Nicolás Ortiz Niño Ladrón de Guevara. H. L. Ortiz was married to an Anglo American woman from Alabama. [Source: *El Nuevo Mexicano*, June 15, 1901.]

Enrique H. Salazar was a native of Santa Fe and was educated at St. Michael's College. He was the son of Josefina Salazar de Manderfield and the stepson of William H. Manderfield, one of the founders of the New Mexican Printing Company, who taught him the newspaper business. At age eighteen, Salazar started his career as a newspaper man. With Nestor Montoya, he founded *La*

Voz del Pueblo, first published in Santa Fe in 1888; after two years they parted ways and the paper moved to Las Vegas. In 1894 Salazar founded *El Independiente* in Las Vegas, a paper with liberal democratic views similar to *La Voz* and equally influential. A longtime resident of Las Vegas, Enrique Salazar was appointed as the city postmaster by President McKinley in 1898—a common political appointment for newspaper editors who had close connections with the communications system—and was reappointed by President Roosevelt in 1902. According to the Santa Fe *New Mexican*, E. H. Salazar was "recognized as a political power in San Miguel county, in fact, throughout the territory." Because he was an ardent supporter of statehood, Salazar switched his support to the Republican party and later served as a secretary of the New Mexico legislative assembly. In 1910 President Taft appointed him receiver of the federal Office of Land Management at Fort Sumner, with jurisdiction over two million acres of public land. Salazar married Agueda López, the daughter of political boss Lorenzo López of Las Vegas, in 1891. He died in 1914. [Sources: *Santa Fe New Mexican*, Feb. 11, 1902; *El Nuevo Mexicano*, Aug. 20, 1910; Read, *Historia Ilustrada de Nuevo México*.]

Enrique J. Sosa was born in Guanajuato, Mexico, in 1856; his father was a native of Spain, who was a hotel owner and sports promoter in Mexico. At the age of fifteen, Enrique Sosa ran away from home and joined the Mexican army, serving for thirteen years and achieving the rank of captain during the war against France. He then went to school in Mexico City and was trained as a civil engineer, in which capacity he worked for several railroad companies, finally moving to El Paso, Texas, and later to Las Cruces, N.M. In Las Cruces he practiced his other vocation, painting, and then moved to Albuquerque, where he founded a weekly newspaper, *La Estrella de Nuevo Mexico*. After five years he sold his interest and moved to Santa Fe, where he founded *La Hormiga de Oro* and also worked as an artist. After becoming a citizen of the United States, Sosa moved to Mora, N.M., where he lived for the rest of his life. For ten years he owned, edited, and published *El Eco del Norte*, a Republican newspaper. He was also a founder and proprietor for a number of years of the Sosa Theater in Mora. In 1895 he married Luz Alderete, a native of Las Cruces, and they had ten children. Sosa was a member of the Methodist Episcopal Church and was a local minister of that church when he lived in Albuquerque. [Source: Coan, *History of New Mexico*.]

Notes

Preface

1. Luis Leal, "Mexican American Literature: A Historical Perspective," 25–26.

Chapter 1

1. Other terms were also used at the time, such as *nuevomexicanos, hispano-americanos, mexicanos, hispanos,* and *nativos*—appellations that were sometimes interchangeable and often politically charged. The term *neomexicano,* rendered in Spanish and with its definitive identification with the New Mexican homeland, is, in my opinion, the most historically accurate and the least politically controversial way to refer to this cultural group in the period under consideration. One finds abundant evidence of the use of the term *neomexicano* in the newspapers: among other examples, both *La Voz del Pueblo* and *El Independiente,* which were ardent defenders of neomexicano culture, used this identifier frequently during the period from 1880 to 1990. Papers that used the term *mexicano* did so in a cultural rather than a political sense; this term was, in fact, protested by an editorial in *El Nuevo Mundo* (November 20, 1897) on the basis that it was too divisive and suggested that Hispanic New Mexicans were not Americans. The term *hispanoamericano* was generally preferred by the elite and those who wanted to identify with historical and cultural roots in Spain rather than Mexico, particularly after the Mexican political and labor unrest of the early twentieth century.

Contemporary literary critics and historians are not unanimous regarding the preferred terminology, an expression in part of their own diverse ideological orientations. I cannot agree, for example, with Juan Gómez-Quiñones's theory that the preferred term across the board should be *mexicanos* because, in his words, "the people's sense of identity led them to consider themselves as Mexicans regardless of citizenship or of the boundary line between countries" and that other terms "were verbal manipulations serving the dominant power's attempt to divide the Mexican people on the generational, national, regional, and local levels." *Roots of Chicano Politics, 1600–1940,* 194–95. In my view, the history of neomexicano culture and the multiple complexities of bicultural interaction during the late nineteenth century argue against generalizations and

219

are not served by the binary, victim/oppressor approach to explaining cultural identity or by the notion that Americanization was a capitalist plot to transform Spanish speakers into a subordinate labor force.

Arthur L. Campa, in *Spanish Folk-Poetry in New Mexico*, perceived the issue of identifiers as inherently ambivalent, and thus misleading in the case of Hispanic New Mexicans, given that terminology on the whole "is based on prejudice and confused notions of race and nationality" (12). "Obviously," he said, "they are not Mexicans, and they have not been since 1848; neither are they natives exclusively. Few can prove conclusively to be of Spanish descent, and none of them are Spanish-Americans, considering that such an adjective applies to people in Spanish-America. On the other hand, there are valid reasons why New Mexicans may claim in part any or all the foregoing appellations. Legally and nationally they are Americans; linguistically, Spanish; Spanish-American, geographically; culturally, Mexican; native by birth, and New Mexican by state boundaries. What are they racially, since that seems to be of so great concern? The answer to that question may be found in the history of the conquest" (15).

2. See Sollars, *Beyond Ethnicity: Consent and Descent in American Culture*, 7, 39.

3. Ronald Takaki, *A Different Mirror: A History of Multicultural America*, 16.

4. Gloria Anzaldúa, *Borderlands/La Frontera: The New Mestiza*, 194.

5. David J. Weber and Jane M. Rausch, "Introduction," in Weber and Rausch, eds., *Where Cultures Meet: Frontiers in Latin American History*, xiv.

6. Carolyn Zeleny, "Relations Between the Spanish-Americans and Anglo-Americans in New Mexico: A Study of Conflict and Accommodation in a Dual-Ethnic Situation," 14. According to Fray Angelico Chavez (who prefers to be called a Spanish New Mexican and whose name in publications carries no accents), "New Mexico got her distinctive name *two hundred and forty years* before there was a Republic called Mexico south of here." Chavez, *Chávez: A Distinctive American Clan of New Mexico*, xiii.

7. Bruce-Novoa, *RetroSpace: Collected Essays on Chicano Literature, Theory and History*, 23, 31. "Chicanismo is the product/producer of ongoing synthesis, continually drawing from what seem to outsiders to be opposing cultural elements. Therefore, the literature proposes an alternative, an 'inter' space for a new ethnic identity to exist" (31).

8. George P. Hammond and Agapito Rey, "Oñate and the Colonization of New Mexico," 22.

9. See Luis Leal, "The First American Epic: Villagrá's History of New Mexico," 47. I take this quote from Leal who, in turn, quotes F. W. Hodge's foreword to an English translation of Villagrá's poem done by a New Mexican, Gilberto Espinosa, and published in Los Angeles in 1933 by the Quivira Society.

10. Hall, 222.

11. Marc Simmons, *New Mexico: An Interpretive History*, 130.

12. The term *American* is used here in the common parlance to refer to the citizens and representatives of the United States of America. Of course, properly defined, all peoples of the Americas are Americans, from Canada to South America. At issue in this study is the definition of what constitutes Americanness within the U.S., and in this context, neomexicanos have a unique narrative to share.

13. Cited in David J. Weber, ed., *Foreigners in Their Native Land: Historical Roots of the Mexican Americans*, 161.

14. On the history of journalism in the United States, see Robert A. Rutland, *The Newsmongers: Journalism in the Life of the Nation, 1690–1972*. For the history of Mexican journalism, see Yolanda Argudín, *Historia del periodismo en México: desde el virreinato hasta nuestros días*.

15. Porter Stratton, *The Territorial Press in New Mexico, 1834–1912*, 21–22.

16. A libel law enacted in New Mexico in 1889 stimulated an increased consciousness of press responsibility. When the libel law was repealed in 1893, under criticism that it was stifling free expression, press association activity decreased. Stratton, *Territorial Press*, 37–38. On press standards in the late nineteenth century, see also Hazel Dicken-Garcia, *Journalistic Standards in Nineteenth-Century America*: "Critics after 1850 struggled to define appropriate journalistic conduct and were more specific than their predecessors in citing abuses and corrections. But by 1890 they were still groping with what had become an immense social institution of overwhelming capabilities" (221).

17. Simmons, *New Mexico*, 12. My focus is on the Hispanic and Anglo ethnic groups in New Mexico as the main interlocutors of a cultural dialogue during this period, but it would be a grave omission not to recognize the importance of Native Americans in the shaping of New Mexico's collective identity as a state. Although the Pueblo Indian tribes after 1692 lived peacefully at some remove, with minimal interaction with the majority populations, the Comanche and Apache tribes resisted pacification and were not subdued by federal troops until approximately 1890. The Navajos surrendered earlier, in 1864, at which time the U.S. government abolished the common practice of peonage and Indian slavery in New Mexico. For the most part, Anglo and Hispano editors in these years showed little concern for the welfare of the exploited and mistreated Native Americans, although occasional editorials called for improvement of living conditions on the reservations and backed the establishment of Indian schools. See also Stratton, *Territorial Press*, 117–26.

18. Cited by Zeleny, "Relations Between the Spanish-Americans and Anglo-Americans," 136.

19. Ibid., 137. The Hispanic population of New Mexico in proportion to that of Texas, California, and Arizona experienced a complete change between 1850 and 1960. In 1850, the estimated figures were: New Mexico, 60,000; Texas and California, about 7,500 each. (Weber, *Foreigners in Their Native Land*, 140). In 1960, the figures were estimated to be: New Mexico, 296,000; Texas, 1,560,000; and California, 1,569,000. The difference is attributable to the larger numbers of Mexican immigrants crossing into the two more populous states after 1910.

20. Charles F. Coan, *A History of New Mexico*, 1:392.

21. Frederick Jackson Turner, "The Significance of the Frontier in American History," in Turner, *The Frontier in American History*, 22.

22. Joseph Franklin Sexton, "New Mexico: Intellectual and Cultural Developments, 1885–1925: Conflicts among Ideas and Institutions," 181. A recent essay by Rudolfo Anaya, the well-known Chicano author who writes about his New Mexico roots, echoes the concept of two New Mexicos by contrasting the traditional harmonious ways of life of the Indo-Hispanic Southwest with the destructive development of a materialistic urban environment. Anaya sees the battle for New Mexico's future as one of epic proportions: "The first step in answering these questions is to realize that we have turned away from our inner nature and from our connection to the earth and old

historical relationships. We have allowed a political and economic consciousness from without to take control. How we engage this consciousness not only describes us but also will inform future generations of our values." Anaya, "Mythical Dimensions/Political Reality," 30.

23. Joshua A. Fishman, *Language Loyalty in the United States: The Maintenance and Perpetuation of Non-English Mother Tongues by American Ethnic and Religious Groups*, 31.

24. Ibid., 27.

25. On the role of the communications media in mediating between tradition and modernity in Latin America, see William Rowe and Vivian Schelling, *Memory and Modernity: Popular Culture in Latin America*.

26. See Jacqueline Dorgan Meketa, *Legacy of Honor: The Life of Rafael Chacón, a Nineteenth-Century New Mexican*; and Genaro Padilla, *My History, Not Yours: The Formation of Mexican-American Autobiography*.

27. The complex nature of New Mexico's political history in the territorial period has been the subject of many studies. Two by Robert W. Larson are recommended to give the interested reader some background in this subject: "Territorial Politics and Cultural Impact" and *New Mexico's Quest for Statehood, 1846–1912*.

28. Bruce-Novoa, in his recent "Dialogical Strategies, Monological Goals: Chicano Literature," points out that the "tribal orientation" of the Chicano movement could not produce a cohesive nationalistic group because a we/they dichotomy does not reflect the dialogical reality of cultural production. "Heteroglossia is the undeniable state of contemporary culture. Dialogized language makes the return to the monological a nostalgic illusion" (241). I would add that even in the late nineteenth century, intracultural dialogism made the idealized theory of monologic anti-Anglo resistance impossible.

29. The association met for several years, mostly with neomexicano and a few tejano editors, and then petered out of existence until 1911, when it was revived and eventually, in 1912, merged with the Anglo press association, which was begun in 1881 and also had a sketchy history. See Stratton, *Territorial Press*, 65–66. A running commentary of the association's evolution can be found in *El Hispano Americano* (Socorro and Las Vegas), the paper owned and edited by Victor L. Ochoa, a Mexican liberal and anti-Díaz activist who lived in exile in New Mexico in the early 1890s. It is interesting to note that Ochoa, an ardent Mexican nationalist, chose this name for his paper after moving upriver from El Paso, and clearly separated the usage of the term *mexicano* to refer to Mexico and Mexicans. His rationale may also have reflected his desire to garner support in areas beyond New Mexico for his anti-Díaz campaign.

A sampling of recent critical studies related to the Hispanic press in other parts of the Southwest in the late nineteenth and early twentieth centuries includes: Luis Leal, "The Spanish-Language Press: Function and Use"; Nicolás Kanellos, "A Socio-Historic Study of Hispanic Newspapers in the United States"; Félix Gutiérrez, "Spanish Language Media in America: Background, Resources, History"; Juan Rodríguez, "Jorge Ulica y Carlo de Medina: escritores de la bahía de San Francisco"; Juan Bruce-Novoa, "*La Prensa* and the Chicano Community" (specifically, San Antonio); Francine Medeiros, "*La Opinión*: A Mexican Exile Newspaper, A Content Analysis of Its First Years, 1926–1929" (in Los Angeles); Richard Griswold del Castillo, "The Mexican Revolution and the Spanish-Language Press in the Borderlands"; Clara Lomas, "The Articulation of Gender in the Mexican Borderlands, 1900–1915" (on women's role in the alternative press during the Mexican Revolution). I refer the interested reader to other collections of studies where further bibliographic information can be found: *Americas Review* 17, no. 3-4 (Fall-Winter 1989) (issue on "La Prensa/Hispanic Journalism"); *Journalism History* 4, no. 2 (1977); Ramon Gutiérrez and Genaro Padilla, eds., *Recovering the U.S. Hispanic Literary Heritage*; and, for a full overview, Rafael Chabrán and Richard Chabrán, "The Spanish-Language and Latino Press of the United States: Newspapers and Periodicals."

30. Rubén Munguía, who grew up in San Antonio in the early 1900s, has written of the impact of the Spanish-language press on working-class immigrants there who never had the means to buy books; however, Munguía says, they sometimes use their earnings to "indulge in the luxury of buying *La Prensa*, and, in slowing picking out the forbidden letters," to "educate themselves." Munguía, "*La Prensa*: Memories of a Boy . . . Sixty Years Later," 131.

31. Clifford Geertz, *The Interpretation of Cultures*, 5.

Chapter 2

1. Aurelio Espinosa, "Spanish Folk-Lore in New Mexico," 143.

2. Ibid., 149.

3. Detailed studies of Spanish folk poetry in New Mexico include the following: Campa, *Spanish Folk-Poetry in New Mexico*; Aurelio M. Espinosa, *Romancero de Nuevo Méjico*; and Aurora Lucero-White Lea, *Literary Folklore of the Hispanic Southwest*. For an overview of folklore in New Mexico from a multicultural perspective, see Marta Weigle and Peter White, *The Lore of New Mexico*. On the nature of early Hispanic settlers and their contacts with Pueblo and nomadic tribes, see Frances Leon Swadesh, *Los Primeros Pobladores: Hispanic Americans of the Ute Frontier*.

4. Campa, *Spanish Folk-Poetry in New Mexico*, 18–19.

5. Espinosa, "Spanish Folk-Lore in New Mexico," 150.

6. John R. Chávez, *The Lost Land: The Chicano Image of the Southwest*, 98.

7. "Apreciaciones de don Benjamin M. Read sobre el Profesor Espinosa y sus estudios nuevomexicanos," *La Revista de Taos*, June 20, 1911.

8. Espinosa, "Spanish Folk-Lore in New Mexico," 151.

9. Some authors signed their names to their work, and I will take this up in later chapters. For more information about neomexicano authors known by name in the latter part of the nineteenth century, see Erlinda Gonzáles-Berry, ed., *Pasó por Aquí: Critical Essays on the New Mexican Literary Tradition, 1542–1988*; and Anselmo F. Arellano, *Los pobladores nuevo mexicanos y su poesía, 1889–1950*.

10. I refer here to the concept of *dialogic discourse* as put forth by Mikhail Bakhtin, the Russian linguist (1895–1975). Although Bakhtin believed that dialogism, or heteroglossia, functions within a given language system (self and other), his concept of dialogic discourse can also apply on the macro-level to the contact between languages/cultures/ideological systems if there is some common ground of communicative understanding. Bakhtin's image of the "borderline" between self and other, where all communication takes place, is particularly apt in the present historical context. See Bakhtin, "Discourse in the Novel," 280–84 and 293–96.

11. Antonio Gramsci, *Selections from Cultural Writings* (1985), cited by Marcia Landy, "Cultural Politics and Common Sense," 118.

12. The earliest known printings in New Mexico were in 1835 by Padre Antonio José Martínez, a Taos priest, on a small handpress that most likely was used a year earlier in Santa Fe to print the first New Mexican newspaper, reputed to be *El Crepúsculo*—no issues of which appear to have survived. Chavez, *But Time and Change: The Story of Padre Martínez of Taos, 1793–1867*, 48–49. The padre's first books were school primers; in 1838 he published his *Relación de mérito*, an account of his life in response to accusations against him. See D. C. McMurtrie, "The History of Early Printing in New Mexico..." and "Some Supplementary New Mexican Imprints, 1850–1860."

13. Américo Paredes, "Folklore and History," 61. "The American historian wishing really to understand the Mexican point of view toward the United States would do well to begin with a study of the Mexican *corridos*" (62). See, for example, Paredes, *"With His Pistol in His Hand": A Border Ballad and Its Hero*.

14. *Cantadores* or *trovadores*, as they were also called in northern New Mexico, would compete in singing contests, "singing as many as 200 different décimas of an evening! In an effort to outdo each other they would sit around the campfire until daybreak. The purpose of the song was entirely lost in tilts of this sort, endurance being the only objective." Authur L. Campa, "The Spanish Folksong in the Southwest," 34. Also, see Weigle and White, *Lore of New Mexico*, chap. 6 ("Namescape: The Verbal Arts").

15. The Otero clan produced many distinguished neomexicano politicians. Mariano Otero (1844–1904) had earlier served as delegate to Congress from 1878 to 1880; he should not be confused with his uncle, Miguel A. Otero Sr. (1829–1882), a territorial representative who was appointed secretary of the territory by President Lincoln; or with his cousin, Miguel A. Otero Jr. (1859–1944), who was territorial governor from 1898 to 1904, appointed by Republican presidents McKinley and Roosevelt. For biographies of these and other notable neomexicanos, see Maurilio E. Vigil, *Los Patrones: Profiles of Hispanic Political Leaders in New Mexico History*.

16. Larson, *New Mexico's Quest for Statehood*, 144–45. For detailed information about the Santa Fe Ring, see ibid., chap. 9, 135–46.

17. "Los condados del Nuevo Mexico" [New Mexico's Counties], *La Voz del Pueblo*, Oct. 11, 1890. All quotations in this and subsequent chapters reproduce the punctuation, orthography, and diacritics of the original newspaper publications. Accent marks were much less frequently used in the newspapers, although the prepositional *á* was customary. Spelling errors were often missed by careless typesetters and editors, although sometimes obvious errors carried satiric intent. My accompanying translations do not attempt to reproduce the poetic rhyme or meter and are included solely to convey content as clearly as possible.

18. "Antonio Joseph fue quien suplicó al Senador Stewart que introdujera los actos..." [Antonio Joseph was the one who urged Senator Stewart to introduce a bill...] *El Nuevo Mexicano*, Oct. 18, 1890. Antonio Joseph de Treviz did have Portuguese blood, but his background and education were purely neomexicano. His father, originally from the Azores, settled in Taos and was a fur trapper whose friends included Kit Carson and St. Vrain. Joseph himself was educated in the school belonging to Padre José Antonio Martínez in Taos and later at St. Michael's in Santa Fe. A five-

term Democratic delegate to Congress from a principally Republican territory (1884–1894), he was eventually unseated in 1894 by T. B. Catron, when Populist voters deserted the Democratic ranks. Stratton, *Territorial Press*, 227 (n. 28).

19. Zeleny, "Relations Between the Spanish-Americans and Anglo-Americans," 225.

20. For a discussion of the situation leading to the enactment in 1889 of a libel law by the territorial legislature and its subsequent repeal in 1893, see Stratton, *Territorial Press*, 48–49.

21. Ibid., 66–67.

22. For further information on the *corrido*, see Vicente Mendoza, *El romance español y el corrido mexicano*; Merle E. Simmons, *The Mexican Corrido as a Source for Interpretive Study of Modern Mexico, 1870–1950*; and María Herrera-Sobek, *The Mexican Corrido: A Feminist Analysis*.

23. Américo Paredes cites William James Entwhistle's *European Balladry* as the source of this observation about "the classic conditions of balladry." *"With His Pistol in His Hand,"* 241.

24. According to an article in *El Nuevo Mexicano*, January 9, 1897, Ortiz was murdered by several men who were competing with him for the affections of a woman.

25. *La Voz del Pueblo* (Santa Fe), Apr. 26, 1890. For the political events that are thought to have motivated Ortiz's murder, see Ralph E. Twitchell, *The Leading Facts of New Mexican History*, 2:511–12, n. 429. The other two *corridos* may be found in *El Nuevo Mexicano* (Santa Fe), Aug. 23 and Sept. 13, 1890.

26. Other examples of "death poems" can be found in *La Revista de Taos*, Oct. 16, 1902, and Jan. 8, 1903; *La Bandera Americana*, Feb. 12, 1904; *El Nuevo Mexicano*, Feb. 4, 1905. They were submitted so frequently and often written so badly that one editor warned readers that they would not be published if they insisted on such absurdities as having the dead rise from their tombs and speak (*La Voz del Pueblo*, Apr. 13, 1905).

27. Campa, *Spanish Folk-Poetry in New Mexico*, 181–82.

28. Campa, "Spanish Folksong in the Southwest," 56.

29. *La Aurora* (Santa Fe) Aug. 9, 1884.

30. *El Hispano Americano*, Feb. 20, 1892.

31. *La Aurora*, Aug. 9, 1884. Even as late as 1917, *El Nuevo Mexicano* (Apr. 19) was protesting the number of unsolicited poems it received that were of mediocre quality and "solo interesan al que los escribe, y puede ser que a media docena de vecinos del lugar"[are of interest only to the one who writes them and maybe to a half-dozen of his neighbors]. Ironically, the paper had to defend itself against the protests of the authors, who believed their work deserved public attention.

32. *La Crónica del Río Colorado*, San Lorenzo, Nov. 4, 1882.

33. *La Aurora*, Santa Fe, Aug. 9, 1884.

34. *La Voz del Pueblo*, Las Vegas, June 25, 1892.

35. Luis Leal, "Truth-Telling Tongues: Early Chicano Poetry," 100. Leal says that the society of the time was "rapidly becoming bilingual," but this does not hold true for New Mexico.

36. *La Voz del Pueblo*, Las Vegas, Feb. 4, 1893.

37. "The conflict was chiefly one between the Spanish-Americans who clung to their traditional capital, and the Anglo-American business interests who stood to profit by its removal, although many Anglos in Santa Fe favored its remaining there." Zeleny,

"Relations Between Spanish-Americans and Anglo-Americans, . . . ," 231. A congressional bill in 1898 determined that the capital would remain in Santa Fe.

38. *El Nuevo Mexicano*, Santa Fe, Feb. 14, 1891.

39. There was an "X," an "X.X.," and an "X.Z." who published in the same paper in the early 1890s, but none of them, if we assume them to be different individuals, were consistent contributors. It should also be noted that for three years, between 1894 and 1897, when Max Frost was not editing the paper, virtually no poetry was published in *El Nuevo Mexicano*; during this time, X.X.X. published one poem in *El Independiente* of Las Vegas, where another of his poems also appeared in 1898.

40. For example, he translated poetry by Byron and Shelley, "Thanatopsis" by W. C. Bryant, and a Provençal verse legend "Mirad los pastores / a Belen caminan."

41. *El Nuevo Mexicano*, Dec. 25, 1897.

42. *El Nuevo Mexicano*, Aug. 5, 1899.

43. *El Nuevo Mexicano*, May 13, 1893. The issue of water rights was increasingly critical as Anglo land-grabbing divested Hispanos of their communal lands.

44. *El Nuevo Mexicano*, Apr. 9, 1898. Colonel Albert J. Fountain and his son were reported missing and presumed killed in February, 1896, near Las Cruces. The crime was never solved but was believed to have been politically motivated.

45. "De vuelta a su pueblo" [Back in his village], *El Nuevo Mexicano*, Aug. 14, 1897.

46. *El Nuevo Mexicano*, Feb. 5, 1898.

47. More of Teddy Roosevelt's Rough Riders were from New Mexico and Arizona than from any other state; it was hoped that this would help secure statehood. See Warren A. Beck, *New Mexico: A History of Four Centuries*, 233–34.

48. *El Nuevo Mexicano*, May 14, 1898.

49. Zeleny, "Relations Between Spanish-Americans and Anglo-Americans," 310–11.

50. For example, see Mabel Major and T. M. Pearce, *Southwest Heritage: A Literary History with Bibliography* (1972). Although this study admits its limitations (no Hispanic literature after 1800 is mentioned), it tries to defend itself by stating: "While civilization here is greatly enriched by contacts with other cultures and languages, today the dominant strain seems clearly to be Anglo-American, with its ever increasing tendency to spread its influence and to absorb its competitors" (2). Recent collective efforts to change this perception include: Gonzales-Berry, *Pasó por aquí*; Ramón Gutiérrez and Genaro Padilla, eds., *Recovering the U.S. Hispanic Literary Heritage*; and Francisco Lomelí, ed., *Handbook of Hispanic Cultures in the United States: Literature and Art*.

Chapter 3

1. The number of books about Vicente Silva testifies to the public fascination with his criminal history and to authors' intentions to discredit him as a moral lesson. The original biography of Silva, written shortly after his disappearance, was by Manuel C. de Baca, *Historia de Vicente Silva y sus cuarenta bandidos . . .* (1896). An English translation of this text was published in 1947: *Vicente Silva and His Forty Bandits*, trans. Lane Kauffmann (1947). Another English version appeared some years before that, by Carlos C. de Baca, *Vicente Silva: New Mexico's Vice King of the Nineties* (1938); it was reissued under another title, *Vicente Silva: The Terror of Las Vegas* (1968), by the same

author. For further accounts of Silva and his gang, see Peter Hertzog, *A Directory of New Mexico Desperados*; Miguel A. Otero, *My Life on the Frontier*, vol. 2; and F. Stanley, *Desperadoes of New Mexico*.

2. In 1895, two years after the crime, Manuel C. de Baca learned the whereabouts of the bodies of Silva and his wife through interviews with Silva's men in jail (*La Voz del Pueblo*, Mar. 23, 1895). Baca, who collected a three-thousand-dollar reward for the discovery, and Miguel. A. Otero, Jr., were among those present in 1895 when the bodies were exhumed from an arroyo near Los Alamos, according to Otero, in *My Life on the Frontier*, 2:179. Silva's men evidently killed him for the money he hoarded and because they suspected Silva might turn on them and kill them at any time. Carlos C.de Baca, *Vicente Silva*, 30. Until these facts were known, local papers carried regular reports of rumors concerning Silva's fate. See *Las Vegas Daily Optic*, April-May 1894.

3. See Stratton, *Territorial Press*, 175–95.

4. *El Sol de Mayo,*, Dec. 10, 1891.

5. *Las Vegas Daily Optic*, Apr. 12, 1894.

6. Carlos C. de Baca, *Vicente Silva*, 5.

7. Robert J. Rosenbaum, *Mexicano Resistance in the Southwest: "The Sacred Right of Self-Preservation,"* 27.

8. For a discussion of this problem, its origins and consequences, see Zeleny, "Relations Between the Spanish-Americans and Anglo-Americans," chapter 7.

9. The Gorras Blancas have been portrayed as common marauders (see Otero, *My Life on the Frontier*, 2:166–67) as well as oppressed "social bandits" in line with the Hobsbawn theory (see Andrew B. Schlesinger, Jr., "Las Gorras Blancas, 1889–1891," 87–143). The most objective commentary is found in Rosenbaum, *Mexicano Resistance*, and in his earlier dissertation, "Mexicano versus Americano: A Study of Hispanic American Resistance to Anglo-American Control in New Mexico, 1870–1900." Rosenbaum points out that "the term White Cap was applied to many vigilante groups in the U.S. in the late nineteenth century" (*Mexicano Resistance*, 204, n. 2).

10. Local juries generally would not convict fence-cutters. See Rosenbaum, *Mexicano Resistance*, 124. The press was divided in its reaction to the Gorras Blancas: "most territorial editors, whether Anglo or Hispano, disapproved of violent methods, but some recognized the justice of the ends of the White Caps and sought to persuade them to use methods that would lead to reconciliation rather than conflict between ethnic groups." Stratton, *Territorial Press*, 131.

11. Robert W. Larson, *Populism in the Mountain West*, 116.

12. Rosenbaum, *Mexicano Resistance*, 126.

13. For information on Romero and López, see ibid., 126–128, and Otero, *My Life on the Frontier*, 2:224–26. In another twist of political–family relationships, López's son-in-law was Enrique H. Salazar, a politically progressive newspaper editor with *La Voz del Pueblo* and, later, *El Independiente*.

14. *Las Vegas Daily Optic*, Sept. 8, l890.

15. Gómez-Quiñones, *Roots of Chicano Politics*, 283.

16. See *La Revista Católica* of Mar. 15 and 22, and July 19, 1891, and *El Defensor del Pueblo* of July 11 and 25, and Aug. 1, 1891. Herrera's responses are signed by him and are rambling diatribes against the Jesuits whom he accused of being threatened by the recent power of the Partido del Pueblo Unido after years of Republican, church-backed

control in New Mexico. Herrera says he deplores criminality and claims that the Caballeros de Labor are not behind the Gorras Blancas; nonetheless he endorses the native people's right to protest the loss of their lands to "Americanos invasores que los custodiaban con armas y bayonetas, como nuevos patrones" [American invaders who guarded them with weapons and bayonets, like new bosses] (Aug. 1).

17. See *The Daily Citizen* (Albuquerque), Aug. 12, 1891.

18. *El Sol de Mayo*, Feb. 25, 1892.

19. Rosenbaum, "Mexicano versus Americano," 267.

20. Otero, *My Life on the Frontier*, 2:263. For confirmation of Otero's assessment of New Mexican politics in 1892, see Howard R. Lamar, *The Far Southwest, 1846–1912: A Territorial History*, 93–94.

21. Rosenbaum, "Mexicano versus Americano," 329–35. Rosenbaum says here that Silva was with the Romero faction, a statement for which there is no proof. It is more likely that he was with López and the Pueblo Unido, as explained in the pages that follow.

22. Otero, *My Life on the Frontier*, 2:167.

23. Schlesinger, for example, calls Otero's theory a "distortion"; he maintains that López was a shrewd politician who was fed up with Republican criticism of his inability to establish law and order as a sheriff and therefore switched to the Pueblo Unido. Schlesinger, *Las Gorras Blancas*, 120 and 216.

24. Carlos C. de Baca, *Vicente Silva*, (1968), 10.

25. See *El Sol de Mayo*, June 12, 1891. An editorial called "One Sided Justice" in the English-language portion of the paper reads as follows: "We know of no law that allows a sheriff to turn his prisoners loose without proper authority. It looks like the work of demagogues or politicians who have a pull that the affable Joe could not withstand when an official elected by the people goes so far as to disregard his official oath. . . . For the sheriff of a county is supposed to defend and uphold the dignity of the law and not to embolden crime by allowing offenders against the highest laws of God and man perfect immunity."

26. For details of the mock trial and subsequent hanging of Patricio Maes, see Carlos C. de Baca, *Vicente Silva*, (1968), 14–17. Also, see *La Voz del Pueblo* (Las Vegas), May 5, 1894.

27. *El Sol de Mayo*, Feb. 18, 1892, in a letter to the editor from a Taos resident, J. Alires. Alires says that Lorenzo López and Juan José Herrera were partners in this endeavor.

28. "El Moro" was the alias of Martin González y Blea, a Silva outlaw. He turned state's evidence after his arrest and avoided the death penalty, serving instead a life sentence in the state penitentiary.

29. On the same page with Rael's poem is a letter from another convicted Silva gang member, Ricardo Romero, who protests public opinion that he should have been given a longer, a life, sentence. He says that some got off even lighter than he "quiza porque portan las pistolas del condado" [perhaps because they are carrying the county's pistols]. This appears to be a reference to Sheriff López, who had his henchmen among the bandit gangs.

30. The witnesses' testimony was published in *La Voz del Pueblo*, Apr. 7, 1894; *El Independiente* (Las Vegas), May 26, 1894; and the *Las Vegas Daily Optic*, Apr. 16, 1894.

31. Manuel C. de Baca, *Silva and His Forty Bandits*, 102. The supposed conversation and its melodramatic representation of Hispanic gender roles is omitted in the adapted English version by Carlos C. de Baca.

32. *La Voz del Pueblo*, May 19, 1894.

33. *Las Vegas Daily Optic*, May 23, 1894, and *La Voz del Pueblo*, May 26, 1894.

34. *La Voz del Pueblo*, May 26, 1894.

35. In his final interviews with reporters, Maestas claimed to have forgiven his wife and he requested, but was denied, permission to see her one last time. It is therefore likely that his poem was written shortly after his sentencing. Maestas had once before turned to writing to express himself: when he broke out of prison to find Rosita, he reportedly left a letter for the sheriff (Lorenzo López), the contents of which were not made public. *Las Vegas Daily Optic*, Apr. 16, 1894. The same newspaper also reported that Governor Thornton turned down many petitions to commute Maestas's sentence (May 21) and that the sheriff received one hundred dollars for the hanging (May 26).

36. See Américo Paredes, *"With His Pistol in His Hand."* In another study, "Folklore and History," Américo Paredes discusses the importance of consulting popular ballads as a source of history. See Paredes, *Singers and Storytellers*, ed. M. C. Boatright, 56–68.

37. Sarah Deutsch, *No Separate Refuge: Culture, Class and Gender on an Anglo-Hispanic Frontier in the American Southwest, 1880–1940*: "In line with their tradition of flexible sexual division of labor, economic autonomy, and a family economy, and with depletions in the land base affecting their purview as it had the men's, the women, too, quickly took advantage of new opportunities for cash income" (33).

Chapter 4

1. According to Carolyn Zeleny: "A high proportion of the people, some estimate about seven-eighths, were illiterate at the beginning of the American era. The few who received any education at all, except those destined for the Church, had to be content with the simplest rudiments. Anyone able to read or write, and having a smattering of arithmetic was considered learned." Cited with source references in "Relations Between the Spanish-Americans and Anglo-Americans," 279.

2. Another regular feature for women readers in the same newspaper was "La semana al vuelo" [The week's overview], signed by "Rubén," who was also most likely Escobar. On popular pen names, see Myra L. Yancey, "Some Mexican Writers and Their Pseudonyms," and Ernest E. Stowell, "More Mexican Writers and Pseudonyms."

3. *El Defensor del Pueblo* had already taken a stance in support of expanded women's education and emancipation. In the fall of 1891 it had published in four installments a long essay by the Colombian feminist writer Soledad Acosta de Samper (see Chapter 7).

4. Francisco R. Almada, *La imprenta y el periodismo en Chihuahua*, 39.

5. *El Tiempo* (Las Cruces), May 29, 1897.

6. The activities of this association, founded in early 1892, are chronicled in the Spanish-language newspapers of the time. See, for example, Escobar's *El Combate*, July 7, 1892, which reported the minutes of one of its meetings in Santa Fe. Both Victor L. Ochoa, its first president, and Pedro García de la Lama, another prominent member, were *antiporfiristas* like Escobar. The association's defense of the dignity of Mexican-Americans in a period of increasing Anglicization, however, crossed party lines separating neomexicanos. Many had recently aligned themselves with the Partido del Pueblo Unido, which attempted to bring Hispanos together after a period of debilitating divisiveness.

7. See Chapter 10, "History and Identity," for a discussion of his efforts as a historian.

8. Escobar was the editor of the following newspapers, during the approximate dates indicated:

El Defensor del Pueblo (Albuquerque), 1891–1892

El Combate (Albuquerque), 1892

La Voz de Nuevo México (Albuquerque), 1893, and again in 1895

El Progreso (Trinidad, Colo.), 1893?

Las Dos Repúblicas (Denver, Colo.), 1894?

El Amigo del Pueblo (Raton), 1895–96

El Nuevo Mundo (Albuquerque), 1897

El Combate (Socorro), 1898

9. From an editorial by García de la Lama in La Opinión Pública (Albuquerque), Feb. 9, 1895.

10. In this newspaper, whose name reflected Escobar's aggressive style of journalism, he denounced political bossism, and particularly the powerful Perea family of Bernalillo County (Jan. 8, 1898). Escobar referred to an offer of five hundred dollars to get him to resign as editor from El Nuevo Mundo and another one he had just gotten to push him out of El Combate. This may have been the final straw that convinced him to return to Mexico.

11. Escobar may have been influenced to return to Mexico by a law concerning citizenship (Ley de Extranjería y Naturalización) passed in Mexico on May 28, 1886, which in Article 823, Section 3, stipulates that no Mexican national may remain out of the country for more than ten years without losing his citizenship unless he has been issued a formal approval by the government. This was widely known and the subject of comment in the Spanish-language newspapers in New Mexico, for example in El Defensor del Pueblo, Feb. 6, 1892. Also, see Joseph Wheless, Compendium of the Laws of Mexico Officially Authorized by the Mexican Government, vol. 2, 523–26. It is possible that the political climate in Mexico was more favorable to Escobar's return in 1898, in spite of the fact that Porfirio Díaz was still in power. Journalists were persecuted by the Díaz regime although opposition viewpoints were intermittently tolerated in the press. See T. Torres, Periodismo, 82.

12. Ricardo Gullón, Direcciones del modernismo, 14–15.

13. El Defensor del Pueblo (Albuquerque), Apr. 2, 1892. Other Mexican poets frequently cited in Escobar's newspapers include Ignacio M. Altamirano, Juan de Dios Peza, Salvador Díaz Mirón, Luis G. Urbina, Ricardo Domínguez, and Antonio Zaragoza, among others. They were among the best known and literarily engaged authors of the time, with many of them contributing to journals such as La República Literaria (1886–1890, Guadalajara), which published the best of the post-romantic writing in the positivistic and modernist modes. H. García Rivas, Historia de la literatura mexicana, 2:217.

14. Max Henríquez Ureña says about Gutiérrez Nájera: "Su influencia en América fue múltiple: modernistas y no modernistas lo imitaron. Escribir 'a la manera de Gutiérrez Nájera' fue casi una moda, y muchas de sus ideas poéticas sirvieron de punto de partida a la inspiración de otros poetas" [His influence in America was multiple: modernists and nonmodernists alike imitated him. To write "in the style of Gutiérrez

Nájera" was almost the fashion, and many of his poetic ideas served as stimuli to inspire other poets]. Henríquez Ureña, *Breve historia del modernismo*, 76–77.

15. *El Hispano Americano* (Socorro), Jan. 30, 1892. Escobar's poems are transcribed here as printed in the newspapers cited, without orthographic or punctuation corrections. In some cases, the poems were dated by the poet, and that date is added at the end wherever possible. In addition to the poems reprinted in this chapter, Escobar's poetry can be found in the following papers, in chronological order:

    El Defensor del Pueblo (Albuquerque),
        "Cineraria" March 12, 1892
        "Negro y blanco" March 19, 1892
        "Mi historia" April 2, 1892
        "Serenata" April 9, 1892
        "¡Calla!" April 16, 1892
        "Crepúsculo" May 21, 1892
        "Ojos negros" May 21, 1892
    La Opinion Pública (Albuquerque)
        "Mis laureles" June 16, 1892
        "Llanto" July 2, 1892
    El Combate (Socorro)
        "Floral" July 7, 1892
    La Opinión Pública (Albuquerque)
        "Mensajera" August 20, 1892
        "Infidencias" August 27, 1892
    El Hispano Americano (Las Vegas)
        "Intima" October 15, 1892
    La Voz del Pueblo (Las Vegas)
        "Aves negras" July 8, 1893
    El Independiente (Las Vegas)
        "¡Cantad!" April 28, 1894
    El Tiempo (Las Cruces)
        "Serenata" October 1, 1896
    El Combate (Socorro)
        "Amame" January 15, 1898
        "Versos y flores" January 15, 1898
    El Labrador (Las Cruces)
        "Te volví a ver" January 23, 1898

Many of these poems were published more than once in different neomexicano newspapers. Reprints of some of them can also be found in my article on Escobar (see Bibliography). I hope to publish his poetry, along with Luis Tafoya's, in a separate publication.

16. These verses by Justo Sierra were imitated by other Mexican poets such as Gutiérrez Nájera, according to Henríquez Ureña, *Breve historia del modernismo*, 73–74.

17. *El Defensor del Pueblo* (Albuquerque), Feb. 13, 1892.

18. *El Defensor del Pueblo*, Feb. 20, 1892.

19. *Defensor del Pueblo*, Feb. 27, 1892.

20. See Stratton, *Territorial Press* (chap. 4, "The Territorial Press and the Politicians," 81–116).

21. *El Nuevo Mundo* (Albuquerque), Oct. 9, 1897.

22. A. Torres Rioseco, *Precursores del modernismo*, 34.

23. For example: "Se sigue hablando de escuelas literarias por confusión o rutina en la crítica moderna, cuando debiera restringirse el término para referirse solamente a hechos históricos anteriores al romanticismo, como póngase por caso la escuela salmantina o sevillana, y no tiene sentido hablar de escuelas modernistas, realistas, surrealistas o expresionistas" [Modern criticism continues to talk about literary schools out of confusion or custom when the term should be restricted to referring only to historical facts prior to romanticism, as for example the Salamancan or Sevillian schools. It makes no sense to talk of modernist, realist, surrealist or expressionist schools]. Bernardo Gicovate, *Conceptos fundamentales de literatura comparada*, 47. See also Gullón, *Direcciones del modernismo*, 8.

24. For a discussion of Mexican literary journals, their founders, and those who contributed to them in the late nineteenth century, see García Rivas, *Historia de la literatura mexicana*, vol. 2. Henríquez Ureña, *Breve historia del modernismo*, 489, points out that Mexican writers absent from their homeland usually kept in touch with literary groups there.

25. The respective dates of their publication are May 1, June 5, July 24, and August 7, 1897.

26. Fray Angelico Chavez, *Our Lady of the Conquest*, 22; quoted in Weigle and White, *Lore of New Mexico*, 317.

27. For a description of the exterior and interior of Cordova's chapel of San Antonio, see Lorin W. Brown, with Charles L. Briggs and Marta Weigle, *Hispano Folklife of New Mexico: The Lorin W. Brown Federal Writers' Project Manuscripts*, 210–26.

28. The titles and dates are as follows. Some are signed by Zig-Zag, others by La Redacción [The Editorials], and some are without attribution; they are all, however, very similar in outlook and language and are undoubtedly by Escobar:

"Algo sobre el nombramiento de gobernador para Nuevo México" [Some thoughts about the appointment of a governor for N.M.] (May 8)

"¡Algunas Causas que Contribuyen al Malestar y Retroceso de las Masas Populares de Nuevo México!" [Some factors that contribute to the discomfort and backwardness of the popular masses of N.M.] (May 15)

"Ayer y hoy: Algo sobre el Pasado y el Presente de Nuevo México" [Yesterday and today: Something about the past and present of N.M.] (May 29)

"Indiferencia del Pueblo Hispano-Americano para la Prensa" [Indifference of the Hispanic-American people toward the press] (June 5)

"Defectos Graves que deben Corregirse: Triste Porvenir de la Juventud Neo-Mexicana" [Grave defects that must be corrected: Sad future for Neo-mexicano youth] (June 12)

"Llegada del Nuevo Gobernador de Nuevo México: Miguel A. Otero" [Arrival of the new governor of N.M.: Miguel A. Otero] (June 19)

"Diferencia del Pasado y del Presente: Plagas Sociales" [Differences between past and present: Social plagues] (July 10). This essay was reprinted in the first issue of *La Golondrina* (Socorro, Feb. 12, 1898), owned and edited by Ignacio A. Gutiérrez, a Mexican expatriate like Escobar. It is likely that

Escobar collaborated with him on this paper after leaving *El Nuevo Mundo*.
"[Illegible first part] Nuevo México será admitido o no como Estado" [. . .
New Mexico will be admitted or not as a state] (July 17)
"Algo sobre la Feria Territorial, su Importancia" [Some thoughts about the
territorial fair, its importance] (July 24)
"Más Sobre la Cuestión de Estado" [More on the question of statehood]
(July 31)
"Urgente Necesidad de Nuestra Unión" [Urgent need for our unity]
(August 7)
"Una Aclaración Importante: Rectitud y Justicia de Nuestra Posición" [An
important clarification: Rightness and justice of our position]
(August 14)
"Deberes de la Prensa Para Con El Pueblo: Responsabilidad de esta en el
malestar de las masas Hispano Americanas de Nuevo México" [Duties of
the press toward the people: Its responsibility for the bad situation of the
Hispano American masses of N.M.] (August 21)
"Inmovilidad que Lentamente nos va llevando a la Retaguardia en toda clase
de Negocios" [Immobility that slowly carries us to the back of the line in
all kinds of business] (September 18)

I have found a few other examples of essays signed by "Zig-Zag," or "Zic-Zac"; one
of them is in *El Defensor del Pueblo*, Feb. 27, 1892, which Escobar edited, and another
in *La Voz del Pueblo*, July 8, 1893, with which he may have been affiliated but was not
named on the masthead. In this latter contribution, "Por Aquí y Allá," Escobar is more
like a roving social reporter who, true to form, comments effusively and romantically
on the lovely ladies of Las Vegas, and even says, of a night at the local Opera House: "La
noche se pasó agradablemente y al fin aunque con gran sentimiento, tuve que abandonar
aquel recinto en que la esplendiente belleza de aquellas rubias *misses*, me hizo soñar
por un momento con aquellas sombras azules que ménos ingratas que las golondrinas
de Bécquer, vuelven de cuando en cuando á pasar varios instantes en su antiguo y
solitario nido: mi alma. . . . !" [The evening passed pleasantly and finally, reluctantly, I
had to leave behind there the dazzling beauty of those blond misses that made me
dream for an instant of those blue shadows who, less ungrateful than Bécquer's swal-
lows, return from time to time to spend a few instants in their former, solitary nest: my
soul. . . . !]

29. From his July 17, 1897, essay.

30. From his May 15, 1897, essay.

31. From his August 21, 1897, essay.

32. It appears that Escobar was known and respected as a writer among his contemporaries in New Mexico to the point that he was quoted by another author, Ignacio A.
Gutiérrez, in his story entitled "Confidencias" [Confidences], published in *El Nuevo
Mundo* (Feb. 15, 1900). This story, told in the first person, refers to a semi-supernatu-
ral experience of the author in which the mythic Hispanic figure of *la Llorona* [The
wailing woman] comes to life. Gutiérrez, whose poetry and prose can be found in
various newspapers but is not as extensive as Escobar's, closes his story with this reference: "¿Sería que, como dice José Escobar, á fuerza de sufrir, llega el corazon á embotarse

á tal grado que no se conmueve ni con el sufrimiento del hombre ni con el fúnebre aparato de la muerte"? No lo podré decir. . . . " [Could it be that, as José Escobar says, "by dint of suffering the heart becomes inured to the point that it is not moved by man's suffering or by the funereal apparatus of death"? I couldn't say. . . .] Certainly Escobar's poetry speaks to this kind of suffering and testifies to its numbing effect.

33. *El Nuevo Mundo*, May 8, 1897.

Chapter 5

1. Various studies have addressed the negative stereotyping common in Anglo travelers' writings in Mexico after the Independence period and in the Southwest after 1846. See, for example, David J. Weber, "'Scarce More than Apes': Historical Roots of Anglo-American Stereotypes of Mexicans in the Border Region"; Cecil Robinson, *With the Ears of Strangers: The Mexican in American Literature*; Arnoldo De León, *They Called Them Greasers: Anglo Attitudes toward Mexicans in Texas, 1821–1900*; Raymund A. Paredes, "The Origins of Anti-Mexican Sentiment in the United States" and "The Mexican Image in American Travel Literature, 1831–1869"; José E. Limón, "Stereotyping and Chicano Resistance: An Historical Dimension,"; Edward Simmen, ed., *The Chicano: From Caricature to Self-Portrait*; D. T. Leary, "Race and Regeneration," in Manuel P. Servín, ed., *The Mexican Americans: An Awakening Minority*; and R. Armando Rios, "The Mexican in Fact, Fiction and Folklore."

2. De León, *They Called Them Greasers*, 4–5.

3. Weber, *Foreigners in Their Native Land*, 60.

4. See Dennis E. Berge, "Manifest Destiny and the Historians," in Michael P. Malone, ed., *Historians and the American West*, for a review of scholarly interpretations of the war with Mexico. Gene M. Brack, in "Mexican Opinion, American Racism and the War of 1846," points out that before the Mexican War, Mexican newspapers expressed awareness of the racist and expansionist attitudes of the United States and feared the conquest of Mexico itself if war was not declared.

5. Rebecca McDowell Craver, *The Impact of Intimacy: Mexican-Anglo Intermarriage in New Mexico, 1821–1846*, 4.

6. Weber, "Scarce More than Apes," 296. Further information on Anglo attitudes toward Hispanic women can be found in Beverly Trulio, "Anglo-American Attitudes toward New Mexican Women," and De León, *They Called Them Greasers* (chap. 4).

7. Robinson, *With the Ears of Strangers*, 25–26. De León, in *They Called Them Greasers*, points out that "greaser" was also probably used for Indians and that "greasers," "niggers," and "redskins" were all terms that southern whites in Texas used to express their contempt for races of color (16–17). The fact that there was a much lower rate of Anglo-Hispano intermarriage in San Antonio than in Santa Fe from 1850 to 1880 has been attributed by Richard Griswold del Castillo, in *La Familia* (69), to the lower numbers of single Anglo-American men relative to women in San Antonio (which was also true in Tucson). It may also be the result of more racial bigotry in Texas, where southern whites anathematized miscegenation.

8. Philip V. Ortega, ed., *We Are Chicanos: An Anthology of Mexican-American Literature*, xix.

9. See chap.12 ("Social Relations and Intermarriage") in Zeleny, "Relations Between the Spanish-Americans and Anglo-Americans," 307–40. Zeleny's observations regarding social relations at the time she was writing, in the 1940s, are particularly interesting as evidence of how informal social segregation played out after statehood.

10. Stratton, in *Territorial Press*, sees the territorial press on both sides as agents of reconciliation, which is generally true. He points out that Anglo editors often defended Hispanics from external attacks and thereby assumed a more knowledgeable and conciliatory attitude in negotiating other ethnic disagreements (129). However, as this chapter will show, I do not accept Stratton's assessment that "Most Hispano editors . . . were moderate in their demands and often apologetic when questions of ethnic differences were raised" (126) or his opinion that "final assimilation was slowed because their numerical superiority in New Mexico encouraged their continued use of Spanish and the old customs. Had this small number of Hispanos been scattered over the United States, assimilation would have been rapid" (126–27). Assimilation did not occur for a variety of reasons, and Stratton's gratuitous speculation simply confirms an ethnocentric perspective in a generally valuable piece of groundbreaking scholarship.

11. See Larson, *New Mexico's Quest for Statehood*, chaps. 9 and 10, which deal with the Ring and the rejected state constitution of 1889 and their relationship to the statehood debate.

12. *El Hispano-Americano* (Albuquerque), Feb. 6, 1892.

13. *El Combate* (Albuquerque), July 7, 1892 ("La Prensa Asociada").

14. Robinson, *With the Ears of Strangers*, 42.

15. One small article in the May 14, 1898, issue of *El Nuevo Mexicano*, quoted here in translation, chastised certain disruptive elements among local Spanish speakers who evidently felt otherwise:

A Warning to Interested Parties

This is a very necessary warning. All citizens and those who reside in the country, whatever their nationality, race or blood ties may be, must remember that they are living under this government and enjoying its beneficent protection. In time of war it is often necessary to make examples. It is said that some people in this territory born elsewhere are those who are promoting the doctrine that the sympathies of the citizens of Mexican origin should be on the side of Spain. This could be construed, in case of necessity, as a crime of treason and the punishment imposed would be very harsh if the authorities of the United States were to get involved in the matter. A warning to those who can read and want to learn is sufficient. Those to whom it applies would do well to avoid difficulties and not expose themselves to the indignation and anger of the many thousands of patriotic citizens that there are in New Mexico.

16. Chicanos involved in the Korean and Vietnam wars have expressed similar sentiments, which show that Mexican Americans continue to fight these stereotypes. For example, see Rolando Hinojosa's novels—in particular, *The Klail City Death Trip Series* (Arte Público Press, 1990)—and José Montoya's poem "El Louie."

17. Deutsch, *No Separate Refuge*, 71.

18. "The key message of the missionaries, then, involved the Americanization of Hispanic gender roles, the replication in the plazas of Anglo gender patterns—women in the home, men outside it—in short, the cult of domesticity." Deutsch, *No Separate Refuge*, 76.

19. Ibid., 67.

20. Robinson, *With the Ears of Strangers*, 31. Illiteracy rates in New Mexico may have been inflated in the nineteenth century by English-speaking census takers who did not take neomexicano literacy in Spanish into consideration.

21. "The Education Law of 1891 established the first school system of any comprehensiveness in the territory. By it the office of Superintendent of Public Instruction, to be filled by the governor's appointment, was created. A territorial Board of Education composed of the governor, the Superintendent of Public Instruction and the Presidents of the University, the Agricultural College and St. Michael's College, was given wide powers for the organization and control of the entire school system and power to decide on the adoption of a uniform system of textbooks." Zeleny, "Relations Between Spanish-Americans and Anglo-Americans," 286. For a discussion of the legislative debate and adoption of this bill, see Stratton, *Territorial Press*, 140–45.

22. *El Independiente*, Sept. 1, 1894.

23. The article mentions by name the history of New Mexico by W. W. H. Davis, *El Gringo, or New Mexico and Her People* (1857) as the Anglo prototype, too often imitated by others. On this subject, see Octavio I. Romano-V., "The Anthropology and Sociology of the Mexican-Americans: The Distortion of Mexican-American History (A Review Essay)," in Romano-V., ed., *Voices: Readings from El Grito, 1967-1973*, 26–39.

24. *El Nuevo Mundo*, June 12, 1897.

25. See, for example, *La Voz del Pueblo*, Feb. 15, 1896.

26. Leopoldo Zea, *The Latin American Mind*, 30.

27. This is stated in an earlier, similar article in the same newspaper, *El Independiente*, Mar. 16, 1895, entitled "Decadencia de nuestro pueblo" [Decadence of our people].

28. See "La condición de Nuevo México" [The condition of New Mexico], which elaborates this thesis, in *El Independiente*, Dec. 28, 1899. The conservative position in Mexico after Independence favored an imitation of the European model for progress that was centralist and authoritarian in comparison to the liberal viewpoint.

29. Argudín, *Historia del periodismo en México*, 100–101.

30. *El Independiente*, Apr. 18, 1907 ("Nuevo México y sus enemigos internos").

31. Larson, *New Mexico's Quest for Statehood*, 276 and 279. Also, see Juan Gómez Quiñones, *Roots of Chicano Politics*, 327–28; Article 7, Section 3., of the constitution guarantees: "The right of any citizen of the state to vote, hold office, or sit upon juries, shall never be restricted, abridged or impaired on account of religion, race, language or color, or inability to speak, read or write the English or Spanish languages except as may be otherwise provided in this Constitution; ... "

32. Américo Paredes has pointed out that in the Texas border region, "The Mexican American is proud to call himself a *mexicano*, but he is often ashamed to be known as a Mexican." See Paredes, "The Problem of Identity in a Changing Culture ... " 87. An assimilated shame regarding what being Mexican meant in the United States is not the essential motivation for rejecting the term in New Mexico in the late territorial period,

where neomexicanos had lived through a different set of historical, political, and cultural experiences with Anglos and their government. Their objection to being called Mexican at this time must be seen in the context of the lengthy struggle for statehood, recently won, and the anticipation of future politics in the state if they were to be identified and stereotyped in the pejorative context that Anglos had given to the term *Mexican*. The neomexicanos and border Texans are different cultural communities who share common ethnic roots, so issues of identity need to be discussed with specific contexts in mind.

33. David J. Weber, *The Spanish Frontier in North America*, 355–56. On this subject, see also Chávez, *Lost Land*, 85–101.

34. Luis Valdez, "Introduction: 'La Plebe,'" Valdez and Stan Steiner, eds., *Aztlán: An Anthology of Mexican American Literature*, xxx. For further information, see Rudolfo A. Anaya and Francisco Lomelí, eds., *Aztlán: Essays on the Chicano Homeland*.

35. Tomás Almaguer has called persuasively for a reconsideration of the impact on Chicano scholarship of nationalist politics of the late 1960s and urged scholars to "enter a debate on issues that will advance our understanding of the complexities of Chicano history." Almaguer, "Ideological Distortions in Recent Chicano Historiography: The Internal Model and Chicano Historical Interpretation," 24.

36. Turner, "The Significance of the Frontier in American History," 3.

Chapter 6

1. Jane McNab Christian and Chester C. Christian, Jr., "Spanish Language and Culture in the Southwest," 300.

2. Edward Sapir, "Language," 15–16.

3. Bakhtin, "Discourse in the Novel," 279 and passim.

4. Alfred Arteaga, "An Other Tongue," 13 and 16.

5. Rosaura Sánchez, *Chicano Discourse: Socio-historic Perspectives*, 58.

6. See Tsvetan Todorov, *The Conquest of America: The Question of the Other*, 80–81 and 251–53; also Stephen Greenblatt, *Marvelous Possessions: The Wonder of the New World*, 9–12.

7. Patricia Nelson Limerick, *The Legacy of Conquest: The Unbroken Past of the American West*, 225.

8. On the origins and lexicon of this regional dialect, see Rubén Cobos, *A Dictionary of New Mexico and Southern Colorado Spanish*. When Aurelio M. Espinosa wrote about New Mexican Spanish and its roots, his work gave academic legitimacy to a dialect of Spanish that had often only been referred to as a "corruption" of the mother tongue. Neomexicanos recognized and celebrated his findings. See *El Nuevo Mexicano*, Oct. 2, 1909 ("Estudios en español mexicano"), and Nov. 5, 1910 ("El español que se habla aquí").

9. Eleanor B. Adams and France V. Scholes, "Books in New Mexico, 1598–1680," 243–46.

10. Weber, *Foreigners in Their Native Land*, 42.

11. See 1877 manuscript copy of Santiago Valdez's "Biografía del Rev. P. Antonio José Martínez," in the William G. Ritch Collection, Huntington Library, Pasadena, Calif.

12. Fray Angelico Chavez, *But Time and Change*, 48–49.

13. Benjamin M. Read, *A History of Education in New Mexico*, 13–14.

14. The historian Hubert Howe Bancroft, showing his ethnocentrism, attributed this to "the apathy of the native population," "the mixture of language and religion," and "all the causes that have hindered progress in other directions." He noted that with immigration from the East came "a healthful sentiment in favor of schools" and "encouraging progress." A different story from the neomexicano perspective has been told by Read in his *History of Education*. See Bancroft, *History of Arizona and New Mexico, 1530–1888*, 774–76.

15. Article 9 of the Treaty of Guadalupe Hidalgo, as reprinted in Ruth Lamb, *Mexican-Americans, Sons of the Southwest*, 62–79.

16. Patricia Nelson Limerick, "Making the Most of Words: Verbal Activity and Western America," 168.

17. Ibid.

18. L. Bradford Prince, *New Mexico's Struggle for Statehood*, 40–41.

19. Larson, *New Mexico's Quest for Statehood*, 151.

20. Called the Kistler school bill, it was also opposed by some wealthy Anglo landowners who objected to the proposed taxes. Some Democrats, like Governor Edmund G. Ross, accused Republican Santa Fe Ring leaders of defeating the bill in order to keep the native peoples ignorant and the Ring in power. See ibid., 146, and Stratton, *Territorial Press*, 140–41.

21. Larson, *New Mexico's Quest for Statehood*, 167; New Mexico Republicans accused Joseph of being complicit in this proposal (see poem cited in Chapter 1). Another congressional attempt to promote rapid "Americanization" was a change suggested in 1892 by the Senate Committee on Territories in the wording of another enabling act for New Mexico. In the section dealing with the language of instruction in the public schools, it was proposed that the phrase "in all of which schools the English language shall be taught" be changed to "the said schools shall always be conducted in English." Prince, *New Mexico's Struggle for Statehood*, 44. Although final action on this act was never taken in the Senate in 1892, nor again in 1894 when similar provisions were sought in a House report, it became more and more clear to informed territorial citizens that national sentiment was strongly in favor of reducing if not eliminating the use of Spanish in the schools, and that the granting of statehood might be contingent upon this factor.

22. Stratton, *Territorial Press*, 143.

23. From Section 1525. Section 1520 reads: "That it shall be his [Superintendent of Public Instruction's] duty to recommend the most approved text books in English, or in English and Spanish for the common schools of the territory . . . and such textbooks, when adopted, shall not be changed for a period of four years." (In 1903, of eighty-seven textbooks ordered, only eleven were in Spanish, or a mixture of Spanish and English.) *Compilation of the School Laws of the Territory of New Mexico*, 3 and 5.

24. Stratton, *Territorial Press*, 144.

25. Ibid., 126–27.

26. Twitchell, *Leading Facts of New Mexican History*, 2:508–9.

27. Cited in Larson, *New Mexico's Quest for Statehood*, 279. This guarantee was an-

other instance of words being undermined by practice. The history of public education in New Mexico since 1910 has been fraught with injustices toward Hispanic children. See E. B. Fincher, "Spanish-Americans as a Political Factor in New Mexico, 1912–1950."

28. Similar articles appear in 1895–97 in the same paper.

29. In several other articles in the 1890s, the neomexicano press called for stricter enforcement of the 1891 law requiring bilingual teachers in districts where Spanish-speaking students were enrolled. *La Voz del Pueblo* (Las Vegas), July 27, 1895, and *La Unión* (Raton), May 21, 1898.

30. Brown, *Hispano Folklife of New Mexico*, 194.

31. *El Independiente*, Feb. 20, 1908 ("Legislación racional sobre escuelas").

32. A description of the schools' objectives and structure is reprinted in *El Nuevo Mexicano* (Santa Fe), Sept. 18, 1909.

33. *La Voz del Pueblo* (Las Vegas), January-March 1915. In 1941 legislation was passed requiring that Spanish be taught in the public schools of New Mexico, but there were loopholes in the law and discriminatory practices in the schools, and Hispanic students were thus not provided with an equal education in the state. See Fincher, "Spanish-Americans as a Political Factor in New Mexico," 72.

34. See "Conferencias con un Colegial," in *El Promotor Escolar* (Las Cruces), Jan. 18, 1892.

35. See "El Beliz," in *El Tiempo* (Las Cruces), June 28, 1894.

36. See the poem "Mi Gusto" in Chapter 2, from *La Voz del Pueblo* (Las Vegas), June 25, 1892.

37. On this subject and the contemporary Mexican American experience, see Eliu Carranza, "Cultural Erosion"; Edwin Casavantes, "Pride and Prejudice: A Mexican-American Dilemma"; and Fernando C. Dominguez, "A Look at Education through an 'Estereotyposcope'"; all in Ralph Poblano, ed., *Ghosts in the Barrio: Issues in Bilingual-Bicultural Education*, 61–69, 71–79, and 88–99, respectively.

38. *La Voz del Pueblo*, May 9, 1914.

Chapter 7

1. Limerick, "Making the Most of Words," 170.

2. Sandra L. Myres, "Women in the West," 369. Myres cites T. A. Larson, "Women's Role in the American West." For revisionist views of Western history from a feminist perspective, see Susan Armitage and Elizabeth Jameson, eds., *The Women's West*; and Ellen Carol DuBois and Vicki L. Ruiz, eds., *Unequal Sisters: A Multicultural Reader in U.S. Women's History*.

3. On Chicana or Southwest Hispanic women's historiography, see Adelaida R. Del Castillo, ed., *Between Borders: Essays on Mexicana/Chicana History*, a collection of studies, both general and specific, which, together, give a good sense of the diversity of this area of scholarship. At the end of her volume is an extensive and very useful Bibliography. An example of a one-sided approach to Chicana history is Irene I. Blea's *La Chicana and the Intersection of Race, Class, and Gender*; although recognizing the uniqueness of Chicana history and the importance of considering more than just gender in its evolu-

tion, Blea's analysis glosses over historical periods and reduces women's role to that of victims (for example, "Spanish Colonial Women in the United States," 43–45.)

4. Turner, "Significance of the Frontier in American History," 38. Turner's thesis, which has undergone much revisionist criticism since his time, was that the frontier era of "perennial rebirth," or social development along a fluid western line of expansion and colonization of "free land," had ended by 1890. He noted that the expansionism of the pioneer years had given way to a period of settled life and demands from westerners that the federal government regulate the national economy to support its needs and democratic ideals.

5. The contemporary Chicana author from south Texas, Gloria Anzaldúa, has captured the conflicted nature of the female Hispanic experience within a bicultural, bilingual historical context in her book *Borderlands/La Frontera*. Another informative study of the socio-cultural and historical context of Chicana experience is Tey Diana Rebolledo's *Women Singing in the Snow: A Cultural Analysis of Chicana Literature*.

6. "Chicano mothers have taught their daughters that men come first, that their brothers are more important, and that women's education is less important. Thus Chicano women have been brainwashed into accepting their subordinate roles by other women." Rosaura Sánchez, "The History of Chicanas: Proposal for a Materialist Perspective," 22.

7. On this subject, see Darlis A. Miller, "Cross-Cultural Marriages in the Southwest: The New Mexico Experience, 1848–1900." Juan Gómez-Quiñones has said that an upper-class Hispano woman who married an Anglo man after 1850 "was more likely to see her children become Anglicized rather than grow up as part of the extended Mexican community" (*Roots of Chicano Politics*, 244). From what I have seen in the world of neomexicano newspapers, this is subject to interpretation based on what is meant by "Anglicized." Two problematic examples of this would be Benjamin M. Read and Enrique H. Salazar, neither of whom were culturally Anglicized to the point that they shed Hispanic social customs or ceased to write in Spanish.

8. Richard Griswold del Castillo, "Patriarchy and the Status of Women in the Late Nineteenth-Century Southwest," 89.

9. On this subject, see Janet Lecompte, "The Independent Women of Hispanic New Mexico, 1821–1846," who bases her research on New Mexico court records as well as Anglo accounts of travels to New Mexico at the time. Lecompte makes the point that it was only during the Mexican period after 1821 that New Mexico began to open up to foreign commerce and gradually shed its character as an isolated frontier where women were less restricted by traditional patriarchal attitudes.

10. On the development of a more progressive, but still segregated and subordinate role for women in greater Mexican society at the time, see Jean Franco, *Plotting Women: Gender and Representation in Mexico*, chap. 4 ("Sense and Sensuality: Notes on the National Period, 1812–1910"). Also, see Josefina Zoraida Vásquez, "Educación y papel de la mujer en México." After 1900, the radical *magonistas* of the PLM (Partido Liberal Mexicano), living in the United States and agitating for anticapitalist revolution in Mexico, favored social equality for women but still equated the female role with the domestic sphere. The PLM newspaper, *Regeneración*, published articles to this effect from 1910 to 1918. See Emma M. Pérez, "'A La Mujer': A Critique of the Partido Lib-

eral Mexicano's Gender Ideology on Women," and Clara Lomas, "The Articulation of Gender in the Mexican Borderlands, 1900–1915"; Lomas finds evidence that in at least one journal of the liberal cause women's voices were fabricated by male authors. On traditional gender role stereotyping in Mexican American culture, see Carmen Ramos Escandon, "Alternative Sources to Women's History: Literature," 203–5, and Douglas Monroy, "'They Didn't Call Them *Padre* for Nothing': Patriarchy in Hispanic California," which also discusses the way wealthy *dons* often married their daughters off to California Anglos for potential economic gain to the family.

11. Ana Lao and Carmen Ramos, "Estudio preliminar," *Mujeres y revolución, 1900–1917,* 18.

12. See, for example, the oral testimony of Guadalupe Lupita Gallegos, recorded in Marta Weigle, ed., *Two Guadalupes: Hispanic Legends and Magic Tales from Northern New Mexico,* 36–52. Born into a well-to-do land-owning family in Las Vegas, N.M., in 1853, she led a protected childhood, cared for by Indian servants in a patriarchal household, received a minimal education, and was married with family consent at age twelve. Her husband, an entrepreneur who often left her at home when he pursued new business ventures in various parts of the territory, spent much of her family money and died when Lupita was forty. She thereafter went to live with her parents and later with her children and grandchildren, and died when she was in her mid-eighties.

13. Swadesh, *Los Primeros Pobladores,* 178.

14. See Sarah Deutsch, *No Separate Refuge,* chap. 2 ("At the Center: Hispanic Village Women, 1900–1914"), 41–62 and passim.

15. Cecil Robinson's *With the Ears of Strangers* recounts plots of several popular novels, such as those by New Mexican author Harvey Fergusson, depicting Hispanic territorial culture in which neomexicano women are portrayed as more sensual and erotic than the average Anglo female. Robinson himself wrote from a decidedly gender-biased viewpoint, however, so his analyses do not elucidate this aspect of negative stereotyping in Fergusson's novels.

16. Deena J. González, "The Widowed Women of Santa Fe: Assessments on the Lives of an Unmarried Population, 1850–1880," 44. This is a very informative and well-documented study based on census and court records of the period.

17. H. V. González was not a female author, as was originally suggested by Tey Diana Rebolledo in her essay "Las Escritoras, Romances and Realities." Professor Rebolledo confirmed this when I spoke with her in August 1995, noting that she was given erroneous information regarding this author, which she discovered too late to correct. She has since located other poems by González, who published quite regularly in neomexicano newspapers at the end of the century.

18. Octavio Paz, *The Labyrinth of Solitude: Life and Thought in Mexico,* 198. This observation obtains cross-culturally in the persistence of myths propagated by American travelers of the past century about New Mexican Hispanic women; see Trulio, "Anglo-American Attitudes toward New Mexican Women." Paz himself has been accused of complicity in the perpetuation of the Malinche mythology.

19. The newspapers have historically been overlooked as a source of information about Hispanic women. For example, Rosaura Sánchez does not mention them in her list of potential sources in an otherwise informative study. See "History of Chicanas," 16.

20. Rosario Castellanos (1925–1974) has described how Mexican women in her generation were acculturated to live only through their offspring and how motherhood is a national mystique in Mexico. See *Mujer que sabe latín. . .* , 15–16.

21. For the interested reader, some other examples are *El Sol de Mayo* (Las Vegas), May 14, 1891 ("A la mujer") and June 4, 1891 ("Pobre mujer"); *La Voz del Pueblo* (Las Vegas), Oct. 6, 1894 ("Y esto arde . . . ") and Mar. 14, 1896 ("A mamá"); *El Nuevo Mundo* (Albuquerque), June 5, 1897 ("El rosario de una madre"); *El Hispano Americano* (Mora), 1905, serial form ("La dignidad de la maternidad"; *El Independiente* (Las Vegas), June 2, 1910 ("Día de las madres"). Many articles were placed in neomexicano newspapers by the Women's Christian Temperance Union (WCTU), which also spoke to the moral virtues within gender-stereotypical roles; it would appear that they were syndicated translations, however, and not necessarily written by Hispanics.

22. David Argüello had previously published at least one poem in the newspapers. I found one he sent as an admiring subscriber to *El Sol de Mayo* (May 19, 1894) which shows he had an above average education as he refers to Victor Hugo although he writes in traditional octosyllablic verse.

23. Deutsch, *No Separate Refuge*, 57.

24. Deena González, "Widowed Women of Santa Fe," 36–38. González uses the term *widowed* to refer also to "the far larger community of women who were divorced, separated, or deserted" (34). She points out that after the U.S.–Mexican War, all women in Santa Fe (and presumably in the rest of New Mexico) faced "generally dismal economic circumstances" as a result of the "dislocation and upheaval of conquest" (35).

25. *El Nuevo Mundo* (Old Albuquerque), Sept. 7, 1899.

26. One woman's name, Dora Laureana Wright, does appear as a "Contributor" on the masthead of José Escobar's Albuquerque newspaper, *El Combate*, in 1892, but the single surviving issue (July 7) contains no pieces signed by her. Wright, also known as Laureana Wright de Kleinhans, was Mexican like some of the other male contributors named with her. Born in Taxco in 1846, she was a poet and liberal journalist, an editor and contributor to *Violetas del Anáhuac* (1887–88), where she first published biographical essays of famous Mexican women that she later published in a book, *Mujeres notables mexicanas* (México, 1910). According to Ana Lao and Carmen Ramos in their "Estudio preliminar" to *Mujeres y revolución, 1900–1917*, Laureana Wright supported women's efforts to achieve social and professional equality (19–20), and García Rivas notes that she was a precursor of feminist journalism in Mexico (*Historia de la literatura mexicana*, 2:190).

27. In Mexico there were ladies magazines of two types: (1)those edited by men for women readers ("devoted heavily to changing styles and fashions for women") and (2) liberal magazines edited by women ("devoted primarily to demands for female emancipation and a voice in national debate"). "The circulation of women's periodicals in Mexico in the mid-1800s compares with that of independent feminist periodicals today [1990]: *La Semana de las Señoritas Mejicanas* (Mexico City, 1851–52) lists almost 1,400 subscribers, of whom only 200 resided in Mexico City; *El Semanario de las Señoritas Mejicanas* (1841–42) lists a high of 1,020 subscribers, with only 196 in Mexico City. Such evidence may point to an international readership for these magazines." From "Toward a History of Women's Periodicals in Latin America: Introduction," in Semi-

nar on Women and Culture in Latin America, *Women, Culture, and Politics in Latin America*, 175.

28. Larson, *Populism in the Mountain West*, 125.

29. Craver, *Impact of Intimacy*, 4, 17, 46. Richard Griswold del Castillo points out in a comparison of southwestern intermarriage patterns that the higher ratio of Hispanic women to Anglo men prior to 1880 in Santa Fe accounts for the larger number of intermarriages there in comparison to San Antonio or Los Angeles. See his *La Familia*, 68–69.

30. Miller, "Cross-Cultural Marriages in the Southwest," 341.

31. Jane Dysart, writing about Mexican women in San Antonio in the 1850s, noted that "only the women and children with Anglo surnames, light skins, and wealth had a reasonable chance to escape the stigma attached to their Mexican ancestry." See "Mexican Women in San Antonio, 1830–1860: The Assimilation Process," 375. In those years racial prejudice was more pronounced in Texas than in New Mexico because of the pro-slavery sentiment that prevailed in that region.

32. *La Revista de Taos*, Feb. 17, 1911 ("Castidad sin modestia").

33. On Gutiérrez Nájera, the modernist aesthetic, and woman's body as a site of pleasure and commodification, see Jean Franco, *Plotting Women*, 95–98.

34. Newspapers often published lists of subscribers to encourage others to follow suit. In 1907, for example, *La Voz del Pueblo* (Las Vegas) listed names for four consecutive weeks and among them I found several dozen females among several hundred male subscribers. Nonetheless, many women probably read papers to which their husbands or relatives subscribed.

35. For an overview of the literary scene in New Mexico and Las Vegas in particular in the 1890s, see Francisco A. Lomelí, "A Literary Portrait of Hispanic New Mexico: Dialectics of Perception."

36. *La Voz del Pueblo*, Mar. 14, 1896. Women were not generally members of other kinds of mutualist societies in the 1890s; an article in *El Indito* (Albuquerque), Dec. 8, 1900, specifically calls for a change in practice to allow women to be members. It points out that a woman is by nature "un agente poderoso moralizador" [a powerful moralizing agent] and that since being charitable is also part of her nature, a woman should have the right to belong.

37. Aurora Lucero, daughter of Antonio Lucero (journalist and school superintendent), attended the Normal School at Las Vegas. Her essay, "Defensa de nuestro idioma" [Defense of our language], was published in *El Mensajero* (Mora) Mar. 3, 1911, and another, "New Occasions Teach New Duties," in *The New Mexican* (Santa Fe), Nov. 25, 1911.

38. For example, I have found single poems by Guadalupe V. Gallegos from Mora, N.M. (*El Nuevo Mexicano*, Mar. 1, 1917), Adela Arriola (*El Nuevo Mexicano*, Apr. 19, 1917), and Carolina Ortega from Truchas, N.M. (*El Nuevo Mexicano*, June 28, 1917).

39. John Sherman, *Santa Fe: A Pictorial History*, 78.

40. Alice Stevens Tipton, "Present Political Status of the Women of New Mexico," republished from *The New American Woman* in the weekly Santa Fe *New Mexican* (Jan. 25, 1917).

41. Pedro García de la Lama edited the paper prior to October 1891 and José Escobar did so beginning in February 1892; both of them were anti-Porfirista political liberals.

42. Some issues among the eleven weeks are missing, but because the letters carry

numbers one can posit a consecutive series of at least this length. I have found only numbers 1, 4, 6–9, 11, and 13, or eight of the eleven letters.

43. Fray Angelico Chavez, *Chávez*, 3. This study does not deal with the time period discussed here. In my efforts to identify the author I spoke with Norah Chavez, sister of Fray Angelico, and Thomas Chávez, director of the history museum of the Palace of the Governors in Santa Fe. Neither of them had any idea who N. Chávez might have been.

Chapter 8

1. Although the book was published in Albuquerque, it was copyrighted by Chacón in Mexico. No mention is made of the printer's name or of the number of copies printed.

2. Philip D. Ortego, in "Backgrounds of Mexican-American Literature," has referred to the territorial period as the "dark ages" of American literary history, recognizing that the contributions of Hispanic Americans have been systematically obscured (50–51).

3. Rafael Chacón's memoirs (preserved by Felipe's children) were recently brought to light, translated into English, and published with insightful commentary on life in early territorial New Mexico. See Meketa, *Legacy of Honor*.

4. Francisco Lomelí has located some of this author's publications, including two *novelitas*. See Eusebio Chacón, *El hijo de la tempestad/Tras la tormenta la calma* (Tipografía de El Boletín Popular, 1892); and Francisco Lomelí, "Eusebio Chacón," 78–82, for further information on his life and work. I have also found a poem, published in a Ratón newspaper, *La Unión* (May 14, 1898), by Antonio E. Chacón; this is most probably Antonio Elías Chacón, Eusebio's elder brother, who was later murdered by a friend in October 1898. See Meketa, *Legacy of Honor*, 328–29.

5. St. Michael's, where all education was in English, was referred to by neomexicanos as "El Colegio de San Miguel." In its early years it was commonly called a college by English speakers translating literally from the Spanish, although more appropriately it would be called an academy or high school, as it is today. It did receive a charter that enabled it to offer higher education, but this was rarely practiced. The street in Santa Fe where it was located came to be called College Street, but then its name was changed back to its original form, Old Santa Fe Trail. Only a residence building of the Christian Brothers remains today at that site, next to the old church of San Miguel; St. Michael's High School has been relocated.

6. I have seen three of F. M. Chacón's poems published in *La Voz del Pueblo* between 1911 and 1912. Two of them, "Mayo" and "La Navidad," appear in his book; a third, "¡Valor, Neo-Mexicanos!" (Oct. 28, 1911), does not. This poem was inspired by the political intrigue surrounding the state election; it shows that Chacón was at that time a progressive, pro-reform Republican. He had supported Democrat Octaviano Larrazolo's candidacy for delegate to Congress in 1906 and 1908, a crossover choice that reflected his support of Larrazolo's pro-native, anti-corruption stance.

7. According to David J. Weber, Carey McWilliams first expressed this concept of being "foreigners in their native land," in *North from Mexico: The Spanish-Speaking People of the United States*, in this way: "[it] is not that Mexicans are slower to accept change than are other ethnics. Rather, it is because Mexican culture continues to be

nourished through continuous immigration and constant contact with neighboring Mexico." Weber, *Foreigners in Their Native Land*, 2.

8. Julián Josué Vigil published, in a limited edition in 1980, his translations of Chacón's stories. See Felipe Maximiliano Chacón, *Short Stories*.

9. Erlinda Gonzáles-Berry, in "Vicente Bernal and Felipe M. Chacón: Bridging Two Cultures," 196–97, has suggested that "Eustacio y Carlota" was written as an allegory of cultural identity in New Mexico. She believes that Chacón's work shows an ambivalence in loyalties (a "push-me-pull-you pose") that does not fit into a "definitive discourse of resistance," but seems more like a double-voiced discourse of resistance and assimilation which she finds curious. I cannot agree with this interpretation. Seen within the context of his other works, Chacón was not ambivalent about his patriotism as a U.S. citizen or about his loyalty to his Hispanic cultural heritage. He believed, as did many educated neomexicanos of his time, that it was possible to combine and integrate these two sentiments compatibly, and indeed that it was essential to do so in order for neomexicanos to be authentically American. The key point is that being a loyal American citizen—a believer in the rights and responsibilities of the U.S. form of government—did not have to mean giving up one's cultural identity. One could learn two languages and *function effectively in a bicultural society* without betrayal of the parent culture. This perspective is, in my opinion, a valuable historical precedent for Latinos today who are concerned about similar issues of cultural identity.

Chapter 9

1. Lomelí, "Literary Portrait of Hispanic New Mexico," 137–38.

2. Ramón Saldívar, *Chicano Narrative: The Dialectics of Difference*, 24.

3. One of his poems was dedicated to his mother, and appeared at the end of her obituary in *El Nuevo Mexicano*, Apr. 29, 1899; she was born in 1830 and was the descendant of an old New Mexico family. The pallbearers at her funeral were well-known men in the Santa Fe Ring and Republican circles.

4. Stratton, *Territorial Press of New Mexico*, 36–37.

5. One of Antonio Ortiz y Salazar's pallbearers at his 1907 funeral was Thomas B. Catron, the leader of the Santa Fe Ring during the 1870s, 1880s, and 1890s (*El Nuevo Mexicano*, Sept. 7, 1907). It is interesting to note that Max Frost and W. H. Manderfield, who were partners in publishing *The New Mexican*, were also affiliated with the Ring. The early connection between E. H. Salazar and Tafoya is easily inferred as Salazar and Tafoya were almost contemporaries and shared the same kind of upbringing in which both were stepchildren. Several of Tafoya's poems were written to Salazar or members of his family.

6. Al Regensberg at the New Mexico State Records Center and Archives helped me locate Luis Tafoya's baptismal certificate and his parents' marriage certificate, dated 1846, in the archives of the Archdiocese of Santa Fe. Mr. Regensberg also traced a genealogical tree for Tafoya back six generations to Juan de Tafoya Altamirano, named as one of the founding fathers of the New Mexico Reconquest period in Fray Angelico Chavez, *Origins of New Mexico Families in the Spanish Colonial Period*, 291–92.

7. The provisions of this constitution prohibit discrimination against Spanish-speaking citizens on civil, political, or religious grounds, regardless of whether or not they are literate in either Spanish or English. The reaffirmation of the rights written into the Treaty of Guadalupe Hidalgo was crucial to the neomexicano representatives at the constitutional convention in view of the fact that they had not been enforced during the territorial period. See Zeleny, "Relations Between the Spanish-Americans and Anglo-Americans in New Mexico," 233–36. This poem by Tafoya was also published in *El Nuevo Mexicano*, Jan. 28, 1911.

8. This is evident in many of his poems and later writings. Also, the papers he wrote for were consistent backers of the statehood movement, as were most neomexicanos who believed that their larger numbers would ensure greater representation under the elective rather than the appointive system of territorial politics. See Zeleny, "Relations Between the Spanish-Americans and the Anglo-Americans in New Mexico," 216. This may clarify why many native writers like Tafoya and Felipe Chacón were patriotic Americans and also ethnocentric Hispanos; full enfranchisement in the political and civil arenas would theoretically make it more difficult to discriminate against the native population and give them more power as an ethnic group. In practice this has not always been the case, although New Mexico has negotiated multicultural coexistence more successfully than other states.

9. The pseudonyms I have identified other than "X.X.X." include "El Padre Panchito," "Pero Grullo," and "El Corresponsal," the last three in *La Revista de Taos*. The papers to which he contributed, as far as I know, were *El Nuevo Mexicano* (1893–1897), *El Independiente* (1898–1903, 1908–1910), and *La Revista de Taos* (1910–1918). I hope to publish his works, along with those of Escobar, in the near future.

10. Américo Paredes has written about "the Rio Grande People" of the Texas border communities in these same years. Similar cultural and societal values would obtain for the upper Rio Grande Valley of New Mexico. See *"With His Pistol in His Hand"* 9–15.

11. Saldívar, *Chicano Narrative*, 24–25.

12. Bakhtin, "Discourse in the Novel," 278–79.

13. Zeleny, "Relations Between the Spanish-Americans and the Anglo-Americans," 225–26.

14. The commonly used expression in Spanish, "Verdad de Perogrullo," indicates that something is universally accepted, a truth "known by all."

15. For an overview of Larrazolo's influence and this movement in particular, see Paul A. F. Walter, "Octaviano Ambrosio Larrazolo"; and Gómez-Quiñones, *Roots of Chicano Politics*, 328–33. Regarding Larrazolo's career, Walter, a Republican supporter and publisher of the Santa Fe *New Mexican*, wrote in 1932: "It can now be said that both defeat and victory, disillusionments and incomplete triumphs, came to him because of intense feeling engendered by his fiery and persistent pleas for race consciousness addressed to the Spanish-speaking people of the state. Whether for good or for evil, it is because of the impress he gave his day that the cleavage between the descendants of the Spanish conquerors and colonists and those who came from other states continues to be accentuated in political life and is felt even in business, in the professions, and in social activities" (97). Larrazolo was elected governor of New Mexico in 1918, after which the native-son movement declined in strength. Another Hispanic

governor would not be elected until more than fifty years later, despite the fact that neomexicanos were in the majority until the 1930s.

16. Gómez-Quiñones, *Roots of Chicano Politics*, 328.

17. Zeleny, "Relations Between the Spanish-Americans and the Anglo-Americans in New Mexico," 239.

18. I have found no mention of foul play in any of the writing on the period, but C. de Baca's sudden death does raise questions when viewed in the context of Tafoya's personal history.

19. Reported in *La Revista de Taos*, Feb. 27, 1914.

20. Porter Stratton notes that personal attacks were common among journalists in the 1880s, but observes a decline in this practice in the more economically depressed 1890s. He adds that by 1900 the territorial press was dominated by politics and had lost the "daring and vitality of pioneers" (49). I question this conclusion as it may apply to the Spanish-language press, which, for the most part, continued to speak out vigorously for its own interests. The nature of the attacks against Tafoya—if one is to believe that they are not overly exaggerated by the victim—transcend the verbal vitriolics of the 1880s and suggest that they were motivated by politics and perpetrated by paid thugs.

21. *La Revista de Taos*, Apr. 26, 1918.

22. Tafoya, like Benjamin Read, was skeptical of the outcome of the upheaval that removed Porfirio Díaz from power. There was no unanimity among neomexicanos on the Mexican Revolution. Some with close ties to Mexico were in favor of it and eager to hear proponents who came to the cities "río arriba" [up river] to give talks and get support; others opposed the ideology behind it and predicted worse times ahead for the Mexican populace. See *La Revista de Taos* (April 1911) for articles and poems by both of these authors on this topic.

23. *La Revista de Taos*, Apr. 26, 1918. The companion dialogue to this piece appeared on Aug. 23, 1918.

24. "The periodical essay did much in forming a taste that the novel, too, could cater for." Ian Watt, *The Rise of the Novel: Studies in Defoe, Richardson, and Fielding*, 31 and 51.

25. Census figures alone show that Anglo immigration (or those indicating "born in other parts of the U.S.") jumped drastically after the arrival of the railroad in New Mexico in 1879, going from approximately 10,000 in 1880 to 120,000 in 1910. Zeleny, "Relations Between the Spanish-Americans and the Anglo-Americans in New Mexico," 136.

26. Weber, *Spanish Frontier in North America*, 346.

27. Genaro Padilla, "Imprisoned Narrative? Or Lies, Secrets, and Silence in New Mexico Women's Autobiography," 52, 59, and passim.

Chapter 10

1. *La Bandera Americana*, Feb. 7, 1902.

2. On the formation of Arizona as a separate territory "controlled by Anglo businessmen who hoped to build railroads and develop the mineral resources of the area without interference from Santa Fe," see Chávez, *The Lost Land*, 56. Also, see Larson, *New Mexico's Quest for Statehood*, 87–89.

NOTES TO PAGES 184–187

3. Larson cites Twitchell as his authority for this information (250). Larson's discussion of the 1902 and 1906 initiatives can be found in chaps. 13 and 14 of *New Mexico's Quest for Statehood*.

4. For an overview of this subject, see Rafael Chabrán and Richard Chabrán, "The Spanish-Language and Latino Press of the United States: Newspapers and Periodicals."

5. Patricia Galloway, "The Archaeology of Ethnohistorical Narrative," 458.

6. In addition to the autobiographical memoirs of Rafael Chacón (see J.D. Meketa, *Legacy of Honor*), other examples include the memoirs of Santiago Valdez and the biography by Pedro Sánchez, both dealing with Padre Antonio José Martínez.

7. Juan Bruce-Novoa, "History as Content, History as Act: The Chicano Novel," 32. The issue of *Aztlán* in which this study appears contains an excellent series of articles dealing with the intersections of history and literature in Chicano writing.

8. See E. A. Mares, "The Wraggle-Taggle Outlaws: Vicente Silva and Billy the Kid as Seen in Two Nineteenth-century Hispanic Documents," 170.

9. The translator of Baca's *Vicente Silva and His Forty Bandits*, Lane Kaufmann, also comments on Baca's motives for writing as "a mixture of righteous morality and the zeal and pride of a local historian" (v).

10. Among the newspapers advertising or commenting on its progress were *El Sol de Mayo* (Las Vegas), *La Voz de Nuevo México* (Albuquerque), *El Independiente* (Las Vegas), and *La Flor del Valle* (Las Cruces). It seems that the project, sponsored by Lama and Escobar, tried to get off the ground earlier but failed financially. *El Sol de Mayo's* editorial of Feb. 10, 1894, attributes this to Eusebio Chacón's withdrawal from it. Apparently, Chacón intended to collaborate with Escobar, then backed off saying he wanted to write his own, more in-depth history of New Mexico. An open letter from Escobar and G. de la Lama to Chacón in *La Opinión Pública*, on Jan. 21, 1894, wishes him well, considering the magnitude of the job, and clarifies that they still intend to write "un pequeño ensayo histórico cuyo principal objeto es, ayudar en algo á la literatura nacional al mismo tiempo que proporcionar á la juventud Neo Mexicano una breve sinópsis de los acontecimientos culminantes de su historia, para que en éllos se enseñe á admirar las virtudes cívicas de sus antepasados" [a little historical essay whose principal objective is to contribute to the national literature and also to give neomexicano youth a brief synopsis of the outstanding events of their history so that they may learn through it to admire the civic virtues of their ancestors].

11. From *El Independiente*, Jan. 12, 1895: "Don José Escobar de Albuquerque desea anunciar a sus patrones y al público en general que ha suspendido sus publicaciones *La Voz de Nuevo México* y 'Nuevo México y sus Hombres Ilustres' mientras se traslada a Los Lunas, condado de Valencia. Promete allí resumirá las publicaciones dentro de poco con grandes mejoras para el beneficio de sus lectores." [Don José Escobar of Albuquerque wants to announce to his patrons and to the general public that he has suspended his publications, *La Voz de Nuevo México* and 'Nuevo México y sus Hombres Ilustres', while he moves to Los Lunas in Valencia County. He promises to resume their publication there soon with great improvements for the benefit of his readers.] In fact, it appears that Escobar headed north at the time, to Raton and Colorado, rather than south. His mobility as an editor was remarkable even at a time when frequent moves were not uncommon. His outspokenness may have had more to do with this than the economic precariousness of his trade.

12. Lomelí, "Eusebio Chacón," *Dictionary of Literary Biography*, 78. Lomelí notes that Benjamin Read mentions this publication of Chacón's in an earlier biographical sketch of him in *Historia ilustrada* (460). I have not personally seen the series.

13. Thoma was only a part-time resident of the territory, having lived earlier in Mexico and later moving to the Philippines, where he worked as a translator. In the late 1890s, before going abroad, Thoma was the proprietor of a dry-goods store, as evidenced by a liquidation sale advertised in *El Labrador* (Las Cruces, June 21, 1899) in anticipation of his imminent departure. Further details of his life have not been found.

14. Francisco de Thoma, "Introducción," *Historia popular de Nuevo México desde su descubrimiento hasta la actualidad*, 5–6.

15. Ibid., 180–81.

16. Russell Steele Saxton, "Ethnocentrism in the Historical Literature of New Mexico," 381. Saxton offers a detailed discussion of Thoma's book and his exaltation of the spiritual superiority of patriarchal Hispano-Catholicism and the nobility of the brave hidalgos who settled New Mexico. A few years later, on Sept. 8, 1900, *El Nuevo Mexicano* published a brief article extolling "Frank" de Thoma's book. A year later, on Sept. 7, 1901, *El Nuevo Mexicano* began running installments of the book. Why it took the paper so long to endorse and promote it is not clear.

17. His editorial of May 29, 1897, "Ayer y hoy: Algo sobre el pasado y el presente de Nuevo México," is reproduced in full in Chapter 5. Articles such as this one appeared in almost every issue of *El Nuevo Mundo* during 1897, until Escobar moved to Socorro to edit *El Combate*. Also worthy of note is the historical consciousness of José Segura of *El Boletín Popular*, who published in *El Nuevo Mexicano* a letter in his possession written by Diego de Vargas in October 1693 to the Spanish viceroy, Conde Galve; this was reported in *El Nuevo Mundo*, Nov. 27, 1897.

18. David J. Weber, "The Idea of the Spanish Borderlands," 4.

19. On this subject, see Saxton, "Ethnocentrism," chaps. 4 (on Bancroft) and 6 (on Lummis). Saxton documents the ethnocentrism in both authors' works with extensive examples from their writings on New Mexico. For Bancroft, or his designated writer of *History of Arizona and New Mexico* (1889), H. L. Oak, New Mexican Hispanic culture represented an impediment to progress and the solution was increased Anglo immigration. In Lummis's case, his characterization of the Hispanic population in *The Land of Poco Tiempo* is shaped more by a nostalgia for the romantic Spanish past than a thorough understanding of the neomexicano present.

20. Biographical information on Read is found among his own papers in the Benjamin M. Read Collection in the New Mexico State Records Center and Archives in Santa Fe, in an obituary in *El Nuevo Mexicano* (Sept. 22, 1927), and in "Necrology of Benjamin M. Read." Read was a Fellow of the New Mexico Historical Society (founded in 1859) and an officer of the Archaeological Society of New Mexico.

21. Gómez-Quiñones, *Roots of Chicano Politics*, 244. Also, see Craver, *Impact of Intimacy*, 6–7, 39.

22. "Necrology of Benjamin M. Read."

23. Benjamin M. Read, *Illustrated History of New Mexico*, 339.

24. *La Opinión Pública* (Albuquerque), Feb. 25, 1893.

25. Saxton, "Ethnocentrism," 410–11. Read would not have accepted characterization of the Protestants as a "menace." He did point out in a 1922 article that Protestants

had a history of bigotry in the United States, but he wrote this to counterbalance the persistence of the Black Legend against Catholics and not to condemn the Protestant faith. See Read, "Review of Bigotry in America."

26. In 1919 Benjamin Read published a "A Short History of Slavery in America" in the *Fortnightly Review* (St. Louis) which was reprinted as *A Short History of Slavery in New Mexico*.

27. "Lo hecho, hecho, seamos francos, seamos hombres," [What's done is done, let's be honest, let's be men].

28. From Sra. Read's obituary in *La Bandera Americana*, Aug. 19, 1904.

29. Read, "El castellano en los E. U."; quoted from a copy of the article in the Read Collection.

30. "Necrology of Benjamin M. Read."

31. See Peter Novick, *That Noble Dream: The "Objectivity Question" and the American Historical Profession*, 47–53. Novick points out that the German model of academic training, with its standardized techniques and pretensions to scientific objectivity, was greatly admired and had led by 1900 to more U.S. professionalization of the discipline; still, "much of the most distinguished historical work continued to be produced by those without Ph.D.'s or professorships" (49). The American Historical Association was founded in 1884; in New Mexico the first historical society was founded in 1859, then disbanded during the Civil War, and reconstituted in 1880. All its founding members appear to have been Anglos. See W. G. Ritch, *The New Mexico Blue Book* (1882).

32. In the Read Collection can be found, for example, the testimony of don Demetrio Pérez, in his own handwriting, of how life was in Santa Fe under the Mexican regime. Read explains that he asked the aged don Demetrio to write this for him while the latter was visiting him in Santa Fe in 1913. This account was later published by Read, with full credit to his informant, in the *New Mexico Historical Review* (January 1927). Another of Read's informants was Rafael Chacón of Trinidad, Colorado. Padilla, in *My History, Not Yours*, criticizes Read as one of the regional historians who treated Chacón as "a colorful character whose memories would supplement the legend of the West" (258). Padilla sees evidence of this in a photo of the aged soldier dressed in military regalia, which was included in Read's *Illustrated History* and later in Chacón's published memoirs; to Padilla the photograph "raises questions about the way Chacón was appropriated as a kind of specimen-object of the Old West by historians" (181). It appears that Padilla did not know about Read's motives or how he came by the photo: in the Read collection is a letter from Rafael Chacón, dated April 6, 1911, when he was seventy-eight, in which he refers specifically to the photo for the book, which he includes with the letter, saying: "El adjunto retrato se lo presento á Don Benjamin M. Read. Fue tomado con el uniforme de coronel de la guardia nacional de Colorado teniendo 70 años de edad" [I present the enclosed portrait to Don Benjamin M. Read. It was taken in the uniform of the Colorado National Guard when I was 70 years old].

33. Among his other works, Read compiled "A Digest of Documentos Inéditos de las Indias," which was his last published work according to his necrology in the *New Mexico Historical Review* but which I have not seen.

34. From "Necrology of Benjamin M. Read," 396.

35. To underwrite the cost of the *Illustrated History*, he sought contributions from wealthy citizens, both Hispano and Anglo. When Rafael Chacón's son Eusebio wrote

him (Apr. 5, 1911) that the price of the book was high for some interested readers, Read responded in a letter to don Rafael (Apr. 7, 1911) that it had been very expensive to produce (an average of four dollars per page), adding that, despite this, "para beneficio de la gente pobre haré una segunda edición (sin los bosquejos) menos costosa" [for the benefit of the poor I will do a less expensive second edition (without the biographies)]. A second edition did appear, from which an English translation was made under Read's direction by Eleuterio Baca (not to be confused with Manuel or Ezequiel).

36. Fray Angelico Chavez, *But Time and Change*, 33–34. There has been speculation that Santiago Valdez (who later changed his name) was the son of Padre Martínez, but Father Chavez argues that it was probably his brother's adulterous child.

37. The manuscript in the Read Collection, clearly dated 1867, appears to be a portion of the original version. A copy of the manuscript, transcribed by Larkin Read and dated 1877, is in the Ritch Collection at the Huntington Library; I have seen a microfilm of this copy and Benjamin Read's translation, which is based on his brother's copy (page numbers correlating with the Spanish copy are in the margin of the translation). Benjamin's signature does not appear on the translation as far as I can tell, but is in his handwriting, not Larkin's. To date, I have not been able to make a detailed comparison with the manuscript in the Read Collection. Father Angelico Chavez cites the Huntington Library copy as his source and gives further details of the papers there in his bibliography to *But Time and Change* (173). I do not believe he is correct in stating that the translation is by Larkin Read or that the original biography was written in 1877 by Valdez. Why Read never published his translation is not clear, considering how often he published other materials at his own expense; he may have been saving it to use in his later historical writings and then neglected it.

38. The Beveridge report stated the illiteracy rate in New Mexico as 33.2 percent, but the report from New Mexico Governor Otero to the secretary of the interior in 1902 listed the figure as 18 percent (Larson, *New Mexico's Quest for Statehood*, 215). It should be noted that Read and other neomexicanos were not alone in pointing out the flaws in the Beveridge report; Anglo editors and politicians were also outraged by its findings, although they could not have felt the insult as personally as the Hispanic population.

39. *El Nuevo Mexicano*, Mar. 13, 1909.

40. It was published in Santa Fe by Compañía Impresora del Nuevo Mexicano, a printing enterprise owned by the publishers of the Spanish and English newspapers of the same name. Read must have subsidized the publication partly out of advance orders and partly out of his own pocket, which would be the case in his future publications as well.

41. Benjamin Read, Guerra *México-Americana*, 4.

42. Twitchell, *The History of the Military Occupation. . .* (1909).

43. Read, *Guerra México-Americana*, 212–13.

44. Ibid, 6. Among the Read Collection papers in the state archives is the typescript of an article by Eusebio Chacón, dated August 24, 1910, praising Read for writing this book with objectivity and in "the unimpassioned style of true history," adding that "it comes from the first native New Mexican who has taken the trouble and time to delve into that most unpleasant subject, the period of disaster when our forefathers received such terrible chastisement from American arms." Chacón also praises Read for his bal-

anced treatment of General Armijo's role in the capitulation to American troops and for "what I consider the most correct and detailed biography of Father Martinez . . . this great man."

45. Ibid., 9.

46. Ibid., 188.

47. Doña Ignacia remarried and had three more sons and a daughter by her second husband, Mateo Ortiz, before her death in Santa Fe in 1878.

48. In his preface, Read pointedly disassociated himself from the type of work done by Francisco de Thoma, the only other neomexicano to publish a history of New Mexico, noting that it was a mere copy of portions of Bancroft's work, which Thoma himself had acknowledged.

49. Read, *Illustrated History*, 5.

50. Ibid., 6.

51. Ibid., 14. I quote from the translation by Eleuterio Baca, commissioned and overseen by Read.

52. Roberto González Echevarría, *The Voice of the Masters*, 13.

53. Cited by Hayden White, *Tropics of Discourse: Essays in Cultural Criticism*, 104.

54. Ibid., 129.

55. In a public speech a few days before the constitution was voted upon by the citizens of New Mexico, Read spoke these words, reproduced in *El Nuevo Mexicano* of Jan. 14, 1911: "diré con todo el énfasis de que soy capaz que si hay un sólo ciudadano en todo el condado de Santa Fé, que, conociendo las ventajas que traerá el estado, esté opuesto á la constitucion y á sabiendas votare en contra de ella, merece que lo suban en un tren que vaya para Las Vegas y lo encierren en el asilo de locos" [I will say with all the emphasis I possess that if there is a single citizen in all of Santa Fe County who, knowing the benefits that statehood will bring, is opposed to the constitution and knowingly votes against it, he deserves to be put on a train to Las Vegas and locked up in the insane asylum].

56. For a detailed discussion of these constitutional safeguards, see Gómez-Quiñones, *Roots of Chicano Politics*, 326–28. This author points out that the term *Spanish Americans* rather than *Mexicans* was used in stating the ethnic identity of neomexicanos in the state constitution (327), with the implication that the latter would have been the more appropriate term. Considering the roots of New Mexican history and the preferred terms of self-identification expressed in the neomexicano press, the choice of *Spanish American* can be justified without attributing it to ethnic capitulation.

57. See Read, *History of Education in New Mexico* (Santa Fe, 1911).

58. "B. M. Read Tells Reasons Why He Thinks Teachers in Spanish-Speaking Districts Ought to Know Spanish," [published in English and Spanish editions] in Santa Fe *New Mexican*, Mar. 1, 1917.

59. Read, "Lo hecho, hecho, seamos francos, seamos hombres" [What's done is done, let's be frank and be men], *Revista de Taos*, Aug. 8, 1922; also published in other newspapers, as were many of his articles, including *El Nuevo Mexicano*, Aug. 31, 1922, and *El Nuevo Estado* (Tierra Amarilla), Aug. 28, 1922.

60. *El Palacio*, a journal of the Archaeological Society of New Mexico, reported that Read's Cortés manuscript had been accepted for publication. Vol. 14, no. 2 (1913): 12.

I have not found further documentation explaining what might have happened to cancel this agreement.

61. This quote is from an article by Read entitled "A Study of New Mexican Folklore." Did Read perceive a superficial resemblance between himself as "lengua" [interpreter] and the Mexican woman who translated for Cortés? Did he feel toward the end of his life, frustrated by his inability to publish more widely, that his intercultural mediation was not fully appreciated?

62. The governor's introduction and the finished nature of the manuscript copy itself indicate that this project too was slated for proximate publication, yet no information to this effect has come to my attention. Read clearly intended this volume for an Hispanic audience; it was probably conceived as a sequel to his earlier book on the Mexican American War, which was also in Spanish.

63. From the "Preface" to his manuscript on Cortés, which reads more fully: "I felt, and feel, that my humble pen was not equal to the occasion, specially when I considered that not being a novelist it was impossible for me to undertake, even if I desired to, the art of 'roving too freely over the field of imagination', which is the artifice employed by many authors who give the world fiction for facts. Thus is it that the reader will be given true facts in the simplest form . . . "

64. Read, *History of Education in New Mexico*, 6–7. I cannot agree with Russell Saxton's interpretation, in "Ethnocentrism," that Read struck a "deadly bargain accepting Angloamerican temporal superiority in exchange for the right to proclaim the purity of Catholic intention" (414). An appreciation of the U.S. system of government does not necessarily include an acceptance of Protestant values. The democratic political process based on the federal constitution is not synonymous with any religion. This explains how Read could espouse the U.S. government while repudiating some of its actions in the past.

65. With regard to contemporary Mexico, Read represented the conservative viewpoint that prevailed in the United States at the time. He did not support the anti-Díaz movement in Mexico, nor did he have much hope for the future when Díaz went into exile in 1911. He believed that Mexico lacked a tradition of political stability and responsible self-government and he anticipated the fratricidal bloodshed that ensued. "El broche" [The Clasp], *La Revista de Taos*, June 2, 1911.

66. "El estado y los hijos de Nuevo México" [The state and the sons of New Mexico], *La Revista de Taos*, Aug. 25, 1911.

Chapter 11

1. My information on Latinos in New Mexico is taken from Rodney E. Hero, *Latinos and the U. S. Political System: Two-Tiered Pluralism* (1992), chap. 6 ("Latinos and State Politics"), 99–115. I have also consulted Victoria Van Son, *CQ's State Fact Finder* (1993), and Kathleen O. Morgan, Scott Morgan, and Neal Quitno, eds., *State Rankings 1992: A Statistical View of the Fifty United States* (1992).

2. Hero, *Latinos and the U.S. Political System*, 101. Although the qualifier "Other Spanish" is too ambiguous to be sure what was understood by each respondent who chose it, New Mexico remains unique in its continued preference for identifying with

Spanish roots, and it is an indication of the traditionalist bent of the state's Hispanic population.

3. Stuart Hall, "Cultural Identity and Diaspora," 235.

4. Henry Giroux, "Resisting Difference: Cultural Studies and the Discourse of Critical Pedagogy," 204.

5. I take this expression from bell hooks's courageous book *Talking Back: Thinking Feminist, Thinking Black* (1989).

6. Giroux, "Resisting Difference," 205.

7. From a taped lecture on neomexicano literary and cultural history given at the University of New Mexico in 1990. I am grateful to the UNM Southwest Research Collection for furnishing me with a copy of the tape and to Francisco Lomelí for his insights in an area of research where we have many parallel interests.

8. Read, *Illustrated History*, 368.

Bibliography

Newspapers

In the following list, I have indicated only the portions of the newspapers that I have read. Gaps in holdings within these years are not noted. For complete information on all New Mexico newspaper titles, their years of publication, and location of holdings, see the *New Mexico Newspaper Project* (March 1994, ongoing); Pearce S. Grove, *New Mexico Newspapers*; and Porter A. Stratton, *The Territorial Press of New Mexico, 1834–1912*. The reader should be aware that the first of these is the most up-to-date bibliographic source, but other information may be found regarding newspaper editors and political affiliations in the listings of the other texts.

ALBUQUERQUE:
La Bandera Americana, 1895–1896, 1901–1908
El Combate, 1892
Daily Citizen, 1891
El Defensor del Pueblo, 1891–1892
La Estrella Mexicana, 1890
El Indito, 1903?
El Mensajero, 1911
La Nueva Estrella, 1910–1911
El Nuevo Mundo, 1897–1901
El Pueblo, 1900
La Opinión Pública, 1892–1894, 1906–1907
La Revista de Albuquerque, 1881
La Unión de Albuquerque, 1893
La Voz de Nuevo México, 1894
The News, 1886

BERNALILLO:
El Espejo, 1879

CLAYTON:
La Unión del Pueblo, 1913

LAS CRUCES:
El Defensor del Pueblo, 1891?, 1892
El Labrador, 1896–1899
El Eco del Rio Grande, 1876
El Eco del Siglo, 1892
El Eco del Valle, 1905–1916
La Empresa, 1896–1897
La Flor del Valle, 1894–
El Fronterizo, 1871
El Observador Fronterizo, 1888
El Promotor Escolar, 1891–1892
El Tiempo, 1882–1899
La Verdad, 1890, 1898

LAS VEGAS:
La Cachiporra, 1888–1890
El Clarín Mexicano, 1890
Daily Optic, 1894
El Hispano Americano, 1892
El Independiente, 1894–1897, 1913
Revista Católica, 1875–1900
El Sol de Mayo, 1891–1894
La Voz del Pueblo, 1890–1924

MALDONADO:
La Estrella, 1897

MORA:
La Crónica de Mora, 1889
La Gaceta de Mora, 1890
El Eco de Mora, 1890
El Hispano Americano, 1905–1908
El Mensajero, 1910–1912

RATON:
El Amigo del Pueblo, 1896
La Unión, 1898

SAN ACACIA:
El Comercio, 1901

SAN MARCIAL:
La Libertad, 1896

SANTA FE:
La Aurora, 1884
El Boletín Popular, 1888–1904
El Clarín Mexicano, 1873
El Gato, 1894

El Guía de Santa Fe, 1886
The New Mexican [various]
El Nuevo Mexicano, 1850, 1863, 1881,
    1890–1927
El Payo de Nuevo México, 1845
El Registro de Nuevo México, 1916
Santa Fe Daily Democrat, 1880
La Verdad, 1844–1845
La Voz del Pueblo, 1889–1890

SAN LORENZO:
La Crónica del Rio Colorado, 1882–1883

SOCORRO:
El Combate, 1898
La Estrella de Nuevo México, 1896–1897
La Golondrina, 1898
El Hispano Americano, 1891–1892

SPRINGER:
El Estandarte de Springer, 1891

TAOS:
El Heraldo de Taos, 1886–1888
El Monitor, 1890–1891
La Revista de Taos, 1902–1917

TIERRA AMARILLA:
El Nuevo Estado, 1911–1912

TRINIDAD, COLO.:
El Progreso, 1899

WAGON MOUND:
El Combate, 1902–1905, 1911

Manuscript Collections

Benjamin M. Read Collection. State Records Center and Archives, Santa Fe, N.M.
L. Bradford Prince Papers. State Records Center and Archives, Santa Fe, N.M.
Mauro Montoya Collection. History Library, Palace of the Governors, Santa Fe, N.M.
Newspaper and Rare Book Collection. Special Collections Division, University of
    New Mexico Library, Albuquerque, N.M.
Newspaper Collection. History Library, Palace of the Governors, Santa Fe, N.M.
William G. Ritch Collection. Huntington Library, Pasadena, Calif.
Woodward Collection. State Records Center and Archives, Santa Fe, N.M.
Works Progress Administration Writers' Files. History Library, Palace of the Gover-
    nors, Santa Fe, N.M.

Books, Articles and Unpublished Monographs

Adams, Eleanor B., and France V. Scholes. "Books in New Mexico, 1598–1680." *New Mexico Historical Review* 17 (1943): 226–70.

Almada, Francisco R. *La imprenta y el periodismo en Chihuahua*. México, D.F.: Publicación del Gobierno del Estado, 1943.

Almaguer, Tomás. "Ideological Distortions in Recent Chicano Historiography: The Internal Model and Chicano Historical Interpretation." *Aztlán* 18, no. 1 (1987): 7–28.

Anaya, Rudolfo A. "Mythical Dimensions/ Political Reality." In *Open Spaces, City Places: Contemporary Writers on the Changing Southwest*, ed. Judy Nolte Temple, 25–30. Tucson and London: University of Arizona Press, 1994.

Anaya, Rudolfo, and Francisco Lomelí, eds. *Aztlán: Essays on the Chicano Homeland*. Albuquerque: University of New Mexico Press, 1991.

Anzaldúa, Gloria. *Borderlands/La Frontera: The New Mestiza*. San Francisco: Aunt Lute Books, 1987.

Arellano, Anselmo F. *Los pobladores nuevo mexicanos y su poesía, 1889–1950*. Albuquerque, N.M.: Pajarito Publications, 1976.

Argudín, Yolanda. *Historia del periodismo en Mexico: desde el Virreinato hasta nuestros días*. México: Panorama Editorial, 1987.

Armitage, Shelley. "New Mexico's Literary Heritage." *El Palacio* 90, no. 2 (1984): 20–29.

Armitage, Susan, and Elizabeth Jameson, eds. *The Women's West*. Norman: University of Oklahoma Press, 1987.

Arteaga, Alfred. "An Other Tongue." In *An Other Tongue: Nation and Ethnicity in the Linguistic Borderlands*, ed. Arteaga, 9–33. Durham, N.C., and London: Duke University Press, 1994.

Ashley, Perry J., ed. *American Newspaper Journalists, 1873–1900. Dictionary of Literary Biography*, vol. 23. Detroit: Gale Research, 1983.

Baca, Carlos C. de. *Vicente Silva: New Mexico's Vice King of the Nineties*. 1938. Reprinted as *Vicente Silva: The Terror of Las Vegas*. Española, N.M., 1968.

Baca, Manuel C. de. *Vicente Silva and his Forty Bandits*, trans. Lane Kauffmann. Washington, D.C.: Edward McLean, 1947.

———. *Historia de Vicente Silva y sus cuarenta bandidos, sus crimenes y retribuciones*. Las Vegas, N.M.: Imprenta La Voz del Pueblo, 1896.

Bakhtin, Mikhail. "Discourse in the Novel." In *The Dialogic Imagination: Four Essays*, trans. Caryl Emerson and Michael Holquist, 259–422. Austin: University of Texas Press, 1981.

Bancroft, Hubert Howe. *History of Arizona and New Mexico, 1530–1888*. San Francisco: The History Company, 1889.

Beck, Warren A. *New Mexico: A History of Four Centuries*. Norman: University of Oklahoma Press, 1962.

Bécquer, Gustavo Adolfo. *Romantic Legends of Spain*, trans. C. F. Bates and K. L. Bates. New York: Thomas Y. Crowell and Co., 1909.

Benedict, Brother Alphonsus, ed. *A Hundred Years of Service: St. Michael's High School Centennial, 1859–1959*. Santa Fe, New Mexico, 1959.

Berge, Dennis E. "Manifest Destiny and the Historians." In *Historians and the American West*, ed. Michael P. Malone, 76–95. Lincoln and London: University of Nebraska Press.

Blea, Irene I. *La Chicana and the Intersection of Race, Class, and Gender*. New York, Westport, Conn., and London: Praeger Publishers, 1992.

Brack, Gene M. "Mexican Opinion, American Racism and the War of 1846." *Western Historical Quarterly* (April 1970): 161–74.

Brown, Lorin W., with Charles L. Briggs and Marta Weigle. *Hispano Folklife of New Mexico: The Lorin W. Brown Federal Writers' Project Manuscripts*. Albuquerque: University of New Mexico Press, 1978.

Bruce-Novoa, Juan. "Dialogical Strategies, Monological Goals: Chicano Literature." In *An Other Tongue: Nation and Ethnicity in the Linguistic Borderlands*, ed. Alfred Arteaga, 225–45. Durham, N.C., and London: Duke University Press, 1994.

———. "History as Content, History as Act: The Chicano Novel." *Aztlán* 18, no. 1 (1987): 29–42.

———. "*La Prensa* and the Chicano Community." *Americas Review* 17, no. 3–4 (Fall-Winter 1989): 150–59.

———. *Retrospace: Collected Essays on Chicano Literature*. Houston, Tex.: Arte Público Press, 1990.

Campa, Arthur L. *Spanish Folk-Poetry in New Mexico*. Albuquerque: University of New Mexico Press, 1946.

———. "The Spanish Folksong in the Southwest." *The University of New Mexico Bulletin* 4, no. 1 (Nov. 15, 1933): 5–67.

Castellanos, Rosario. *Mujer que sabe latín . . .* México, D.F.: SepSetentas, 1973.

Chabrán, Rafael, and Richard Chabrán. "The Spanish-Language and Latino Press of the United States: Newspapers and Periodicals." In *Handbook of Hispanic Cultures in the United States: Literature and Art*, ed. Francisco Lomelí, 360–83. Houston, Tex.: Arte Público Press, 1993.

Chacón, Eusebio. *El hijo de la tempestad/Tras la tormenta la calma*. Santa Fe, N.M.: Tipografía El Boletín Popular, 1892.

Chacón, Felipe Maximilano. *Obras de Felipe Maximiliano Chacón, "El cantor neomexicano": Poesía y prosa*. Albuquerque, N.M.: Felipe M. Chacón, 1924.

———. *Short Stories*, trans. Julián Josué Vigil. Las Vegas, N.M.: Editorial Telaraña, 1980.

Chavez, Fray Angelico. *But Time and Change: The Story of Padre Martínez of Taos, 1793–1867*. Santa Fe, N.M.: Sunstone Press, 1981.

———. *Chávez: A Distinctive American Clan of New Mexico*. Santa Fe, N.M.: William Gannon, 1989.

———. *Origins of New Mexico Families in the Spanish Colonial Period*. Santa Fe, N.M.: William Gannon, 1975.

———. *Our Lady of the Conquest*. Santa Fe, N.M.: Historical Society of New Mexico, 1948.

Chávez, John R. *The Lost Land: The Chicano Image of the Southwest*. Albuquerque: University of New Mexico Press, 1984.

Christian, Jane McNab, and Chester C. Christian, Jr. "Spanish Language and Culture in the Southwest." In *Language Loyalty in the United States: The Maintenance and Perpetuation of Non-English Mother Tongues by American Ethnic and Religious Groups*, ed. Joshua Fishman, 280–317. The Hague: Mouton and Company, 1966.

Coan, Charles F. *A History of New Mexico*, 3 vols. Chicago and New York: American Historical Society, 1925.

Cobos, Rubén. *A Dictionary of New Mexico and Southern Colorado Spanish*. Santa Fe: Museum of New Mexico Press, 1983.

Compilation of the School Laws of the Territory of New Mexico. Santa Fe, N.M.: El Boletín Popular Printing Company, 1903.

Condit, Dr. Lester D.. "Early Printing in New Mexico." *Inventory of American Imprints* 2 [Checklist of New Mexico Imprints and Publications, 1784–1876]: v–xiii.

Craver, Rebecca McDowell. *The Impact of Intimacy: Mexican-Anglo Intermarriage in New Mexico, 1821–1846*. El Paso: Texas Western Press, 1982.

Davis, W. W. H. *El Gringo, or New Mexico and Her People*. New York: Harper and Brothers, 1857.

Defouri, James H. *Los mártires de New México*. Las Vegas, N.M.: Revista Católica Printing Office, 1893.

De León, Arnoldo. *They Called Them Greasers: Anglo Attitudes toward Mexicans in Texas, 1821–1900*. Austin: University of Texas Press, 1983.

Del Castillo, Adelaida R., ed. *Between Borders: Essays on Mexicana/Chicana History*. Encino, Calif.: Floricanto Press, 1990.

Deutsch, Sarah. "Landscape of Enclaves: Race Relations in the West, 1865–1900." In *Under an Open Sky: Rethinking America's Western Past*, ed. William Cronon, George Miles, and Jay Gitlin, 110–31. New York and London: W. W. Norton and Company, 1992.

———. *No Separate Refuge: Culture, Class, and Gender on an Anglo-Hispanic Frontier in the American Southwest, 1880–1940*. New York and Oxford: Oxford University Press, 1987.

Dicken-Garcia, Hazel. *Journalistic Standards in Nineteenth-Century America*. Madison: University of Wisconsin Press, 1989.

Dobie, J. Frank. *Guide to Life and Literature of the Southwest*. Austin: University of Texas Press, 1943.

DuBois, Ellen Carol, and Vicki L. Ruiz, eds. *Unequal Sisters: A Multicultural Reader in U.S. Women's History*. New York and London: Routledge, 1990.

Dysart, Jane. "Mexican Women in San Antonio, 1830–1860: The Assimilation Process." *Western Historical Quarterly* 7 (October 1976): 365–75.

Ellis, Richard N., ed. *New Mexico Past and Present, A Historical Reader*. Albuquerque: University of New Mexico Press, 1971.

Escandon, Carmen Ramos. "Alternative Sources to Women's History: Literature." In *Between Borders: Essays on Mexicana/Chicana History*, ed. Adelaida R. Del Castillo, 201–12. Encino, Calif.: Floricanto Press, 1990.

Espinosa, Aurelio M. "Spanish Folk-Lore in New Mexico." *New Mexico Historical Review* 1, no. 2 (April 1926): 135–55.

————. *Romancero de Nuevo Méjico*. Madrid: Consejo Superior de Investigaciones Científicas, 1953.

————. *The Spanish Language in New Mexico and Southern Colorado*. Santa Fe: Historical Society of New Mexico (Publication 16), 1911.

Fernández, José Emilio. *Cuarenta años de legislador o biografía del Senador Casimiro Barela*, with introduction by Benjamin M. Read. Trinidad, Colo., 1911; reprint, New York: Arno Press, 1976.

Fincher, E. B. "Spanish-Americans as a Political Factor in New Mexico, 1912–1950." Ph.D. diss., New York University, 1950.

Fishman, Joshua A. *Language Loyalty in the United States: The Maintenance and Perpetuation of Non-English Mother Tongues by American Ethnic and Religious Groups*. The Hague: Mouton and Co., 1966.

Franco, Jean. *Plotting Women: Gender and Representation in Mexico*. New York: Columbia University Press, 1989.

Galloway, Patricia, "The Archaeology of Ethnohistorical Narrative." In *Columbian Consequences*, ed. David Hurst Thomas, 453–69. Washington, D.C.; Smithsonian Institution Press, 1991.

García, Mario T. *Desert Immigrants: The Mexicans of El Paso, 1880–1920*. New Haven, Conn.: Yale University Press, 1981.

García Rivas, H. *Historia de la literatura mexicana*, vol. 2. México, D.F.: Textos Universitarios, 1949.

Garry, Patrick M. *Scrambling for Protection: The New Media and the First Amendment*. Pittsburgh and London: University of Pittsburgh Press, 1994.

Geertz, Clifford. *The Interpretation of Cultures*. New York: Basic Books, 1973.

Gicovate, Bernardo. *Conceptos fundamentales de literatura comparada*. San Juan, Puerto Rico: Ediciones Asomante, 1962.

Giroux, Henry A. "Resisting Difference: Cultural Studies and the Discourse of Critical Pedagogy." In *Cultural Studies*, ed. Lawrence Grossberg, Cary Nelson and Paula A. Treichler, 199–212. New York and London, 1992.

Gómez-Quiñones, Juan. *Roots of Chicano Politics, 1600–1940*. Albuquerque: University of New Mexico Press, 1994.

González, Deena J. "The Widowed Women of Santa Fe: Assessments on the Lives of an Unmarried Population, 1850–1880." In *Unequal Sisters: A Multicultural Reader in U.S. Women's History*, ed. Ellen Carol DuBois and Vicki L. Ruiz, 34–50. New York and London: Routledge, 1990.

Gonzáles-Berry, Erlinda. "Introduction" and "Vicente Bernal and Felipe M. Chacón: Bridging Two Cultures." In *Pasó por Aquí: Critical Essays on the New Mexican Literary Tradition, 1542–1988*, ed. Gonzáles-Berry, 1–11 and 185–98. Albuquerque: University of New Mexico Press, 1989.

González Echevarría, Roberto. *The Voice of the Masters: Writing and Authority in Modern Latin American Literature*. Austin: University of Texas Press, 1985.

Greenblatt, Stephen. *Marvelous Possessions: The Wonder of the New World*. Chicago: University of Chicago Press, 1991.

Griswold del Castillo, Richard. *La Familia: Chicano Families in the Urban Southwest, 1848 to the Present*. Notre Dame, Ind.: University of Notre Dame Press, 1984.

————. "Patriarchy and the Status of Women in the Late Nineteenth-Century Southwest." In *The Mexican and Mexican American Experience in the 19th Century*, ed. Jaime E. Rodríguez O., 85–99. Tempe, Ariz.: Bilingual Press/ Editorial Bilingue, 1989.

————. "The Mexican Revolution and the Spanish-Language Press in the Borderlands." *Journalism History* 4, no. 2 (Summer 1977): 42–47.

Grove, Pearce S., Becky J. Barnett, and Sandra J. Hansen. *New Mexico Newspapers: A Comprehensive Guide to Bibliographical Entries and Locations.* Albuquerque: University of New Mexico Press, 1975.

Gullón, Ricardo. *Direcciones del modernismo.* Madrid: Gredos, 1963.

Gutiérrez, Félix. "Spanish-Language Media in America: Background Resources, History." *Journalism History* 4, no. 2 (Summer 1977): 41–43, 65–68.

Gutiérrez, Ramon, and Genaro Padilla, eds. *Recovering the U.S. Hispanic Literary Heritage.* Houston, Tex.: Arte Público Press, 1993.

Hall, Stuart. "Cultural Identity and Diaspora." In *Identity: Community, Culture, Difference*, ed. Jonathan Rutherford, 222–37. London: Lawrence and Wishart, 1990.

Hammond, George P., and Agapito Rey, "Oñate and the Colonization of New Mexico." In *New Mexico Past and Present, A Historical Perspective*, ed. Richard N. Ellis, 17–29. Albuquerque: University of New Mexico Press, 1971.

Hernández, Guillermo E. *Chicano Satire: A Study in Literary Culture.* Austin: University of Texas Press, 1991.

Henríquez-Ureña, Max. *Breve historia del modernismo*, 2nd. ed. Mexico, D.F.: Fondo de Cultura Económica, 1962.

Hero, Rodney E. *Latinos and the U.S. Political System: Two-Tiered Pluralism.* Philadelphia, Pa.: Temple University Press, 1992.

Herrera-Sobek, María. *The Mexican Corrido: A Feminist Analysis.* 1990; reprint, Bloomington: Indiana University Press, 1993.

Hertzog, Peter. *A Directory of New Mexico Desperados.* Santa Fe, N.M.: Press of the Territorian, 1965.

Hodgson, Ila D., and Elloyse M. Garthwaite. "New Mexico's Early Elections: Statehood to New Deal, 1912–1932." *New Mexico Historical Review* 70, no. 1 (January 1995): 29–46.

Hooks, Bell. *Talking Back: Thinking Feminist, Thinking Black.* Boston: South End Press, 1989.

Illustrated History of New Mexico. [No author or editor identified.] Chicago: The Lewis Publishing Company, 1895.

Jiménez Rueda, J. *Letras mexicanas en el siglo XIX.* México, D.F.: Fondo de Cultura Económica, 1944.

Kanellos, Nicolás. "A Socio-Historic Study of Hispanic Newspapers in the United States." In *Recovering the U.S. Hispanic Literary Heritage*, ed. Ramón Gutiérrez and Genaro Padilla, 107–28. Houston, Tex.: Arte Público Press, 1993.

Kanellos, Nicolás, and Claudio Esteva-Fabregat, eds. *Handbook of Hispanic Cultures in the United States*, 4 vols. Houston, Tex.: Arte Público Press, 1994.

Karolevitz, Robert F. *Newspapering in the Old West.* Seattle, Wash.: 1965.

King, Anthony D., ed. *Culture, Globalization and The World System: Contemporary Conditions for the Representation of Identity.* Binghampton, N.Y.: State University of New York, 1991.

Lamar, Howard R. *The Far Southwest, 1846–1912: A Territorial History.* New Haven, Conn.: Yale University Press, 1966.

Lamb, Ruth. *Mexican-Americans, Sons of the Southwest.* Claremont, Calif.: Ocelot Press, 1970.

Landy, Marcia. "Cultural Politics and Common Sense." *Critical Studies* 3, no. 1 (1991) [Special issue, "Cultural Studies: Crossing Boundaries"]: 105–34.

Lao, Ana, and Carmen Ramos, eds. *Mujeres y revolución, 1900–1917.* México, D.F.: Instituto Nacional de Estudios Históricos de la Revolución Mexicana, 1993.

Larson, Robert W. *New Mexico's Quest for Statehood, 1846–1912.* Albuquerque: University of New Mexico Press, 1968.

———. *Populism in the Mountain West.* Albuquerque: University of New Mexico Press, 1986.

———. "Territorial Politics and Cultural Impact." *New Mexico Historical Review* 60, no. 3 (1985): 249–69.

Lea, Aurora Lucero-White. *Literary Folklore of the Hispanic Southwest.* San Antonio, Tex.: Naylor Company, 1953.

Leal, Luis. *Aztlán y México: Perfiles literarios e históricos.* Binghamton, N.Y.: Bilingual Press/Editorial Bilingue, 1985.

———. "The First American Epic: Villagrá's History of New Mexico." In *Pasó por Aquí: Critical Essays on the New Mexican Literary Tradition, 1542–1988,* ed. Erlinda Gonzáles-Berry, 47–62. Albuquerque: University of New Mexico Press, 1989.

———. "Mexican American Literature: A Historical Perspective." In *Modern Chicano Writers: A Collection of Critical Essays,* ed. Joseph Sommers and Tomás Ybarra-Frausto, 18–30. Englewood Cliffs, N.J.: Prentice-Hall, 1979.

———. "Truth-Telling Tongues: Early Chicano Poetry." In *Recovering the U.S. Hispanic Literary Heritage,* ed. Ramon Gutiérrez and Genaro Padilla, 91–105. Houston, Tex.: Arte Público Press, 1993.

———. "The Spanish-Language Press: Function and Use." *Americas Review* 17, no. 3–4 (Fall-Winter 1989): 157–62.

Leary, D. T. "Race and Regeneration." In *The Mexican Americans: An Awakening Minority,* ed. Manuel P. Servín, Beverly Hills, Calif.: Glencoe Press, 1970.

Lecompte, Janet. "The Independent Women of Hispanic New Mexico, 1821–1846." *The Western Historical Quarterly* 12 (January 1981): 17–36.

Limerick, Patricia Nelson. *The Legacy of Conquest: The Unbroken Past of the American West.* New York: W. W. Norton and Company, 1987.

———. "Making the Most of Words: Verbal Activity and Western America." In *Under an Open Sky: Rethinking America's Western Past,* ed. William Cronon, George Miles, and Jay Gitlin, 167–84. New York: W. W. Norton and Company, 1992.

Limón, José E. "Stereotyping and Chicano Resistance: An Historical Dimension." *Aztlán* 4, no. 2 (1974): 257–69.

Lomas, Clara. "The Articulation of Gender in the Mexican Borderlands, 1900–1915."

In *Recovering the U.S. Hispanic Literary Heritage*, ed. Ramón Gutiérrez and Genaro Padilla, 293–308. Houston, Tex.: Arte Público Press, 1993.

Lomelí, Francisco A. "A Literary Portrait of Hispanic New Mexico: Dialectics of Perception." In *Pasó por Aquí: Critical Essays on the New Mexican Literary Tradition, 1542–1988*, ed. Erlinda Gonzáles-Berry, 131–48. Albuquerque: University of New Mexico Press, 1989.

———. "Eusebio Chacón." In *Chicano Writers (First Series). Dictionary of Literary Biography*, ed. Francisco A. Lomelí and Carl R. Shipley, 82:78–82. Detroit: Gale Research, 1989.

———. "Eusebio Chacón: An Early Pioneer of the New Mexican Novel." In *Pasó por Aquí: Critical Essays on the New Mexican Literary Tradition, 1542–1988*, ed. Erlinda Gonzáles-Berry, 149–66. Albuquerque: University of New Mexico Press, 1989.

Lomelí, Francesco, ed. *Handbook of Hispanic Cultures in the United States: Literature and Art*. Houston, Tex.: Arte Público Press, 1993.

Lummis, Charles F. *The Land of Poco Tiempo*. New York: Charles Scribner's Sons, 1893.

Major, Mabel, and T. M. Pearce. *Southwest Heritage: A Literary History with Bibliography*. Albuquerque: University of New Mexico, 1972.

Mares, E. A. "The Wraggle-Taggle Outlaws: Vicente Silva and Billy the Kid as Seen in Two Nineteenth-Century Hispanic Documents." In *Pasó por Aquí: Critical Essays on the New Mexican Literary Tradition, 1542–1988*, ed. Erlinda Gonzáles-Berry, 167–82. Albuquerque: University of New Mexico Press, 1989.

McMurtrie, D. C. "The History of Early Printing in New Mexico, with Bibliography of Known Issues, 1834–1860." *New Mexico Historical Review* 4 (October 1929): 372–410.

———. "Some Supplementary New Mexican Imprints, 1850–1860." *New Mexico Historical Review* 7 (April 1932): 165–75.

McWilliams, Carey. *North from Mexico: The Spanish-Speaking People of the United States* (1948). New York: Greenwood Press, 1968.

Medeiros, Francine. "*La Opinión*: A Mexican Exile Newspaper, A Content Analysis of Its First Years, 1926–1929." *Aztlán* 11, no. 1 (1980): 65–87.

Meketa, Jacqueline Dorgan, ed. *Legacy of Honor: The Life of Rafael Chacón, A Nineteenth-Century New Mexican*. Albuquerque: University of New Mexico Press, 1986.

Mendoza, Vicente. *El romance español y el corrido mexicano*. México, D.F.: Ediciones de la Universidad Nacional Autónoma, 1939.

Meyer, Doris. "Anonymous Poetry in Spanish-Language New Mexico Newspapers (1880–1900)." *Bilingual Review/La Revista Bilingue* (September-December 1975): 259–75.

———. "Banditry and Poetry: The Verses of Two Outlaws of Old Las Vegas." *New Mexico Historical Review* 50, no. 4 (October 1975): 277–90.

———. "Early Mexican-American Responses to Negative Stereotyping." *New Mexico Historical Review* 53, no. 1 (January 1978): 75–91.

———. "Felipe Maximiliano Chacón: A Forgotten Mexican-American Author." *New*

Scholar 6 (1977): 111–26. Reprinted in *New Directions in Chicano Scholarship*, ed. R. Romo and R. Paredes. San Diego: Center for Chicano Studies, University of California, 1984.

———. "The Language Issue in New Mexico, 1880–1900: Mexican-American Resistance against Cultural Erosion." *Bilingual Review/La Revista Bilingue* (January-August 1977): 99–106.

———. "The Poetry of José Escobar: Mexican Emigré in New Mexico." *Hispania* 61, no. 1 (March 1978): 24–34.

Meyer, Michael C., and William L. Sherman. *The Course of Mexican History*, 5th ed. New York: Oxford University Press, 1995.

Miller, Darlis A. "Cross-Cultural Marriages in the Southwest: The New Mexico Experience, 1846–1900." *New Mexico Historical Review* 57, no. 4 (October 1982): 335–59.

Monroy, Douglas. "'They Didn't Call Them *Padre* for Nothing': Patriarchy in Hispanic California." In *Between Borders: Essays on Mexicana/Chicana History*, ed. Adelaida R. Del Castillo, 433–45. Encino, Calif.: Floricanto Press, 1990.

Morgan, Kathleen O., Scott Morgan, and Neal Quitno, eds. *State Rankings 1992: A Statistical View of the Fifty United States*. Lawrence, Kans.: Morgan Quitno Corporation, 1992.

Morrissey, Katherine G. "Engendering the West." In *Under an Open Sky: Rethinking America's Western Past*, ed. William Cronon, George Miles, and Jay Gitlin, 132–44. New York and London: W. W. Norton and Company, 1992.

Munguía, Rubén. "La Prensa: Memories of a Boy . . . Sixty Years Later." *Americas Review* 17, no. 3–4 (Fall-Winter 1989): 130–35.

Myres, Sandra L. "Women in the West." In *Historians and the American West*, ed. Michael P. Malone, 369–86. Lincoln and London: University of Nebraska Press, 1983.

"Necrology of Benjamin M. Read." *New Mexico Historical Review* 2, no. 4 (October 1927): 394–97.

New Mexico Newspaper Project: New Mexico Newspapers (March 1994). Online Computer Library Center, 1978–1994.

Nostrand, Richard L. *The Hispano Homeland*. Norman: University of Oklahoma Press, 1992.

Novick, Peter. *That Noble Dream: The "Objectivity Question" and the American Historical Profession*. Cambridge: Cambridge University Press, 1988.

Ortego, Philip D. "Backgrounds of Mexican-American Literature." Ph.D. diss., University of New Mexico, 1971.

Ortega, Philip D., ed. *We Are Chicanos: An Anthology of Mexican-American Literature*. New York: Washington Square Press/Simon and Schuster, 1973.

Otero, Miguel Antonio. *My Life on the Frontier*, vol. 2. Albuquerque: University of New Mexico Press, 1939.

Padilla, Genaro M. "Imprisoned Narrative? Or Lies, Secrets, and Silence in New Mexico Women's Autobiography." In *Criticism in the Borderlands: Studies in Chicano Literature, Culture, and Ideology*, ed. Hector Calderón and José David Saldívar, 43–60. Durham, N.C., and London: Duke University Press, 1991.

————. *My History, Not Yours: The Formation of Mexican American Autobiography.* Madison: University of Wisconsin Press, 1993.

Paredes, Américo. "Folklore and History." In *Singers and Storytellers*, ed. M. C. Boatright, 56–68. Dallas, Tex.: Southern Methodist University Press, 1961.

————. "The Problem of Identity in a Changing Culture: Popular Expressions of Culture Conflict Along the Lower Rio Grande Border." In *Views Across the Border: The United States and Mexico*, ed. Stanley R. Ross, 68–98. Albuquerque: University of New Mexico Press, 1978.

————. *"With His Pistol in His Hand": A Border Ballad and Its Hero* (1958). Austin: University of Texas Press, 1988.

Paredes, Raymund A. "The Mexican Image in American Travel Literature, 1831–1869." *New Mexico Historical Review* 52 (January 1977): 5–29.

————. "The Origins of Anti-Mexican Sentiment in the United States." *New Scholar* 6 (1977): 139–65. Reprinted in *New Directions in Chicano Scholarship*, ed. R. Romo and R. Paredes. San Diego: Center for Chicano Studies, University of California, 1984.

Paz, Octavio. *The Labyrinth of Solitude: Life and Thought in Mexico*, trans. Lysander Kemp. New York: Grove Press, 1961.

Pérez, Emma M. "'A La Mujer': A Critique of the Partido Liberal Mexicano's Gender Ideology on Women." In *Between Borders: Essays on Mexicana/Chicana History*, ed. Adelaida R. Del Castillo, 459–82. Encino, Calif.: Floricanto Press, 1990.

Perrigo, Lynn I. *Hispanos: Historic Leaders in New Mexico*. Santa Fe, N.M.: Sunstone Press, 1985.

Poblano, Ralph, ed. *Ghosts in the Barrio: Issues in Bilingual-Bicultural Education*. San Rafael, Calif.: Leswing Press, 1973.

Prince, L. Bradford. *New Mexico's Struggle for Statehood*. Santa Fe: The New Mexican Printing Company, 1910.

Read, Benjamin M. *A History of Education in New Mexico*. Santa Fe: The New Mexican Printing Company, 1911.

————. *A Short History of Slavery in New Mexico*. St. Louis: "Amerika" Print, 1919. Offprint from the *Fortnightly Review*, 1919

————. "A Study of New Mexico Folklore." *Fortnightly Review* (May 1, 1922).

————. *A Treatise on the Disputed Points of the History of New Mexico*. Santa Fe: New Mexico Publishing Corp. 1919.

————. "El castellano en los E. U." *The Southwestern Catholic* 3 (October 1921).

————. *Guerra México-Americana*. Santa Fe: Compañía Impressora del Nuevo Mexicano, 1910.

————. *Historia ilustrada de Nuevo México*. Santa Fe: Compañía Impresora del Nuevo Mexicano, 1911.

————. *Illustrated History of New Mexico*, trans. Eleuterio Baca. Santa Fe: New Mexican Printing Company, 1912.

————. "Lo hecho, hecho, seamos francos, seamos hombres." *La Revista de Taos* (August 25, 1922).

————. "Review of Bigotry in America." *The Southwestern Catholic* (September 1,

1922). This article was published in Spanish in *La Bandera Americana* (December 14 and 21, 1923).

Rebolledo, Tey Diana. "Las Escritoras, Romances and Realities." In *Pasó por Aquí: Critical Essays on the New Mexican Literary Tradition, 1542–1988*, ed. Erlinda Gonzáles-Berry, 199–214. Albuquerque: University of New Mexico Press, 1989.

———. *Women Singing in the Snow: A Cultural Analysis of Chicana Literature*. Tucson and London: University of Arizona Press, 1995.

Rio-McMillan, Nora. "A Biography of Man and His Newspaper." *Americas Review* 17, no. 3–4 (Fall-Winter 1989): 136–49.

Rios, R. Armando. "The Mexican in Fact, Fiction and Folklore." *Voices: Readings from El Grito, 1967–1971*, ed. Octavio I. Romano-V., 59–73. Berkeley, Calif.: Quinto Sol, 1971.

Ritch, W. G. *The New Mexico Blue Book, 1882*. Facsimile ed. Albuquerque: University of New Mexico Press, 1968.

Robinson, Cecil. *With the Ears of Strangers: The Mexican in American Literature*. Tuscon: University of Arizona Press, 1963.

Rodríguez, Juan. "Jorge Ulica y Carlo de Medina: escritores de la bahía de San Francisco." *La Palabra* 2, no. 1 (Spring 1980): 25–46.

Romano-V., Octavio I. "The Anthropology and Sociology of the Mexican-Americans: The Distortion of Mexican-American History (A Review Essay)." In *Voices: Readings from El Grito, 1967–1973*, ed. Romano-V., 43–56. Berkeley, Calif.: Quinto Sol, 1973.

Rosenbaum, Robert J. *Mexicano Resistance in the Southwest: "The Sacred Right of Self-Preservation."* Austin: University of Texas Press, 1981.

———. "Mexicano versus Americano: A Study of Hispanic American Resistance to Anglo-American Control in New Mexico Territory, 1870–1900." Ph.D. diss., University of Texas at Austin, 1977.

Rowe, William, and Vivian Schelling. *Memory and Modernity: Popular Culture in Latin America*. London and New York: Verso, 1991.

Rutland, Robert A. *The Newsmongers: Journalism in the Life of the Nation, 1690–1972*. New York: Dial Press, 1973.

Saldívar, Ramón. *Chicano Narrative: The Dialectics of Difference*. Madison: University of Wisconsin Press, 1990.

Sánchez, Pedro. *Memorias sobre la vida del presbítero Don Antonio José Martínez/ Recollections of the Life of the Priest Don Antonio José Martínez* (1903), trans. Ray John de Aragon. Santa Fe, N.M.: The Lightning Tree, 1978.

Sánchez, Rosaura. *Chicano Discourse: Socio-historic Perspectives*. Houston: Arte Publico Press, 1994.

———. "The History of Chicanas: Proposal for a Materialist Perspective." In *Between Borders: Essays on Mexicana/Chicana History*, ed. Adelaida R. Del Castillo, 1–29. Encino, Calif.: Floricanto Press.

Sapir, Edward. "Language." In *Culture Language and Personality*, ed. David G. Mandelbaum, 1–44. Berkeley: University of California Press, 1949.

Saxton, Russell Steele. "Ethnocentrism in the Historical Literature of Territorial New Mexico." Ph.D. diss., University of New Mexico, 1980.

Schlesinger, Andrew B. "Las Gorras Blancas, 1889–1891." *Journal of Mexican-American History* 1 (Spring 1971): 87–143.

Seminar on Women and Culture in Latin America. "Toward a History of Women's Periodicals in Latin America: Introduction." In *Women, Culture, and Politics in Latin America*, ed. Seminar on Women and Culture in Latin America, 173–81. Berkeley: University of California Press, 1990.

Sexton, Joseph Franklin. "New Mexico: Intellectual and Cultural Developments, 1885–1925: Conflicts among Ideas and Institutions." Ph.D. diss., University of Oklahoma, 1982.

Sherman, John. *Santa Fe: A Pictorial History.* Norfolk, Va.: The Donning Company, 1983.

Simmen, Edward, ed. *The Chicano: From Caricature to Self-Portrait.* New York: New American Library, 1971.

Simmons, Marc. *New Mexico: An Interpretive History.* Albuquerque: University of New Mexico Press, 1977; reprint, 1993.

Simmons, Merle E. *The Mexican Corrido as a Source for Interpretive Study of Modern Mexico, 1870–1950.* Bloomington: Indiana University Press, 1957.

Sollars, Werner. *Beyond Ethnicity: Consent and Descent in American Culture.* New York and Oxford: Oxford University Press, 1986.

Stanley, F. *Desperadoes of New Mexico.* Denver: World Press, 1953.

Stowell, Ernest E. "More Mexican Writers and Pseudonyms." *Hispanic Review* 11 (1943): 164–74.

Stratton, Porter A. *The Territorial Press of New Mexico, 1834–1912.* Albuquerque: University of New Mexico Press, 1969.

Swadesh, Frances Leon. *Los Primeros Pobladores: Hispanic Americans of the Ute Frontier.* Notre Dame and London: University of Notre Dame Press, 1974.

Takaki, Ronald. *A Different Mirror: A History of Multicultural America.* Boston, Toronto and London: Little, Brown and Company, 1993

Tatum, Charles. *Chicano Literature.* Boston: G.K. Hall, 1982.

——. "Some Examples of Chicano Prose Fiction of the Nineteenth and Early Twentieth Centuries." *Revista Chicano-Riqueña* 9 (Winter 1981): 58–67.

Thoma, Francisco de. *Historia popular de Nuevo México desde su descubrimiento hasta la actualidad.* New York: American Book Company, 1896.

Todorov, Tzvetan. *The Conquest of America: The Question of the Other*, trans. Richard Howard. New York: Harper and Row, 1984.

Torres, T. *Periodismo.* Mexico: Ediciones Botas, 1937.

Torres Rioseco, A. *Precursores del modernismo.* New York: Las Americas, 1963.

Trulio, Beverly. "Anglo-American Attitudes toward New Mexican Women." *Journal of the West* 12 (April 1973): 229–39.

Turner, Frederick Jackson. *The Frontier in American History.* New York: Henry Holt and Company, 1947.

Twitchell, Ralph Emerson. *The History of the Military Occupation of the Territory of New Mexico from 1846 to 1851 by the Government of the United States.* Danville, Ill.: The Interstate Printers and Publishers, 1909.

——. *The Leading Facts of New Mexican History*, 5 vols. Cedar Rapids, Iowa: The Torch Press, 1910–1917.

Urbina, Luis G. *La vida literaria de México.* México, D.F.: Editorial Porrúa, 1946.

Valdez, Luis. "Introduction: 'La Plebe.'" In *Aztlán: An Anthology of Mexican American Literature*, ed. Valdez and Stan Steiner, xiii–xxxiv. New York: Vintage Books, 1972.

Valdez, Santiago. "La Vida del Presbítero Antonio José Martínez." Manuscript copy, Dec. 4, 1967. Benjamin M. Read Collection.

Van Son, Victoria. *CQ's State Fact Finder*. Washington, D.C.: Congressional Quarterly, 1993.

Vazquez, Josefina Zoraida. "Educación y Papel de la Mujer en México." In *Between Borders: Essays on Mexicana/Chicana History*, ed. Adelaida R. Del Castillo, 377–98. Encino, Calif.: Floricanto Press, 1990.

Vigil, Maurilio E. *Los Patrones: Profiles of Hispanic Political Leaders in New Mexico History*. Washington, D.C.: University Press of America, 1980.

Walter, Paul A. F. "Octaviano Ambrosio Larrazolo." *New Mexico Historical Review* 7 (April 1932): 97–104.

Watt, Ian. *The Rise of the Novel: Studies in Defoe, Richardson, and Fielding*. Berkeley: University of California Press, 1967.

Weber, David J. "The Idea of the Spanish Borderlands." In *Columbian Consequences*, ed. David Hurst Thomas, 3:3–20. Washington, D.C.; Smithsonian Institution Press, 1991.

———. "'Scarce More than Apes': Historical Roots of Anglo-American Stereotypes of Mexicans in the Border Region." In *New Spain's Far Northern Frontier: Essays on Spain in the American West, 1540–1821*, ed. Weber, 295–307. Albuquerque: University of New Mexico Press, 1979.

———. *The Spanish Frontier in North America*. New Haven and London: Yale University Press, 1992.

Weber, David J., ed. *Foreigners in their Native Land: Historical Roots of the Mexican Americans*. Albuquerque: University of New Mexico Press, 1973.

Weber, David J., and Jane M. Rausch, ed. *Where Cultures Meet: Frontiers in Latin American History*. Wilmington, Del.: Scholarly Resources, 1994.

Weigle, Marta, ed. *Two Guadalupes: Hispanic Legends and Magic Tales from Northern New Mexico*. Santa Fe, N.M.: Ancient City Press, 1987.

Weigle, Marta, and Peter White. *The Lore of New Mexico*. Albuquerque: University of New Mexico Press, 1988.

Wheless, Joseph. *Compendium of the Laws of Mexico Officially Authorized by the Mexican Government*, vol.2. St. Louis: The F. J. Thomas Law Book Co., 1910.

White, Hayden. *Tropics of Discourse: Essays in Cultural Criticism*. Baltimore and London: The Johns Hopkins University Press, 1978.

[Whitman, Walt.] "The Spanish Element in Our Nationality." *El Palacio* (Sept. 17, 1918): 164–65.

Yancey, Myra L. "Some Mexican Writers and Their Pseudonyms." *Hispanic Review* 10 (1942): 347–49.

Yúdice, George, Jean Franco, and Juan Flores, eds. *On Edge: The Crisis of Contemporary Latin American Culture*. Minneapolis: University of Minnesota Press, 1992.

Zea, Leopoldo. *The Latin American Mind*, trans. J. H. Abbott and L. Dunham. Norman: University of Oklahoma Press, 1963.

Zeleny, Carolyn. "Relations Between the Spanish-Americans and Anglo-Americans in New Mexico: A Study of Conflict and Accommodation in a Dual-Ethnic Situation." Ph.D. diss., Yale University, 1944.

Index